THE HI

The History of Tears

Sensibility and Sentimentality in France

Anne Vincent-Buffault

MACMILLAN

Editions Rivages, 1986
5–7, rue Paul-Louis Courier–75007 Paris
10, rue Fortia–13001 Marseille
English translation
© The Macmillan Press Ltd, 1991

First published as *Histoire des larmes XVIIIᵉ–XIXᵉ siècles*
by Editions Rivages 1986

First published 1991

Published by
THE MACMILLAN PRESS LTD
Houndmills, Basingstoke, Hampshire RG21 2XS
and London
Companies and representatives
throughout the world

Printed in Hong Kong

British Library Cataloguing in Publication Data
Vincent-Buffault, Anne
The History of Tears, Sensibility and Sentimentality in France.
1. France. Society, history. Behavioural aspects
I. Title
944
ISBN 0–333–45594–0
ISBN 0–333–45595–9 pbk

Contents

Contents

Introduction

Between silence and speech tears flow. Through eyes damp from floods of tears, through a gaze misted by weeping, they are the manifestation of emotion. Discreet or demonstrative in style, reserved for intimacy or shed in public, they can be the mark of a fine sensibility as well as pass for a woman's weakness. They also possess a history which can be read at a visual level. Roland Barthes, studying the attitudes of the audiences of the plays of Racine, who so liked to use emotion, asks: 'In which societies, in which times did people cry? Since when have men (and not women) ceased to cry? Why, at a certain moment, did sensibility turn into sentimentality?'

It was through reading the novels of the eighteenth century, in which the male characters cry with a confident delectation, that I encountered, for my part, this amazing question of tears. The scenes of effusion range themselves in subtle dance figures where the turbulence of the passions is in contention with the delicious transports of ecstasy. These attitudes are not restricted to fiction: the hyperbole, the Greuze-like poses, appear in correspondence, in theatre reviews. Fiction returns to real life: lovers bathe their letters with tears, friends embrace weeping, and spectators open their hearts with delight. It appears that the same is not true of the nineteenth century: a new economy of body language was gradually becoming established which altered the way in which emotion was displayed. By following the trail of tears, one can grasp the different forms of this transformation.

From the best known literary evidence to the most obscure creation, I searched for a means of approaching this fluid objective whose trace is so fragile. Literature is of its nature included, as are letters, memoirs and private journals which, without being simple reflections of reality, form an area of appropriation of a language where the proper noun is committed. The behaviour of the theatre public from the eighteenth to the nineteenth centuries also furnishes indications, as Roland Barthes noted. Determined not to favour normative writings, instead dealing with borderline states which are the description of the limits of the bearable, the acceptable, or the pathological, I studied medical and scientific

The History of Tears

writings, treatises of *savoir-vivre* and education manuals as a necessary complement to my other sources. Novels and personal
accounts offer a more varied palette of situations, and contain
different levels of speech within the same text, forming registers
which are sometimes contradictory but important to envisage.
Finally, the story of the French Revolution exists as a favoured
vignette of tears shed in public: newspapers, archival documents
and memoirs bear witness to this.

As one interprets these various sources there are traps to avoid:
above all we should not apply our contemporary psychological
criteria to the tears of the past; we would run the risk of coming
up against a dead end. The experience of tears, both general and
deeply personal, can call our own time into question, providing
that we avoid the mirages of the regressive illusion, *bête noire* of
the history of the mind. That being the case, the 'remote view'
of the anthropologists offers a way out. Marcel Mauss did in
fact, in 1922, expose the enigma of tears in a clear-sighted way.
Pondering 'the oral funeral rituals of the Australian population',
he showed that the obligatory but nevertheless spontaneous use
of collective tears confers on them symbolic status. Through
these rites, tears become a language, and reveal a system of
signs. Several months later, and in the same publication, Marcel
Granet developed this analysis observing the language of pain in
Chinese civilisation. These works led me to adjust my notions of
sincerity and spontaneity in relation to the demonstrative use of
tears – a contemporary view which no doubt comes to us from
the nineteenth century, but which is not central to all societies –
towards a concept of the network of communication which they
reveal. What is striking in the rhetoric of tears in the eighteenth
century, is the extent to which the interchange of tears recurs:
they are exchanged, shared and mingled with delight.

'In the seventeenth century, men could cry in public, today
it has become both more difficult and more rare. Women alone
have preserved this right. For how much longer?' writes Norbert
Elias. The demonstrative use of tears characterises the behaviour
of theatre-goers of the eighteenth century, while the playwrights
see in it an indication of the approval of the stalls. This public
aspect of tears is in contrast to a specifically private experience
of them which developed in the nineteenth century, and which
was accompanied by a re-allocation of the male and female roles.
In the eighteenth century, it is true that men and women were

to be seen in tears, while the pleasures of private emotion were extolled. But men did not fear to cry for admiration, tenderness or joy, and often liked to let it be known, an attitude which at that time had no connotations of femininity. An individual moment in the history of tears, the eighteenth century combines the public and private aspects of emotional demonstration.

The bourgeois demands of good behaviour would, in the nineteenth century, abandon the demonstrative aspect of tears, and go so far as to call it into question. The development of individual expression finds its realisation in tears, but unlike the eighteenth century, they are reserved for the intimate and private world. Romanticism, in reaction, with its passions and its weeping, was opposed to a system of restraint and prudishness, tears became a favoured experience, but could equally be denied. For men, the wish to cry was no longer enough, tears were hoped for, but were veiled in irony. Feminine sensibility was celebrated: the tears, fleeting signs which were difficult to read because they could be a pretence, revealed suddenly a profound femininity which was constantly exalted.

It was in the second half of the nineteenth century that the scarce tear became the ultimate evaluation of masculine sensibility whereas women, dominated by an excessive emotionalism, were hardly considered glorious, quite the opposite. Writers mocked the sentimentality of women who loved to feel moved by the worst of clichés, as they mistrusted or denigrated their strategic ability to cry at the right moment. It was at this time that a slow passage from sensibility to sentimentality occurred. It was in the name of this that the bourgeois theatre-goer abandoned the melodrama, and that the audience which still came to cry over the Boulevard of Crime was regarded as brutish and primitive in the eyes of the knowledgeable. The lowering of the value of tears was as much social as sexual. On the other hand painful sobs which could not be suppressed were the cause of disquiet: they were sometimes a sign of illness.

Men of letters and scholars were not the only ones to set the tone. During the same period, there were many different rules of behaviour, the history of tears is made up of images and dreams which are as revealing about those who cry as those who witness the demonstration of their emotions. The novelists of the nineteenth century participated in the invention of the 'maiden' whose tears were pure and easily provoked. In their

personal diaries, young women were battling with this imaginary
ideal. If surprised in tears, they would shrink from giving others
a picture of the young innocent, but in private they were glad
to weep.

I have attempted to find room for these many instances, the
entwined glances, the contradictory accounts, in order to leave
free the path of tears, and call into question these tears shed in
darkened rooms, discreetly wiped away before the lamp is relit.

Part I

The Taste for Tears, An Exchange of Sensibilities

1 Crying and Reading

NOVELS BATHED WITH TEARS

In the search for tears we soon encounter the book: the practice of reading provoked mild demonstrations of emotion in the eighteenth century. People enjoyed crying, the women in their boudoirs, the men in their studies, but tears were also shed when people read together.

Already, in the seventeenth century, the readers of Madame de La Fayette's *La Princesse de Clèves* were moved to tears.[1] The Marquise de Sévigné took pleasure in telling her correspondents of the tears which she shed in reading Corneille's play *Pulchérie*.[2] From the epistolary evidence the taste for tears, which first affected female readers, was already well developed. Fénelon's *Télémaque* was judged to be moving: both the heroes and heroines of the novel shed many tears as well as their readers. The history of reading practices uncovers a new motif: that of the sentimental reader. It was through his emotions that he took in the text he was reading and he wished to make this special occasion known to his friends, to his correspondents and even to the author.

At the beginning of the eighteenth century, the novels of the Abbé Prévost were a triumph of tears. In 1728, Mlle Aïssé wrote to one of her many correspondents: 'There is a new book entitled *Mémoires d'un homme de qualité retiré du monde* [Memoirs of a retired gentleman]. It is not worth much but despite this one spends the one hundred and eighty pages dissolved in tears'.[3] However much Mlle Aïssé may have wept, her emotion did not prevent her from passing a severe judgement on the Abbé Prévost's work. She cried as a connoisseur and her critical distance limited any sentimental participation. However, the novels of Prévost, published between 1728 and 1740, were quite an event. They renewed the rules of the genre through their tragic dimensions, their moral philosophy and the analysis of the passions which was developed in them, and the violent emotions which animated their characters. We need look no further than the work of the Abbé Prévost to prove that one cannot make a distinction between a rational beginning of

3

the eighteenth century and an emotional end; that era of sensitive spirits turned the period following the Enlightenment into
nothing but a shadow of the previous age.[4] As the movement
asserted itself, the vogue for sentiment affected the major writers
as well of those of lesser stature, above all in the novel, although
none of them after Prévost had a monopoly on the genre. In the
course of the eighteenth century the practice of tears appears to
have become the most common denominator among the literary
public. It is possible that men of letters were involved in this
process, but a fashion can escape from its own initiators who
consider themselves to be responsible for maintaining it. Famous
writers who have often been considered to be the promoters of
this fashion, were not the most widely read. The romantic novels
of Mme de Graffigny and Mme Riccoboni, the volumes of sentimental turgidity by Baculard d'Arnaud, which caused many tears
despite the lack of philosophical content, took Rousseau, Diderot
and Voltaire to check and mate on the shelves of libraries, whose
catalogues have been the object of systematic studies.

If readers had picked up a taste for tears in the pages of
the novel, one can imagine that they finally looked for them
there. In revealing the spread of a pattern in literature these
sought-after tears reinforced it. The desire in certain writers to
cause tears became explicit from then on.

The invitation to tears is to be found in many prefaces
to books. But literary figures did not use the same ploys to
bring them about. In the foreword to *Malheurs de l'inconstance*
[Troubles of inconstancy] Dorat explained his choice of emotions
in precise terms. The pleasure of crying provided the opportunity
to receive a moral education in an agreeable fashion, without the
intervention of reason. This showed an optimism characteristic
of the Enlightenment which liked to combine the useful with the
enjoyable and exultation with finer feelings:

> Above all, I have attempted to be true to life, to portray only
> events which are possible, to offer to readers a small part of the
> great canvas which they have before their eyes every day and
> to make it useful while surrounding the teaching with charm
> and feeling. The lesson which is instilled through tears is not
> regretted. It is made clear and enters the mind unperceived,
> in this the mind is betrayed by the spirit so that it should not
> be contradicted in its pleasures.[5]

The moving forces of this moral and sentimental proselytism were available to those who wished to hear.

But the author did not consider that he had used the simplest methods. Rather than oppressing the spirit with terror and 'soothing it with tears', (he was criticising the Gothic novel), he wished to touch the heart by combining sensibility, taste and reason, for the methods of causing tears could be an illustration of the aesthetic and ethical issues. The delicatesse of the method and a finer sensibility were a presage of worthier tears, because they did not relieve the anguish, but engraved moral precepts on the soul in a pleasurable way, without making use of philosophical speculation. He also informed the reader that this work took him years.

Baculard who, unlike Dorat, was happier working in the horrific and black genre, made use of a different argument to present the tale of the guilty lovers who met in a park: 'There is no point in casting a veil over the picture which will follow. The intolerant inflexible reader will be outraged; but the feeling man will allow the scene some tears, and will say: "perhaps I would have behaved like them".'[6] The reader was called on to choose one stance or the other. Cold reason was here dismissed in favour of a tender indulgence which was asserted unequivocally and which called more for identification with the lovers than for pity. The two authors made use of the slender metaphor of the felicitous picture to induce tears. An aspect of the sensibility of the contemporary public can be seen, who pictured the situations, using the same terms of reference as the theatre which was producing touching scenes on stage. But with Baculard, tearful moralising gave way to the fashion for feeling which loved to cry over love, and which excused moral deviations. Baculard achieved the effect he was looking for since, according to Fréron, his novels made readers shed 'floods of tears'.[7] The novels of Baculard were nevertheless considered by Grimm to be just about good enough for 'seamstresses and modistes'.[8] He was not a part of the philosophers' movement, and was not so concerned with moralising as with making use of a process of moving the reader without fear of excess and grandiosity, which he flogged to death.

The effects which were caused by reading, on the other hand, were not ignored, and all the evidence leads us to believe that they were sought by calling on an emotion which

was more or less refined. The task of the writer in this was
to determine the degree of emotion: of course, tears must be
evoked, but different methods were used to achieve this and
had different values. Soon, the habit developed of judging the
success of a work by the quantity of tears shed by the public:
Rousseau's publisher informed him of the success of the first
volumes of *La Nouvelle Héloïse*, which appeared individually, by
evaluating their respective qualities according to the tears shed
by the public.[9] The written accounts of *La Nouvelle Héloïse* which
are more numerous, have slightly distorted the perspective: the
public did not wait for Rousseau to cry while reading. Rousseau,
on the other hand, evoked a process of identification with the
text in the anonymous reader which had no real precedent, and
which is worthy of special attention.

THE NOVEL WITHIN THE NOVEL OR THE PLACE
OF THE READER

The activity of reading played a role within eighteenth century
novels themselves. The tears brought about by reading occupy
a position which was sometimes central to the narrative. The
reading scene of the two lovers thus allowed Mme Riccoboni
to stage an encounter between two hearts:

> At each moment the secret of our hearts seemed ready
> to escape us: our eyes had already spoken of it, when
> one day, on reading a touching story of two lovers who
> were cruelly separated, the book fell from our hands, our
> tears were mingled, and, both seized by some fear, we
> looked up at each other. He put his arm around me, as
> though to support me, I leaned towards him and breaking
> the silence at the same moment, we cried out together 'Ah,
> how unfortunate they were!' A whole confiding followed these
> tender feelings.[10]

This episode consigned reading to a *mise en abîme*, but also
introduced the adventures which the two protagonists would
endure. The echo of their two voices, of their eyes which
wept over a moving novel, suggested to the readers that it
was a good thing to read together with a loved one. The

tears were the authorisation for the two tender heroes to avow their mutual love, and to prove the communion of their souls to themselves, without making their declaration according to the accepted formulae, this event was no less touching for the reader, or 'narratee', to distinguish him from the fictional readers. Making up for the insufficiency of language, the dignity of tears shed over a novel was then the result of what they allowed to be revealed freely, and following the delicate formulae of sensitivity. There was no fear of being caught, since one cried from a feeling of compassion, which was part of virtue.

The technique of the epistolary novel which was used by Mme Riccoboni was much employed in the eighteenth century. It made the illusion of truth which the novels suggested easier to sustain. In this type of work, the lovers made their letters moist while writing or reading, to the point of obliterating the writing: these formulae became commonplaces in literature. This model of behaviour affected real love letters, as though, between the letter novel and the love letter there was a phenomenon of imitation, of impregnation. The pages, whether printed or manuscript, appeared well sprinkled with tears. Mme Riccoboni herself, filled with passion for a young Scot, Sir Liston, bathed her letters with tears like the heroines of her novels.[11] Private writings were not exempt from this either. Lucile Duplessis, writing in her red book to her future husband Camille Desmoulins, left the traces of tears which have been detected by André Monglond: 'Shall I one day be your wife? Will we one day be united? Alas! perhaps at the very moment at which I give shape to these wishes, you have forgotten me . . . With this cruel thought my tears dampen the paper'.[12]

READING AND SELF-REVELATION

The eighteenth century settled into a new age of individual, private reading. It was the creation of a moment and of an exclusive space: it began to take place in *déshabillé*, in the home, surrounded by a certain degree of comfort, by appropriate furnishings.[13] But of the effects produced by solitary reading much was said: the tears, sighs and sobs caused by a work were recounted with a wealth of detail. Correspondence reveals a whole circulation of stories of emotions aroused by literature. This predilection for tears could not at any rate be separated from the discussions which followed reading, whether shared or individual during which the moral and aesthetic aspects of the work were tackled. This practice of a society of readers is indispensable to an understanding of the taste for tears. Even when gained in private, the knowledge of a novel led to discussions in which the ability to arouse emotion was explored at length. A particularly moving scene which led to tears would be analysed.

Certainly this behaviour at first affected a limited group who frequented the *salons*, and which set the tone through its critical activity. In these *salons*, men of letters tested the lachrymal power of their texts. To make fine eyes weep was already a consecration of their work. Marmontel at Mme Geoffrin's suppers would read his little tales out loud: 'What delighted me personally was to see the most beautiful eyes in the world offer tears to the little scenes in which I made nature and love moan'.[14] Here sensibility became mingled with seduction. Voltaire thus read aloud his *Mérope* to several friends gathered at Cirey. Mme de Graffigny who attended his readings, which were spread out over several evenings, would often weep, but her capacity to be moved in no way held back her critical enthusiasm. She wrote, to Devaux on 10 December 1738: '[Voltaire] read two acts of *Mérope*: I was crying during the first; they are always fine lines, fine sentiments, but the drawn-out scenes don't work; he normally fails in them'.[15] Tears shed between friends in no way inhibited aesthetic judgements. This ability to display emotions in front of others at the time of reading did not at all imply a lack of discernment or an eclipse of reason. In Mme de Graffigny, mind and sentiment made good partners.

This *salon* practice blended sentiment with analysis, favourable feelings with mockery. Sensibility was a society practice which had its rules. In the *salons*, the performance of the pitiful tale, which was a genre in itself, or that of reading aloud, provoked collective tears. Tender feelings were developed there to the finest degree. The art of story-telling nevertheless required a mastery of the tale which precluded personal emotion and its ridiculous features: the smothered words, the facial contortions. It was necessary to know how to tell about a sad event or a particularly touching but not personal human characteristic with ease: each individual could thus display his or her sensibility while sharing the experience with others.

On this point, the *salon*, a half public meeting-place, was different from the small community of friends who would meet in the country, in a non-family intimacy. There too, it was rare to tell of one's personal life in order to create feeling, and it was not without reluctance that Mme de Graffigny, during a stay at Cirey agreed to tell of her misfortunes, although there were constant tears on reading tragedies, or on telling touching stories. She wrote to her friend on 22 December 1738:

So it was, that from one question to the next, and constantly resisting, I was made to tell the story of my life, about which they knew nothing. Ah! What a fine heart! The beautiful lady (Mme du Châtelet) laughed in order to prevent herself from crying, but Voltaire, the human Voltaire, broke into tears, for he is not ashamed of appearing sensitive: as for myself, I acted as the beautiful lady did, I wished to stop speaking: but there was no way to do it; I was constantly urged to continue. Mme Dorsin behaved like Voltaire; in the end they were so moved, that my efforts were in vain, I cried as well.

Mme de Graffigny who was not afraid to weep in floods of tears over a book, or at the theatre, feared to cry over her life in front of three people. The taste for public emotion was not about the exposure of individual misfortunes, or of private sufferings. The signs of sensibility were the better if worn in public, and even in private, it was rather better to weep over grand principles and generalities. This distinction displeased some, who wished for stronger emotions, more charged with a personal meaning.

THE EFFECT OF READING

Reading was considered to be a living and pleasing teaching of morals. L.S. Mercier affirmed this:

What a host of exquisite pleasures come from reading a good book! You must remember that you have all cried to a greater or lesser degree, or you may have been the recipient of a consoling, guiding idea which you would not have had without a book to inspire you.[16]

Whether it was moral conversion or simple enjoyment of tears, the degree of reader participation varied. In this respect, Richardson and Rousseau are the two authors who are reference points for sensitive and participating readership. The effects which they brought about were fully reported and exceeded the expression of emotion which had been allowed until that time. The emotion which was aroused by the reading of their novels released a torrent of tears which achieved a moral revolution among their readers and gave them a personal commitment. Diderot described a friend reading Richardson: the delightful troubles of the readers sometimes took on major proportions.

> At this point he seized the notebooks, withdrew into a corner and read. I watched him: first I saw tears running down his face, he interrupted himself, he sobbed; suddenly he got up, he wandered aimlessly, he cried out as though he were devastated, he reproached the Harlove family in the most bitter way.

What an expressive pantomime! At this level of emotion, where the reader was beside himself, where his body was driven by pain and indignation, nothing remained to distinguish the novel from reality. Diderot himself was amazed, when reading forced tears from him, that his very surroundings, the stones, walls, and floor did not join their cries to his. These were moments where fiction attained the level of truth, where the whole world should be drawn in by the emotion which overwhelmed the reader, placing him in a state of 'innocence'.[17] Held in a perpetual state of distress, the spirit of the reader became good and just. He was as happy as if he had just done some virtuous act. To remain unmoved by *Clarissa Harlove* was, for Diderot, an indication of the greatest misfortune, he would rather have seen his daughter die than that she should be struck by it. Should we read this as one of the theatrical effects of which Diderot was an acknowledged master? Indeed we should, but were his daughter not to cry over the misfortunes of so virtuous a heroine, she would be untrue and without compassion, incapable of doing good, with no reason to live. Reading and life were no longer separated.

The publication of *La Nouvelle Héloïse* was probably a great moment in the history of reading and readers: it was also a key event in the history of tears. Letters were filled with accounts of tears shed, letters which did not only come from literary circles who were accustomed to analysing texts, but which were from average readers, provincial townsfolk whose evidence is precious. The letter novel made many cry; it was not new, nor were emotional outbursts caused by reading. But readers so identified themselves with the fictional characters or with the author himself, that they felt that they had to write to Rousseau to let him know of their emotion and their enthusiasm. It may be surprising that a novel should have caused such strong reactions. It is true that Rousseau himself favoured this phenomenon of identification with the story since, in his preface, he described himself just as the editor of letters exchanged between the two famous lovers and not as their author. Some people were taken in by this, and believed the story to be true. In addition, Rousseau declared that he did not address himself to people of society, but to isolated individuals, who reflected on their readings and were filled with them.[18] This appeal was heard, a new bond was established between the author and his public. Loiseau de Mauléon, a young lawyer, declared in a letter to Rousseau: 'That I love to blend the tears which flow from my eyes on behalf of the worthy object who is constantly in my heart with the tears of your virtuous characters'. For his feelings, his thoughts, his principles and his situation all so closely resembled those which were described in *La Nouvelle Héloïse* that he communicated directly with the heroes of the novel through his tears. 'In truth, Sir,' he adds, 'I do not know if you will find a reader more worthy of you than me'.[19] From reality to fiction, from true feelings to the passionate novel, from author to reader, the proximity is such that all distinctions are wiped away to give way to the tears shed. On this point of similarity, de Mauléon asks Rousseau to recognise him as the ideal reader.

Alexandre de Leyde was in transports over the novel and established a special contact with the author.

> You have a soul which penetrates and forms a bond with the reader, who feels it pass through himself when reading your work, he weeps with admiration, regret and desire, he becomes fascinated by goodness, he sometimes does good, he at least believes possible and true something which he has never achieved himself.[20]

This moral reform operated through the tears which indicated the transmigration of Rousseau's spirit into that of the reader. The liquid of cordial expansiveness, in Roland Barthe's words, tears allowed this confusion, this mingling of souls which urged them to do good and incited them to virtue.

Pierre Gallot, a citizen of Rouen, also felt the need to avow his gratitude to Rousseau, and furthermore, he became his spiritual son, living according to the precepts of the author:

> Rousseau, my worthy friend, my tender father [. . .] who could portray my situation, the emotion which I experience in reading your charming works. I think that it would be satisfying for you to see me with a copy of *Émile* or *Héloïse* in my hand. With what attention I read, I can hardly breath in or out, it seems to me that I am alone in the world, I see nothing, I can no longer hear, tears of emotion flow from my eyes and I think that, in these moments, enraptured by the charming simplicity of the nature I have discovered, I have a taste of perfect happiness. This gentle indulgence of the senses has in no way the emptiness of boisterous pleasures.[21]

The books, but also the principles which they developed, the exaltation of nature in particular, are part of that delicious emotion which the reader attempted to recreate for himself, as a perfect disciple. This 'Rousseau effect' relied to a great extent on the propensity of average readers to use it as a model for life, following a kind of conversion through tears.

But reading *La Nouvelle Héloïse* was not always a pleasure, for the tears which were shed could become painful. Cahagne, in a letter which took the form of an extended dissertation, wrote: 'We must suffocate, we must desert the book, we must cry, we must write to you that we are suffocating and crying'.[22] The intensity of emotion forced him to stop reading but drove him to write. He thus abandoned the book at Part Three, then tears overtook him again at the end of the book. There, the attack was violent, painful:

> It is true that I love very much to express emotion, I love to cry. But no one could love too strong a pain, which is oppressive, which smothers or which tears one apart, and that is certainly the continual effect of everything which concerns the death of Julie.[23]

Smothered, oppressed, torn apart, Cahagne no longer felt any pleasure in crying. Even as he thought over Saint-Preux's ideas of suicide from the moral point of view, he asked himself whether the emotion caused by Julie's death might not be injurious to the reader. Some readers, however, adapted themselves to the too-bitter sadness which was aroused by *La Nouvelle Héloïse*. François feared Julie's death scene to the extent of postponing his reading of it:

> I spent three days without daring to read the last letter from M. de Wolmar to Saint-Preux, I could feel how interesting the details it contained would be, and Julie dead or dying was not an idea which I could bear. I had to suppress my reluctance, however, I have never shed such delightful tears, the reading itself had such a strong effect on me that I think that I would, in that moment, have contemplated death with pleasure.[24]

Pain was transformed into pleasure at the price of a complete commitment to the fate reserved for the heroine, which became for the reader, the acceptation of his own death.

Sensitive spirits allowed themselves to be moved, but some judged tears which are shed on the ethical and aesthetic level of order in life. Thus Mirabeau the elder preferred Richardson to Rousseau because of the different qualities of the tears which they brought about:

> Being over fifty years old, I have at present the *Héloïse* on my desk, and when I feel my over-tense spirit begin to become clogged with your ideas and go numb in the shadow of their apparel, I take up Richardson, the most useful of all men to me, and I do not quit him until I have wept. It is the habit of gentle tears which I would like to teach to you, for they are true goodness here below, and I am sorry but you know only burning tears.[25]

This pleasure in weeping was then looked for by making a choice in reading matter.

In a later age, that is, the period when Rousseau had disappeared, his readers extended their delightful emotions by visiting his grave in Ermenonville. This popular excursion would finish with tears shed in the company of others, with the additional pleasure of providing the spectacle of sensitivity in a group. Mirabeau the younger wrote thus to Lafage:

> You are trying to imitate Jean-Jacques? Oh, if you had succeeded in one such emulation, what a man you would be! This Jean-Jacques is a sublime and virtuous man: go when you can to weep on his tomb; perhaps I will lead you there and you will return a better man.[26]

The future Tribune of Provence was also a man of feeling who extended an invitation to weep over the ashes of Jean-Jacques as though this act in itself could inspire virtuous behaviour. Rason, the 'ordinary' reader of Rousseau, of whom a detailed analysis has been given by Robert Darnton, also wished to go to Ermenonville to weep, and he put up a print of the tomb on the wall of his study.[27] This young protestant trader from La Rochelle wished to read the entire works of Rousseau with care, but also to know everything about his life, and to apply his educational principles. In his letters, his family life was mixed with his questions on the great man who was thus a figure of 'day to day rousseauism' for whom a profound reading of Jean-Jacques coloured the fabric of everyday life.

The evidence of these unknown readers, like Diderot's praise of Richardson, led to the drawing of distinctions in the degree of intensity in this taste for tears. The pleasure of crying while reading, already popular in the seventeenth century, took on a more accentuated turn, a more intense existential value. Sensitive reading changed its form from the taste for tears shed with feeling in the boudoir, to the exaltation of the reader which involved moral reform and the blending of souls. To the descriptions of a spectacular physical reaction, there was added a reader's identification with the text, such as there had never been before, and perhaps would never be again, which involved his way of life and thought.

2 The Exchange of Tears and its Rules

In reading these novels which caused so many tears, and these letters which speak of tears, one finds oneself surprised at the formulations used to give an account of the expression of emotion. These tears shed without moderation described a movement which was not arbitrary. By crying, a relationship was established, a reply was expected. The language used in these writings reveals, in itself, that the tears were to be seen and exchanged. Tears shed at home distributed rights and duties in their own way. Love, which made tears flow was the occasion for tender expressions of emotion, but it also caused unshared tears which were on the scale of the tragedy lived out by lovers. One sympathised with strangers, cried with them, experienced the gentle feelings of humanity, sampled the charms of charity. In exploring these bonds forged by tears, little by little an imaginary space took shape in a singular form.

THE TERMS OF THE EXCHANGE OR THE LANGUAGE OF TEARS

In the abundance of statements which are made to us by the novels of the eighteenth century, from the first reading, the frequency of certain expressions related to tears draws the attention. Most of them are now strange to us and are more likely to make us smile than cry. This rhetoric of tears was readable, that is, acceptable, and taken as such by the readers of the eighteenth century. It probably appealed to their imaginations since the same terms were used in their letters. These rhetorical figures, which have become outdated, indicate that the codes of emotional communication were part of the literature of the eighteenth century, but were also part of a broader practice of writing: letters, memoirs, accounts of performances.

Certain recurrent expressions convey a taste for spectacular displays of tears. There was in the first place the excess of

15

emotion which was given to reading. The paroxysm of emotion
was expressed by the use of hyperbole: one would shed torrents
or streams of tears, one would sprinkle or dampen with tears. At
a period when the presence of bodies in novels was very discreet,
this abundance of secretions, with all its agreed principles,
allowed characters' sensibilities to be made of flesh and blood
and gave a physical appearance to emotion, which compensated
for a language which shied away from such expressions, for the
strongest of emotions could only be conceived with the aid of
its external manifestations. It was not the material nature of
the body which was the object of the description, but the movement of the passions which disturbed it. There was no fear of
injuring verisimilitude. The face became a country, across which
rain, streams and torrents flowed. The image of nature was
especially present, as though it alone could give an account
of the strength of emotion. The secretion of tears was sublimated
by these metaphors. The excess of tears acquired, with these
pictures, a dimension which fitted the signals of the human body
in the world which surrounded them. One wonders whether the
use of these images was not connected with a representation of
the body which Robert Muchembled evoked in the case of the
peasants of Artois in the sixteenth and seventeenth centuries, who
considered that their fleshly envelope was a microcosm directly
bound to the outside world: 'a symmetry exists between the tears
shed by an individual, to take one example, and the rain or the
fog'.[1] The history of tears is also that of the limits of the body
and of their greater or lesser accessibility. The passage of a body
belonging to the world and being traversed by its currents, to being
a personally controlled body, which was separate from things, did
indeed mark an 'extraordinary change in the culture of the body'.[2]
These metaphors come from an age which was before the barrier
between the human being and his environment.

One can suppose, more simply, that the use of these expressions
makes the state of the characters in the drama readable within
the economy of the story. It is a very well-known technique of
the theatre to enlarge a gesture to make it obvious. This very
excess allows the reader to see clearly the moment of emotion,
when a more restrained expression might not have given a clear
indication of it. The grasping of the signs of emotion, a natural
ability because it comes from the body, thus finds itself made
easy through hyperbole.

But, even more, tears were signs which travelled. There is no quantitative measure for an exchange which is only conceived in profusion. On the other hand, this economy put into play a whole series of expressions which differentiated between the modes of effusion. When the terms of the exchange were not reciprocal, the drama built up towards a climax, inhumanity revealed itself. But between the fusion in tears, and the refusal to share, a whole range of possibilities allowed the definition of relationship.

At the height of emotion, *they cried together, they shared their tears,* and even more, *they mixed their tears* with those of others. These expressions were part of an ideal encounter thanks to the liquid element, despite the irreparable separation of the bodies. The necessary sharing of signs of emotion and in a certain type of relationship the mingling of tears referred to a model for the art of living between intimates where transparency was a requirement.

In the face of the tears of a human being, it was appropriate to participate and sympathise. It was rare to find someone who was not *touched by the tears of others,* who could hold back his tears in the face of those which were shed. This propensity to be moved by the pain of others provoked curious phenomena of contagion. From one close relation to another, everyone was won by tears. Thus, *tears were drawn out of the most hardened.* To a visible pain, one responded with tears. It was often the case, in novelistic declarations that *one would console, one would receive the tears, one would wipe away the tears of others, one would take the tears to one's breast.* There was a novelistic obligation of compassion and consolation. The frequent occurrence of the remarks is evidence of a suitable response to the tears shed, of gestures appropriate to the situation. It would appear that one could not leave another to cry without acting, that is, without drawing near to him and taking account of his tears.

This movement, this exchange of tears is also expressed by recourse to an economic analogy: *one gives tears, one owes tears* to another or even *one pays one's tribute of tears, one buys with tears.* The worst would probably be to *cost someone tears.* If in the novels of the eighteenth century there were many tears,[3] they were not shed in vain, or at a loss. Respect, love, or simply the feeling of being part of humanity invited everyone to keep an account of what had been expended. By making someone cry, a debt of tears was contracted. Novels developed a strange management of the ebb and flow of the liquid commodity.

Mingling, sharing, exchanging, the liquid economy of tears: the recurrence of this group of literary expressions permits us to discern a code of emotional impulse which made an almost theatrical reading of the fit of tears necessary, causing a scaled response to the outbursts, but which was nevertheless just as physically expressive. It seems then that the rhetoric of tears was evidence of a logic of tearful communication, which the extended study of relationships between the characters of novels will allow us to approach. The specific ties which were sustained between characters were distinguished on a textual level through the regulated movements of tears. This logic appeared however to be self-contained and gave little evidence of the tears which were really shed. If the novel allowed one to grasp the bonds fostered between characters and to identify standard situations from one book to another, letters and memoirs demonstrated how those who wrote for themselves could take over these images. The similarity between the two modes of expression were disturbing: they often came from literary figures but spread also to the wider circle of their readership. The use of this rhetoric of tears reinforced the theory of this imaginary distribution of sensibility.

The shared experience of fiction and non-fictional accounts was to occupy primarily the realm of metaphor. It only remained to the readers to cry a little with the words and images of the times.

THE LIMITED EXCHANGE: THE PRIVATE WORLD AND RELATIONSHIPS BETWEEN INTIMATES

It is through the filter of the novel and of intimate writing that I propose a reading of the tears shed in private. The transformation of literary genres made this possible. This is because of the development of the emotional and sentimental novel from the end of the seventeenth century and above all in the eighteenth century. The best-known authors of this novel genre: Mme de La Fayette, Richardson and Rousseau had many followers. According to Bakhtin's analyses they wrote 'the moving into the intimate',[4] and caused familiar genres to intervene in the narrative of the novel: letters, intimate diaries, daily conversations. This type of novel sought also to ennoble the daily language of feeling, and the tenderness which they described bore witness to a taste among the literary public for edifying scenes of private life. Three main types of intimate relationship attracted my attention in studying these novels of the eighteenth century [translator's note: *La Princesse de Clèves* was written in the seventeenth century]: love, friendship, and of course the family, each of which had their own model where tears were concerned. The search for intense emotional exchanges gave a prominent place to the manifestation of tears. Although not reserved only for them, they did take on a special shape in these situations. These small communities of souls which were bound by sentiment appeared haunted by a search for fusion which led to the mingling of tears and caused bodies to draw near each other. The establishment in the eighteenth century of a private sphere which is highlighted by the analyses of Philippe Ariès, was expressed in its own way in the scenes of tears in novels. The rise of intimacy and of literary history maintained a link in this. Thus in novels and in letters, details of private surroundings in the material sense of the term were quite rare. The description of interiors did not occupy the place which it took in the nineteenth century. The correlation between space and relationships was in any case not apparent. What should one think of a man who embraced his friend, weeping, in the street? This attitude demonstrated the acceptance of public tears, but this emotion was very different from that of strangers who cried together in the theatre auditorium. In a novel by Duclos, a man received, while still in bed, the visit of two unfortunates, a mother and her daughter, who were not known to him, and the tale of their unhappiness led to a general scene of emotion.[5] The situation was intimate, but the characters were at first strangers to each other. The scenery was not as simple as this in a society where the ties of intimacy, which followed a model, exhibited themselves in a new light in novels. The characters propose a bedroom scene of pity, but incongruous situations and moving encounters could sometimes open it up onto the street, just as the street could break into the house.

CRYING WITHIN THE FAMILY

Through literature and memoirs, an ideal bourgeois family was sketched out which found in effusiveness a privileged means of expression. A father came upon his two children who were overcome by the financial difficulties of their parents:

Come, follow me, he added, taking us by the hands; we shall
go and tell your mother what I know of you, come and reward
her for her tears. I know her! What happiness for her! What a
repayment for her pain! [And in front of the mother . . .] Your
daughter was saying earlier to her brother, as they wept, that
since we loved them so much, we well deserved that they
should attempt to calm our worries [. . .] My mother, at this
speech, shed further tears, but of joy.[6]

The unhappy tears of the mother were redeemed by those shed
by the children, and tears of joy succeeded those of pain. The
impulse of tears was beneficial and was evidence of the intensity
of familial affection.

Novels expressed the blossoming of family feeling: many tears
were shed over them, and attempts were made at mutual consolation. This environment of the emotions, where these multiple
tender considerations were in play, was however not without
categorisation: the fraternal relationship, filial piety and paternal
and maternal love each gave their own flavour to the exchange
of tears. Respect, the sense of duty and the honour of families
was mixed with the love between parents and children, giving a
significant character to tears, following subtle measures.

The figure of the father thus acquired a new impact through
the exchange of tears. In the novel, children, who were generally
lovers, cried over the misfortunes of their father, imprisoned, sick
or ruined. Lady Sidley spoke of her father thus: 'My first tears were
shed in a cell over an old man who deserved a throne'.[7] She made
a touching figure of filial piety for a father who was unjustly
punished: this was a picture to provoke tears. But a father was
not of the sort that allowed himself to be moved by the tears of
a child who did not respect his will, or who was not virtuous.
An outraged father would abandon compassion for severity and
distance, when the conduct of his son led to dishonour. Certain
values won over paternal feelings. This is what led to the Chevalier
des Grieux's cry of despair, clasping the knees of his father: 'Ah!
If you have any more [. . .] do not harden yourself against my
tears'.[8] In Prévost's novel, although paternal love was sometimes
expressed through a gesture, it remained bound to authority and
to the enforced obedience of children. It was for this reason that
his tears, rarer than those of a mother, made a stir.

In *La Nouvelle Heloïse* the father's tears were of the type that no virtuous daughter could resist. When Julie refused the marriage which her father proposed with his friend M. de Wolmar for love of St-Preux, he threw himself at her feet while dissolving into tears. 'This most severe of fathers' did not make use of his authority but, fixing damp eyes on his daughter, he begged her to respect his silver hair. By changing from a mood of severity to tears he disarmed Julie. You may judge her state:

> I let myself go, half-dead, into his arms, and it was only after many tears which oppressed me that I could answer him in a distorted weak voice: 'Oh my father! I had defences against your threats, I have none against your tears; it is you who will be the death of your daughter.'[9]

Julie sacrificed herself to her duty on seeing her father's tears fall.

Letters and memoirs suggest that this image of the father in tears was a popular theme. Rousseau in the *Confessions* presented to us a tender father who cried with his son evoking together the picture of a wife and mother who was dead: 'When he said to me: "Jean-Jacques let us speak of your mother", I would say to him "Ah well! In that case, my father, we are going to cry" and these words alone already drew tears from him'.[10] Mirabeau, who was imprisoned by his father in the fort of Vincennes and with whom he fought relentlessly, through occasional vengeful memoirs, wrote to the lady he had been trying to seduce since his arrival in prison: 'At last, my father now conducts himself with a belated and slow generosity; and if I can extract a tear from him, I shall thus be repaid for all that his despotism has made me lose and suffer'.[11] The enemy of paternal authority, made real through the famous 'lettres de cachet', dreamed of paternal sensibility and of weeping. When the despotic authority was replaced by a tear of emotion, balance was restored and with it, family peace.

In *La Vie de mon père* [my father's life], Edmé Rétif de la Bretonne (father of Nicolas) told his children about a memory which he could not evoke without being moved to tears. It concerned the tears which his father Pierre shed after having whipped him too soundly. Perceiving him thus for the first time, it seemed to him that 'nature would be overturned'. He threw himself to his knees and 'said to himself': 'Oh my father! I cost you tears; you love me

my father, I am so happy'. The few tears caused by a paternal love
still in its early stages, took on a symbolic power through their very
rarity.[12] The tears of the father bore witness to a new exchange of
sentiments which overwhelmed his children. By the replacement
of paternal authority, violence and arbitrary decisions with the
gentle appeal of the emotions, filial obedience was given a natural
foundation.

The mother was most often, in the novels of the eighteenth
century, a touching and consoling figure. Her indulgence
towards the errors of her offspring was most often interpreted
by tears which she could not restrain in the face of the misery of
her own children. At first moralising, she would finish by being
unable to resist the distress of her tearful daughter who vowed to
her that she was in love: her softening would even appear to be a
consent although she might disapprove of the guilty passion. But
a daughter could not shed impure tears in the presence of her
mother, maternal compassion was too revered for her to allow
herself to appeal to it at every turn. Respect stifled the daughter's
cries but her tears did not flow any less freely onto a heart which
was rendered all-seeing by maternal love.[13] If the dishonour was
too flagrant for tears to be shared, the mother drew apart in
order to be able to weep in total freedom for the fault which
would cause the death of its perpetrator in the extremes of her
misery.[14] The flow of tears around the family, a subtle balance
between duty, morality and feeling, took the form, from mother
to daughter, of a predominance of the heart which they attempted
to moderate at the same time. This ounce of respect mediatized
emotion, created twists and transformed gestures. Restraint and
modesty functioned like second nature (which at that time was
called Nature) and made a skilfully regulated picture of the act
of weeping. There was no fear in novel writing of presenting the
effusions of a son for his mother, as they indicated the return
to virtue. The hero of Cazotte after his misadventures with the
infamous 'loving Devil' behaved thus at his mother's feet: 'Ah! I
cried out, my eyes filled with tears, my voice rough with sobs,
my mother! my mother! I wished to speak but I could not, I flung
myself at her hands bathing them with tears, and covering them
with the most impassioned caresses'.[15] The excess of emotion
over the image of the mother was to be found also in memoirs. If
mothers gave tears to their beloved children, they returned them
in full. They would rush to console her over her unhappinesses,

and it was sometimes enough to evoke her name for them to shed tears of tenderness. It was also a means of displaying one's goodness of spirit, but nobody at the time thought to find any fault in it. The sensitive Marmontel promoted the cult of the mother who constantly caused him emotion to such an extreme, that he would share it with anybody who was prepared to share it. Thus, in the company of the headmaster who, out of pure generosity, was giving him individual tutoring: 'At the very name of my mother, of whom I spoke to him sometimes, he appeared to breath in her soul and when I told him of her letters where maternal love led her to express her gratitude to him, his eyes overflowed with tears'.[16] Later, when he became famous after his first tragedy, he rushed to cry over his mother who would have been so happy to live such a moment. He found for the time a substitute mother in the person of Mme Harenc whom he covered in tears: 'Ah, madame! I said to her melting into tears, does she not live again, that tender mother you remind me of'.[17] Maternal love was shared with select souls. This sentiment was a sort of model which moved feeling hearts in an intimacy which was not confined to the family. The evocation of the mother was a moving theme in itself, and signified the goodness of the soul.

These family demonstrations can appear to be made up of an edifying sentimentality. These ideal ties, which tears perfected and which were regulated by morality, have lost their appeal. But the taste for sentiment which accompanied the blossoming of family feeling provided a relatively varied palette of modes of conduct. This bourgeois and healthy naturalism had found in tears a mode of expression which could be used freely in novels and personal writings. It operated through tears because they had the value of being a natural sign, just as at the time, one spoke of having the guts of a father or mother to express one's feelings towards one's children. However this nature is not uncategorised. The children have compassion, and must necessarily display this sign of attachment to their parents. Reciprocity, if it sometimes existed, was not always possible: fathers hardened themselves sometimes, unworthy tears were hidden from the mother. If maternal tears could cause emotion, those of a father wiped out all will and made the world tremble. The terms of liquid exchange proposed a micro-anthropology of the mythical family in the eighteenth century. The recourse to 'natural' signs, which were strongly mediatized, appeared to permeate the imaginary institution of the domestic world. It allowed a place for sentiment but regulated its impulses. If the heart had its reasons, it was because duty and virtue supplied it. We are not in full emotional display, but in the preregulated exchange of family affection.

IN THE BOSOM OF FRIENDSHIP

In novels, friendship remained the unconditional refuge where tender spirits could shed tears. The friend, always compassionate, forgave all errors of conduct, or at least never refused the tears which the impassioned friend shed in his arms. Thus the Marquise of Syrcé who knew all the torments of a guilty love assuaged her pain in letters which she sent to her friend: 'I spend the nights in crying, the days in controlling myself, in devouring my tears; you alone my friend, you alone receive the outpourings of my heart'.[18] Her role of confidante, useful for the progress of the narrative, required that she should not be hardened, that the friend's tears should not be rejected. Encouraging a respect for duty, Tiberge shed delicious tears over the conversion which was nevertheless without a future, of an over-enamoured friend: the sober friend of des Grieux thus shed his tears over the virtuous metamorphosis of his friend.[19] But when the latter renewed his mistakes and his torment, in spite of the advice he was offered, he did not receive any fewer tears. In this way the Chevalier de Gérac, protesting against the conduct of his friend, assured him that he would never be severe and that he would always be ready to weep for his weaknesses.[20] Indulgent towards the sinner but not towards the sins, he preferred to know all, and to console his friend constantly over the very fate from which he had attempted to deter him, rather than not be the recipient of the tears shed by the unhappy lover. It was not the friend but the guilty lover who refused an undeserved consolation: this was the tragic end for which the hero of *Les Malheurs de l'inconstance* [The misfortunes of inconstancy] destined himself, who would weep in solitude, refusing too gentle a comfort in expiation of the tears which he had caused to flow.[21]

Generally, tears were not hidden from friends. In the *La Nouvelle Héloïse* Julie reproached her cousin Claire, who had lost her husband, for keeping her unhappiness to herself alone:

I blame you for having denied your Julie, after spending your finest days in crying with her, the sweetness of crying in turn with you, and to wash away, with more worthy tears, the shame of those which she shed upon your breast. If you take some sort of pleasure from it, why do you not want me to share it? Are you unaware that the communication of hearts leaves the imprint of something on sadness which is gentle and touching and which is not to be found in contentment? And was friendship not specially given to the unhappy to ease their pain?[22]

The communication of hearts through the sharing of emotion was the most gentle of sentiments and exceeded simple joy. It could purify less virtuous tears, give hope and consolation to those who suffered. Friendship seemed then, for sensitive hearts, to have the value of a refuge. From a certain point of view, it was a rare type of circulation of tears which nothing could deflect from its course. In addition, the gentle language of friendship had less need for words than for shared tears, the search for transparency found a true metaphor in action by way of the writing desk, thanks to this blending: the image of the fusion of hearts. The friend consoled, shared, received tears, but never cost any tears of unhappiness, being the lovable and intimate, but not familial shape of compassion.

These friendly emotions are also to be found in correspondence. The capacity to be moved was the measure of friendship: Vauvenargues, learning of the illness of his friend Saint Vincens, and despite assurances of his recovery, wrote to him in these terms: 'I am still left with a worry which I cannot dispel, and all my thoughts move me to tears'.[23] Without these novelistic references, it would be hard to understand the exchange of letters between Rousseau and Diderot, at the time of their dispute, in which tears were used as a stake in a totally surprising way. At this point, the dreamed for terrain of transparency was left behind. Expressions of emotion did not require the mutual presence of the two friends, correspondence made up for it very well, if Rousseau was to be believed. He wrote on 16 March 1757: 'I have never written to you without emotion and my last letter was bathed in my tears; but at last the dryness of yours, has reached me. My eyes are dry, and my heart is closed as I write to you.' The drying up of a once liquid correspondence indicated the deep disagreement between the two friends: the change of feeling provoked some unlooked for effects of style. Diderot replied to him on 22 March: 'Oh! Rousseau you are becoming wicked, unjust, cruel, wild, and I cry with pain at it'. After these insults, the tears of Diderot were not of the type which asked for mercy. Rousseau retorted to him on the 23rd:

> Unfeeling and hard man! Two tears shed on my breast would have meant more to me than the throne of the world; but you refuse me this and content yourself with extracting them from me. Ah well, keep all that remains, I no longer want anything from you.

On 21 October he complained once more of Diderot for 'making so cheap of my tears'. It is necessary to distinguish in the rhetoric of the times, the painful tears, those which had a cost, which were exacted but not exchanged, from those which fell deliciously through tender emotion. In the final attempts at reconciliation under the auspices of Mme d'Houdetot, to whom Diderot wrote on 10 November 1757, he expressed himself thus: 'Abandon two friends to all the freedom which you would wish for in their place. If their tears do not flow or mingle without constraint, their hearts will remain sick.' This friendship which was being torn apart, between two men who could manipulate the language wonderfully well, brought into play all the liquid movement of their previous relationship and all the violence which its interruption caused, with the shedding of how many tears, with such different qualities. All this rhetoric of tears, fully used in the epistolary exchanges between the two men, gave the value of a sign to this display of feeling when the relationship was on bad terms. Tears gave an account of the suffering, opposed to past tenderness, but above all, and this was their offensive characteristic, they were evidence of the barbarity of the other. The dreamed of and legendary scene of reconciliation is recounted to us by Marmontel, who had it from Diderot himself, who confided thus: Rousseau 'was eloquent, and was more touching in his pain than he had ever been in his life. Pierced by the state in which I saw him, my eyes filled with tears. On seeing me cry, he softened and received me in his arms. We were thus reconciled'.[24] It is possible to question the degree of accepted literary formulae and the degree of reality in this second-hand account, but it is significant that the rediscovered affection should have passed through such gestures and such tears, which, especially for men, were evidence of the times.

LOVE AND LIBERTINAGE

Love affairs and the manoeuvres of seduction caused a circulation of tears in the novel which suggested a certain coherence. It was above all the lovers who shared their tears, but through the clashes and misfortunes of the protagonists, there was a whole subtle play of received tears, of tears which it was wrong to cost others, of tears which threatened to be hidden in the desert, which bore witness to the misfortunes of the pair of lovers. The ways of crying indicated the different stages of the love story: the first feelings were manifested by a teardrop which escaped, such as 'the furtive tears' of Julie and Saint-Preux.[25] The tears of the man proved the sincerity of the loving feeling. The Marquise de Syrcé explained it thus: 'See, a sigh, a tear, an expressive silence must have more power to affect us than this vain array of gallantries which have seduced only women who were not worth the trouble'.[26] A reciprocal love was declared in the mingling of tears.[27] The tears then shed for love were delightful, and were loved as the lover was loved.[28] When fate separated the lovers, they suffered tears which cost them something, and which could not be received.[29] Letters or a portrait, were bathed with tears.[30] The lover who considered herself abused and abandoned shed solitary tears, which she held back, or hid, and did not wish to be comforted, proving the depths of her despair.[31] The logic of the production of tears, thermometer of the love affair, illustrated a logic of exchange. The ideal remained the binding of the souls through tears, a dreamed-of exchange which fate caused to fail. The tragedy was on the scale of a sharing of impossible tears and of tears shed without being received, a sort of short circuit in the network of lovers' tears. Fiction sometimes presented a truth which was wiped out by the speeches of reconciliation, associating virtue with the delightful sensation of gentle tears which made its practice so comfortable. The novel reserved indeed, a broad place for the victims of virtue, for the tearing apart through passion and duty which led to painful sobbing, where tears were hidden so as not to betray a love condemned by morality, where the separated lovers suffered because they could not mingle their tears. Emotion was not always expressed, and even worse, it could sometimes be a tragic misunderstanding. The Comte de Mirbel, who was no longer attached to Sidley because of his love for the Marquise of Syrcé, visited the former to shed the

cruel tears 'which the loss of a cherished emotion can cause to
flow' at her knee, but Sidley, rather than taking fright, only saw in
them another proof of love.[32] Nothing was more terrible than this
false communication through tears. Novels, though they extolled
virtue with emphasis and tears, were only rarely sentimental: the
young women drowned in tears in the depths of their convent,
unhappy lovers saw their mistresses die while bathing them with
their tears, betrayed women ended their lives in the desert in
unshared tears, virtuous wives devoured them beside a husband
who was unfaithful. Novel writers did not use the happy ending
excessively. The indestructible goodness of the human heart was
far from always having its just reward on this earth: prejudices,
vices and betrayals made its life hard. However, it was the events,
the requirements of duty which put tearful communication into
jeopardy: those who loved would one day mingle their tears.

In the novel of the heart, the libertine, often present, was
the opposite figure to the lover. He fed on the tears of his
victims like a vampire. This category of male parasitic behaviour
revealed itself to be all the more dangerous because the seducer
made use of tears to achieve his ends. The fortune hunter knew
how to seduce women with false tears, shed at the feet of the
victims whom he would abandon after they had given in to
him. It mattered little that they ended their days weeping in a
desert. 'They resemble conquerors, like them, they revel in tears
and would shed blood like them if they were not on the whole
more cowardly than they are vain'.[33] He who cruelly caused the
shedding of tears was thirsty for blood: these two essential fluids
would often be associated with each other in the rhetoric of the
denunciation of cruelty. In the network of the communication
of feelings, the libertine short-circuited the exchange, paying out
tears as one pays lip service, costing tears which his indifference
allowed to flow without feeling any need to staunch them. He
also knew how to cause tears, in order to soften his prey which
he then only had to harvest. Gallantry from that moment became
confined to barbarity. The seducer manipulated the codes while
perverting them for his personal gain. His mastery was such that
he displayed the signs of sensitivity without being affected by
them just as the courtesan fitted her movements to a strategy, but
in order to benefit, not from royal generosity, but from the charms
of a woman who was often virtuous and sensitive. This practice of
libertinage was not an easy thing, if Versac, the little master, was to

be believed when he initiated the hero of the *Egarements du coeur et de l'esprit* [aberrations of the heart and soul] in the manoeuvres of the seducer: 'To be impassioned without emotion, to cry without being moved, to torment without being jealous; these are all the roles which you must play, this is what you must be'. For this it was necessary to have a sufficiently astute mind to 'be always, and without constraint, the character which the moment demands of you'.[34]

These were the required qualities to be a perfect man of the court. Versac, the little master, made use of aristocratic manners to obtain the favours of a lady. They were the same which, as we shall see, ridiculed tearful women in the theatre. At a time when, in the playhouses, aristocrats and bourgeois shed tears, when the *Cour* no longer set the tone for the *Ville*, the little master, the libertine, caricatured the morals of the clergy in the seduction and mockery of the sentimental model. Expressing his mental agility in the tearful ritual, he benefited without giving compensation from a network whose conduct he adopted without sharing its beliefs. In addition, through his direct intervention, or through his pernicious counsels, he would often bring about death and desolation. Sometimes, however, tears were refused and he could not bring his strategy to fruition. This is what happened to Valmont when he attempted to seduce the virtuous Présidente de Tourvel: 'I declare', he wrote to his accomplice in libertinage, 'that in giving myself to this extent I had greatly counted on the help of tears: but either through a bad state of mind, or perhaps because of the effect of the difficult and continuous attention which I gave to everything, it was impossible for me to cry'.[35] The self-control which the libertine imposed on himself sometimes failed as did the plan of conduct which he had decided on, because tears which were deliberately brought about did not always respond to an infallible technique, especially when an attempt was made at perfect self-control. It was not always possible to imitate sensibility, and it was the revenge of Nature over purely strategic self-control, and one of the ruses of Laclos' novel to make the dividing line waver between morality and immorality, libertinage and feeling.

Of the love letters which were written, those of men in particular are worth retaining because they are those which are most surprising today. In 1729, Du Pont de Veyle wrote to Mlle Aïssé: 'I left you, Madame, with much grief. Your letters caught at my heart and renewed my tears'.[36] It was a good thing at that time to admit to crying over the letters of one's mistress and one did not deprive oneself of the pleasure of doing so. When Diderot wrote to Antoinette Champion, who was not a noble but a seamstress, he evoked his tears as proof of his love. 'You cherish me a lot, no doubt, but my gratefulness, my probity, [. . .] the tears which I shed when I was about to lose you, my avowals, your love, the attributes of your body, your heart and your mind, all must assure you on my behalf of an eternal return'.[37] On the occasion of a quarrel, when he returned to the formal 'vous', Diderot reproached Antoinette for not allowing him to cry freely, an attitude which he openly claimed:

> I take the step of writing to you; because in the state to which you have brought me I could not speak to you without weeping, and I have noticed that my tears bothered you. Here my sadness troubles nobody, and to devote myself to it I have no need to hide behind a door.[38]

Contrary to Antoinette Champion, that savage who obliged Diderot to cry behind closed doors, Mme Roland binds her husband to come to weep in her bosom: 'Come my friend, come to my side with confidence: allow me to collect your sighs, your tears, to share your pains'.[39] If even these tears were only ornaments of the pen, they were no less the proof of a development of masculine tears, when it was a question of proving one's love, and of an image of the couple as a unit which shared tears. Philippe Ariès has underlined the appearance, in private correspondence, of the use of the nickname and of a more familiar tone: the account of tears was no doubt part of the same movement. The new couple of sensitive souls liked to cry for love, and to tell each other of it.

The judicial archives occasionally supply evidence of a portrayal of the tears of love in popular Parisian circles. The tale in these cases was born of drama, when pregnant women were abandoned by their lovers. These women who complained to the law that they had been seduced went back in time to recreate a story of love betrayed. Their tears were a part of the idyll and were evidence. The tears demonstrated the sincerity of the man's love: those who made use of them, and who later abandoned their lover were classed as odious seducers. Arlette Farge[40] quotes as follows:

> Françoise Anne Leclerc lodged a complaint against Etienne Devillard, citizen of Geneva, working in Paris, declaring that he pretended to burn with a true flame and made use of the finest arts of seduction in order to touch her heart: politeness, honesty, prayers, tears, promises

or for another the act played by a gentleman's valet for a kitchenmaid:

> he did not omit to speak to her on every possible occasion, imperceptibly he allowed her to infer that he thought of her as a future wife and forgot nothing in persuading her, he wept, calling her his dear wife, telling her that she was pretty, fresh as a rose.

Beside these gentle words and avowals, the tears provided the proofs of love on which these young women relied. But their lovers did not keep their word, their tears were nothing but artifice and ruse.

These rules of intimate circulation in which parents and children, lovers and libertines, confidants or estranged friends feature, translated, in the ways of weeping together, the different types of private relationship. Mingled or hidden, exchanged or exacted, tears pointed out the strategies as the duties and the rights of the heart. Sentimental novels, letters and memoirs constantly drew the new *Carte du Tendre*, which, tragic, passionate or familial, could not exist without emotional expression. The language of tears offered appropriate combinations for the description of natural attraction between intimates and of the obstacles they encountered. Thermometer of emotional temperatures, these tears opened up the network of ties and the quality of feelings to be read.

GENERALISED EXCHANGES

The sharing of emotion exceeded the circle of familiar faces. The propensity to cry over the misfortunes of a stranger, which was considered natural, led to charity. Compassion brought about phenomena of contagion: tears were communicated to a large or small assembly. Even if they were a human virtue, tears circulated like a universal language all over the surface of the planet. The exchange of tears spread and became generalised, relationships were established in favour of emotion.

At trials, the talent of the lawyer appeared to stem largely from his ability to move his listeners. People would allow themselves to be moved as a group by the suffering of others and liked to show their emotion in this. It would grow in a group of strangers, and induce a contagion of tears to great effect. The young lawyer, cousin of Edmé Rétif, even managed to make the judge weep. Defending a mother neglected by her children, he declared: 'She wishes only for bread, her weeping will moisten it if what they give is too hard'. Rétif de la Bretonne then went on to his commentary and explained the effect of this high-flown metaphor: 'these words, far more touching and full of life for the country folk than a town dweller can imagine, aroused the tears of the entire assembly: only the children had dry eyes'.[41] From the weeping gathering only the unworthy children who lacked the most simple filial piety were excluded. In both cases, pity was the essential spring of action on collective emotion. The victims of injustice and of insensitivity thus saw themselves surrounded by the tears of public opinion. Liquid circulation appeared to bind these ephemeral gatherings.

Still further, the language of tears and of pain was supposed to have a universal significance. No human being should have been able to remain unmoved by it. The unhappy Zilia in *Lettres d'une péruvienne* [letters of a Peruvian woman], a priestess kidnapped from the Temple of the Sun by the Spaniards, wrote to her lover Aza:

Far from being moved by my cries, my ravishers are not even touched by my tears; deaf to my language, they can hear the cries of my despair no better. What people is savage enough to remain unmoved by signs of distress? What arid desert saw the birth of such humans so insensitive to the voice of trembling nature?[42]

The level of savagery was demonstrated by this contempt for tears, the natural language. This human appeal had the value of a categorical command and by its yardstick the savage was not always the one we might expect. This implicit philosophy which sustained the success of tales of travel was often made use of. 'It is barbarous to cause tears in another', it was often written, but the barbarian was not the savage here.

How many gentle tears have flowed as a result of charity! 'There is no comparable luxury to that of the experience of damp eyes after having given relief to the unfortunate' declared L.S. Mercier.[43] In giving succour to the unfortunate, characters would experience a pleasant emotion which demonstrated to each of them that virtue carried its own reward. In novels of feeling, the charitable scene took the form of a touching scene which brought about obligatory movements: compassion, help, gratitude of the unfortunate in tears, delightful emotions on both sides. In *Dorval ou Mémoires pour servir à l'histoire des moeurs au XVIIIe siècle* [Dorval or a contribution to the History of Manners in the eighteenth century], the scene of charity lasted for many pages. A woman was weeping, Dorval wished to aid her and the tears which filled his eyes were evidence of his warm and honest interest. A change of scene, the sick husband wept over his children who were dying of hunger. His wife who had just received Dorval's aid, told him of the good news, her face bathed with tears. Dorval entered, filled with emotion, moved to tears, the husband bathed his hand with tears and so on.[44] The charitable scene changed tears of unhappiness to those of pleasure: nobody feared to linger over each stage of this marvellous transformation.

The libertine himself could not contain his tears when he took part in a scene of charity. Thus, Valmont, who was playing at good morals in order to seduce the virtuous Présidente de Tourvel, could not resist the sight of the family whom he had just rescued with the sole aim that the said Présidente should know about it: 'A few tears of gratitude fell from the eyes of the ancient head of the family and ornamented his patriarchal face [. . .]. I will admit to my weakness; my eyes were damp with tears, and I felt inside myself an involuntary movement which was nevertheless delightful'.[45] Surprised at the pleasure which doing good could bring, he was divided between this unmastered feeling and his libertine's logic, his icy self-discipline which made a weakness of it. These remains of sensitivity in a man who despised virtue were a flaw into which the human element slipped, distinguishing him from La Merteuil who had long exercised herself in suppressing all signs of joy and sorrow, and in whom, as Baudelaire said, 'All which is human has become fossilised'.[46] This delightful turmoil caused by tears was the sign of a natural pity. But the episode was ambiguous as Valmont was playing on two levels: he experienced pleasure in doing good while thinking of evil as he wished to make the virtuous Présidente de Tourvel succumb to him by creating for himself the reputation of a sensitive benefactor.

Diderot presented rather ironically the feeling of charity born of pity when presented by sorrow, as a physical impulse which could not be resisted: 'My guts were filled with compassion, tears came to my eyes', declared Jacques le Fataliste in his account of the help he gave to a poor family, to the point of ignoring his own needs and finding himself pretty stupid when he could not pay his own surgeon.[47] Charity resembled a performance where the spectator who was moved became an actor. This theory of compassion and of natural sympathy came from Shaftsbury and from the Abbé du Bos who made it one of the bases of society. Thus he wrote, 'the tears of a stranger move us even before we know the reason for them. The cries of a man who is bound to us only by humanity make us fly to his rescue in a mechanical movement which precedes all thought'.[48]

The principle of compassion was fully examined. In his essay on the origin of languages, Rousseau insisted on the fact that language was more striking than the vision of suffering: 'Imagine a perfectly known situation of pain; in seeing the afflicted person you will find it difficult to be moved to the point of tears, but leave him the chance to tell you of all that he feels, and you will soon dissolve into tears'. Sounds made us shiver and penetrated to the depths of our hearts. For him, aural sensitivity was superior to vision when it was a question of emotion: it would 'strike with redoubled force'.[49] This is why scenes of tragedy were effective. The natural sense of pity was then degraded by the habit of theatre in corrupt societies. In the New Héloïse, Julie compared the beggar to the actor: 'If we wish to consider him according to talent why should I not reward the eloquence of this beggar who stirs my heart and moves me to help him as I pay an actor who makes me weep?'[50] Julie tended to prove that there was no more reason to pay an actor than a beggar. The proposition was here considerably less euphoric, since the unfortunate had to give a performance of poverty likely to cause the same effects as the eloquence of an actor. Pity was subordinated to self-esteem, to appearance: the simple cry of nature was no longer enough, art had to be brought into play in order to cause emotion in others. Beside a charity which remained dominated by a relationship between two individuals, I seem to detect the emergence of a sensitivity to organised charity, a response to a social problem as it was treated at the time. The diary of the Abbé Mulot bore this out in 1782:

> I saw a most moving picture, souls who were affected by the sight of it could not prevent themselves from shedding several tears over it. M. Bureau, building entrepreneur, a thoroughly honest and too little-known man took me to Vaugirard, to the hospice where they receive women and children infected by venereal disease.[51]

We may marvel at these remarks found together: the delightful emotion and the centre for venereal disease associated in this way, give a strange effect. But this capacity to be moved by good administrative works was to be found, according to Tocqueville, in the correspondence of the assistant commissioners to their superiors in the reign of Louis XVI. One of them complained at experiencing 'in the exercise of his duties a pain which was poignant to a sensitive soul'. And these transports, far from displeasing, rather increased one's standing in the halls of power.[52] Speaking of Necker's *Compte rendu* [report], when he was called to administer the finances of France, Rabout-Saint-Etienne expressed himself thus:

> This book passed into everybody's hands; it was read in villages and in hamlets. It was looked through with curiosity, its brief pages on which at last the expenditure of the French nation was set down were devoured by the people. Tears dampened those pages which a citizen minister had imprinted with luminous and consoling reflections, where he took care of the happiness of the French with a sensitivity worthy of all their gratitude. In this mixture of effusiveness and good administration, which rings strangely to our ears, we must no doubt perceive the association of a model of charity with an ideology of the common good. The speeches which date from the French Revolution furnish us with other, more aggressive, examples, but the first fruits of this tendency were not lacking in salt, and above all not in tears.[53]

It was a compassion which was made general to embrace the whole of humanity and which made L.S. Mercier weep copiously: 'All the misfortunes which beset the human race, all the troubles which ruin it and devour it, were retraced in a crowd in my memory; I sighed and the bittersweet blade of pity wounded my heart deliciously. Burning tears flowed down my cheeks'.[54] This representation of collective sorrow, in the solitude of the man of letters' study, allowed L.S. Mercier to invest himself with a mission by weeping hot tears. The sensation, simultaneously delightful and sharp, was only developed in the context of its universal value of shared suffering made sublime. This damp grandiloquence was not immodest because it included the whole of humanity.

In enlarging the circle of the exchange of tears, one could see a certain philosophy of human sentiments being sketched out, which demanded that we should be moved by the sorrows of others through expressive signs. In novels, this social aptitude was translated by precise situations. They illustrated the notion of sociability which was used in the writings of the eighteenth century, whose shape was vast, if not vague. Its semantic field associated it with nature, with virtue, with happiness: sociability was natural: 'Virtue is really no more than sociability', and finally, sociability was a tendency to consider the happiness of others to be as important and indispensable as one's own happiness.[55] It was thus natural to be virtuously moved by a being which was suffering. Charity was related to the natural sociability of the human being; it was, Robert Mauzi told us, 'sociability which has become system and action',[56] indispensable to social and individual happiness. The manifestation of emotion was developed to the point of invading writings where one might not expect to find it. This propensity to weep over strangers or humanitarian principles, which has since then been somewhat ridiculed, was then an affirmation of a new sensitivity to unhappiness and pain. It found in effusiveness the proof of its natural foundation. In this perspective, compassion, charity, the infection of a gathering, a feeling of humanity, which led to the flow of so many tears in the eighteenth century, were all part of the same field of thought where sociability could not be conceived without the notion of pity, in all its philosophical dignity, which overwhelmed the hierarchies of a society of order. 'What is generosity, clemency, humanity, if it is not pity applied to the weak, to the guilty, or to the human race in general?' wrote Rousseau in the *Discours sur l'origine et les fondements de l'inégalité parmi les hommes* [Discourse on the origin and the foundations of inequality among men].[57]

This participation through tears in the suffering of others which, once the remedy was supplied, were transformed to delightful tears, this more general emotion concerning the ills of humanity indicated a new relationship with others regulated by emotional identification. Philanthropic optimism was not yet controlled by modesty: it produced demonstrative signals. The model of natural sociability, this was an age of pity in which the visibility of emotion remained central.

3 On the Polite Code of Emotion

Sensibility and its obligatory procession of tears in the eighteenth century made up a nebulous entity whose contours are hard to distinguish. Certainly 'it is sweet to cry' and we allow ourselves to exalt this pleasure. But it was not always bathed in pure euphoria. Mlle de Lespinasse suffered from her capacity to be moved and shed painful tears. Some distinguished the bittersweet character of the tears they shed, others leaned towards the extreme states where sensitivity borders on deficiency: weakness, crisis and convulsions. The triumphant praises which were certainly numerous, were accompanied by rarer but more discussed concern. Men of letters sought to define a polite code of tears and distinguished their respective qualities with precision. The art of crying had its nuances, its stakes and its limits. One should not necessarily give in to a child which demonstrated its will through tears. A woman could shed the tears of a coquette, or have attacks of the vapours. Beside the beautiful exalted emotions which were described with a great wealth of detail, medical and educational discourses, or, more simply, worldly mockery, traced the limits of acceptability.

THE PLEASURE OF TEARS

Shared tears were delightful: solitary emotion also had its dignity. These tears shed in isolation formed a favoured experience which accounted for the impulses of the spirit, thanks to the voluptuous sensations which they brought about. This type of demonstration represented a relationship within the self which had no real precedent. To cry was 'a sort of sweetness', 'when the heart is truly touched, it takes pleasure in all which provides it with proof of its own sensitivity', wrote Mme du Tencin in 1735, in *Les Mémoires du comte de Comminges*, a novel which was later adapted for the theatre. This emotion in a happy heart required a witness and the act of crying to be revealed. Even when alone this trace of a secretion, with a delightful sensation, extracted a noble humour

38

from the body and acted as an indication of the spirit. This out-pouring seems to indicate that at that time, there was little question of a pure unmoving interiorisation of the emotions, with no external manifestations and that psycho-physiological fiction was superbly disregarding of such a thing. The subjective experience of tears presented pleasure as a blend of the body and the mind, both sensation and internal movement, it was the discovery of the self, the happiness of feeling one's existence. To cry in private was also to know how to 'take pleasure in oneself'. In 1728, Prévost made a subtle definition within the combined sensation of pain and pleasure.

> If tears and sighs cannot bear the name of pleasures, it is nevertheless true that they have an infinite sweetness for someone who is mortally afflicted. Each moment which I devoted to my pain was so dear to me that I took no rest so that I could prolong them.[1]

This deliberate seeking out of the impulses which upset the heart was not only a magnification of pain. In the midst of torments a gentle impression born of affliction and agreeable to maintain grew up. It did not act so much as an outlet but rather as a delight in the self which was revealed through sweet sensations. The taste for tears, even in private was already widespread in the first half of the eighteenth century. Long considered in the light of pre-romanticism, Monglond describes this phenomenon as the appearance of a 'masturbation of the emotions' accompanied by the classic 'it was Rousseau's fault'. Men and women of learning did not wait for Rousseau in their celebration of the tears shed by a sensitive spirit 'into a crystal fountain' in a private place. On the other hand, the 'Rousseau effect' was evidence of the spread of such a model among anonymous readers. This fashion was not accepted by all: in the eighteenth century Mme du Deffand and Mme de Genlis despised the Rousseau-like flights and did not hesitate to say so.

In the *Confessions*, Rousseau mingled emotion with pain. Paul Trahard has enumerated the different sorts of tears to be found in this work, and concluded that the writer's capacity for suffering was infinite.[2] Music, a son or the visit to a favourite place, would awaken a childhood memory which would make him weep. This dive into the history of a subject was part of the autobiographical enterprise and indicated a different relationship with the emotions. He has often been accused of complacency, and in his account of his journey to Vevey, he presented himself with a certain humour:

> My heart ardently flung itself into a thousand innocent pleasures; I was moved, I sighed and wept like a child. How many times, when I halted to cry at my ease, seated on a large stone, did I take pleasure in watching my tears fall into the water.[3]

This light and untroubled joy led him to play with tears, to observe the bodily humour and the natural element become one. This pleasure in a walk which evoked his delightful tears led to strange attitudes which were not put on. Contact with nature was a return to innocence. Rousseau developed the idea of sweetness caused by tears in the midst of moral suffering in the *Nouvelle Héloïse*, through the voice of Saint-Preux. 'There my lively unrest began to take a new course, a more gentle emotion entered my mind, emotion overcame despair, I began to weep torrents of tears, and this state, compared with that which I had just left, was not without a few pleasures'.[4] Emotion soothed the contradictory impulses and led to the mixed sensation already analysed by Prévost. Rousseau's originality came at the end of his text, where he told of his profound rapture born of the combination of the two separate emotions:

> I cried loud and long, and was soothed. When I felt quite recovered, I came to Julie, I took her hand. She was holding her handkerchief, I could feel that it was very damp 'Ah!', I said to her very quietly, 'I see that our hearts have never ceased to understand each other!'

Even more than mingled tears, this encounter of two hearts who wept in solitude at the same moment, was a summit, a suspension in subjective transparency. The damp communication through the medium of the handkerchief created a delicious moment. For solitary emotion was sometimes a compensation for the impossibility of encountering a spirit with whom to share the experience. Replying to one of those solitary readers, Rousseau demonstrated both the inadequacy of an unshared emotion and the comfort which it could give. He knew to what extent 'the need for attachment means that the sensitive heart is afflicted by the impossibility of forming one' but this sad idea has its sweetness: it 'leads to the flowing of a stream of tears, it leads to a melancholy which tells us about our own characters'.[5] This gentle feeling of being one's own representative to the self was only possible through an outpouring which proved one's existence through the sensations which it excited.

The letters exchanged between sensitive hearts constantly analysed these delicate emotions. In his correspondence the Prince de Ligne told of a solitary meditation on a high promontory of the Crimea which led him to tears.

> My reflections, which take me out of time, return me to the time of my heart. I find that nothing down here can remain in perfect stagnation and that once an empire, a power is no longer expanding, it diminishes in the same way that on the day on which we do not love more, we love less. My heart! What have I said? Is it the sight of my heart or that of nature which transports me outside myself? I melt into tears without knowing why; but how sweet they are! It is a common emotion, it is an outpouring of sensibility, which cannot identify its object. At this moment where so many ideas meet, I cry without sadness.[6]

Starting with a traditional discourse on the ravages of time and the ruins which are left to us by history, the Prince de Ligne was diverted towards the transient state of his being. This subjective experience of an individual dissolving into gentle tears seems to me to indicate a concept of the intimate which was perhaps initiated by Rousseau: the experiencing of existence was accompanied by the impression of not belonging to oneself. Between the heart and Nature the boundaries were no longer distinct. People would cry for no reason, they could not find out what the object of their emotional outburst was, they saw the meeting of ideas, they were transported beyond themselves, but they still wrote of it and described it with lyricism, as though this favoured moment had a fundamental significance for subjectiveness.

The physical expressions of solitary pain could certainly result occasionally in a demonstrative hypertrophy, accompanied by excessive remarks praising th pleasure of tears in an exaggerated fashion, but this impulse was the sign of a strong demand from the literary public. Baculard d'Arnaud, indeed, reached new heights

in speaking directly of 'the expression of the pleasure of the soul'.[7]
Following in the steps of Rousseau's novel of the feelings, he
accentuated this characteristic: feelings were putting on weight.[8]
Loaisel de Tréogate made his hero Milcourt say, on the death of his
lover, that he remained alive because: 'if I were to die, then I would
no longer cry, and it is a pleasure to weep'.[9] The taste for shadows
for the dark and for tears which fell on tombs accompanied this
'sensational' fashion of the final years of the *Ancien Régime*. This
novelistic genre was contemporary with the fashionable pilgrimage to Ermenonville, where people came to shed delightful tears
over Rousseau's ashes. The few years which preceded the Revolution developed the pretentions of tears to such a point, it is true,
that such an exaltation moved away from all the nuances which
had been developed until that time. Just as Darnton's studies on
the literary gipsy show the spread of philosophical ideas, simpli-
fied and exaggerated by many lampooners, we may imagine that
the model of the feelings spread without gaining in finesse.

THE PHYSIOLOGICAL DETERMINATIONS OF SENSIBILITY: THE FAINTING WOMAN AND THE MECHANICAL MAN

We should not read, in this overflow of tears, a cult which
was given over to bodily expression in all its forms. Some
extreme states were disquieting because the excess of pain
could bring about death, or more simply make life meaningless.
From illness to mediocrity, the loss of balance between body and
soul permeated the writings of the eighteenth century. In this,
certain critical states could appear worrying. The body of the
virtuous Présidente de Tourvel was transformed in this way by
the torments of her guilty love. Valmont described her thus:

> Imagine a seated lady, remarkably stiff, and with an unchanging
> face, who appeared neither to think, listen, nor hear, whose
> staring eyes allowed almost continuous tears to escape but
> which flowed effortlessly [. . .] after this apparent apathy
> there followed terror, suffocation, convulsions, sobs, and a
> few occasional cries, but without a word spoken.[10]

Passing from apathy to convulsions, the Présidente withdrew
from herself, her body was as though possessed by a strange force

which nothing could hold back. The inability to feel, followed
by the fury of a body which rebelled following a paroxysm of
moral and emotional despair, did not allow for self-analysis or
for the agonies of a tormented soul. The collapse of reason was
complete under flowing tears and smothering sobs. All presence
of humanity disappeared, others could not give comfort, language
vanished. This exteriorisation of the self which referred back to the
episode of the convulsions at Saint-Médard, was apparently part of
a creation which was soon to disappear. The excess of suffering
warned of the approaching end of the Présidente.

In memoirs or correspondence we encounter a far more
benign phenomenon in the vapours. Marmontel's lover was
subject to them, and at the time would shed abundant tears:

> When she was at her most brilliant in playfulness and health,
> the attacks would take the form of bursts of uncontrolled
> laughter; after the laughter, all her limbs would become rigid,
> she would tremble and move convulsively and this would end
> in tears. These troubles were more painful to me than her; but
> they made her even dearer and more fascinating to me.[11]

This passage from laughter to tears was a sign of nervous
disorders.[12] For Mme de Graffigny and Voltaire, her host at Cirey,
who were both sufferers, this problem was most annoying: 'I do
not know where these vapours come from, for it is certainly not
from the mind. Ah! My friend, why were we born sensitive?'[13] In
her search for the source of her ills, Mme de Graffigny complained
of her sufferings, but by situating them in the domain of sensibility,
she reserved them for élite spirits, who of course had all their wits.
The changing nature of Voltaire's moods was indeed a subject on
which they constantly asked questions: was it connected to his
genius, to his humanity? Marmontel very much enjoyed the sight
of Voltaire passing from laughter to tears and distinguished 'in
this great man, the ease of the child in passing from one extreme
to another in the passions which troubled him'.[14] Rousseau, in
the *Confessions* told of similar nervous crises and made certain
observations concerning them which were not without subtlety:

> The vapours are the illness of contented people, they were
> mine. The tears which I shed, often without reason, the lively
> fears at the sound of a leaf or of a bird, the uneven nature of

my humours in the peace of the best life, all this showed the
disgust of well-being which made me, so to speak, wildly exaggerate my sensibilities.[15]

The vapours which led to tears without cause provoked a state
of hyper-aesthetics of the senses, of sudden changes of mood.
Sensitivity wandered, both from the point of view of the emotions
and the sensations. This extravagance was born of ennui aroused
by too comfortable a state of happiness.

Diderot took pleasure in defining the status of emotions and
little by little he built up an organic vision of sensitivity for
himself, starting from the theories of Bordeu and of the doctors
of the Montpellier school. This scientific picture was constructed
on the pattern of the circulation of the blood. Moreover Diderot
wanted a reformation of morals and revolted against the practices
of a vaporous nation suffering from an excess of refinement. He
therefore relied on his medical knowledge to support his analysis
of the emotions. Excessive instability of emotions did not appear
to him to be very dignified. In *Le Rêve d'Alembert* [D'Alembert's
dream], Bordeu also demonstrated to Julie de Lespinasse that in
spending her time laughing and weeping she was condemning
herself to remaining no more than a child. The sensitive being
who placed himself at the mercy of his diaphragm, of the extreme
movements of the nerve endings which were attached to this centre of mobility, was condemning himself to mediocrity. Mme de
Lespinasse recognised herself in this portrait. Immediately moved
by a word or a touching sight which would provoke an interior
tumult of tears, shivering and suffocation, the sensitive person
lost all his or her faculties. Emotion would rise from the bowels
to the head, from the diaphragm to the brain which was no longer
the controlling centre. 'The originator of the impulses no longer
knows what is happening to him'.[16] The vapours then, for Diderot,
were a sort of anarchy of the fibres which particularly affected
women, and made up 'the picture of a feeble administration, in
which everyone takes over the authority of the master'. Harmonic
souls led to men whose fibres would tremble quickly and with
vivacity: 'They are like those weak spirits who cannot listen to
a tale of misfortune without shedding tears over it and for whom
there is no bad tragedy'.[17] The man who was born sensitive must
also learn to direct his impulses: his fibres which entered too easily
into resonance with the exterior elements would deprive him of

all capacity for judgement and reason and threaten him with a meaningless and sterile life. But conversely, the man who had an inflexible diaphragm had a hard heart. 'The head makes wise men; the diaphragm gives compassion and moral sense', wrote Diderot in his refutation of the work of Helvétius.[18] Sensitivity might need to be directed, but it was also indispensable to the dignity of man and to the communication between a man and his fellows. Tears revealed sociability and the true nature of relationships. An extreme sensitivity did not make great men, but with the help of emotion it was possible to create moral and 'sentimental' habits which led to kindness. Sensitivity thus had a dual status: we shall see the effects of it on his theory of theatre.

The digestive theory was taken up again by Fouquet, for the article on Sensibility in the *Encyclopédie*. The sensation of pleasure caused an expansion of the sensitive spirit throughout the body increasing its perceptive surface and receiving a surfeit of experience, whereas pain concentrated the sensitive spirit in the kernel of the body 'whose functions it left to decline'. One could then consider that tears of joy, according to this article, were an expansion of the soul and body which exceeded their 'normal limits' while causing a feeling of voluptuous pleasure. Tears of sadness were, on the other hand, a contraction whose effects on health appear to have been negative. Women and children were more sensitive because of the 'suppleness, the freshness and the slenderness of their mucous tissue', more compact than in the adult male. The excessive sensibility of children made them subject to convulsions and spasms. That of women, whose constitution was similar to that of children, was very acute. One of these nervous centres was the womb, which caused fits in women. This illness, reserved by nature for this sex, had affected men because of their habits of 'luxury and softness'. The physical constitution, determined by age and sex, but also transformed by moral behaviour, mapped out the limits of the developed sensibility.

An evil which, according to L.S. Mercier, was to be feared even more than emotional excesses, was the absence of the tears which are part of melancholy.

Who can know the sufferings of the unfortunate being whose nerves are too strained or too relaxed, and have lost their stability? [. . .] sombre melancholy withers his heart, no more tears, no more laughter, no more emotion; the hours of life are slow and cruel for him; he can literally neither live nor die.[19]

This distress, combined with a lack of balance of the nervous fibres, produced a kind of living dead. Here, the neuro-physiological model, unlike that of Diderot, was more mechanistic than animistic in nature. It remains that illnesses of sensibility were related to the state of the body, to the disharmonious tension which reigned between the forces which inhabited it.

In the eighteenth century, weeping might be popular, but it was not without discernment. A balance was sought between cold lucidity, apathy and the convulsive movements of an unstable temperament. It was important that the constitution of the fibres of the body should not determine its sensitivity. Its aim, which was not without a certain mastery, gave it value. Some saw in this controlled sensibility the signs of a superior status. It was perhaps this thought which guided Delisle de la Sales when he wrote: 'A man who has the gift of great sensitivity is often more master of himself than the man whose temperament is as cold as cold reason'.[20]

A CHILDHOOD OF SENSIBILITY AND SENSIBILITY TOWARDS CHILDHOOD

In the novel, the figure of the unhappy child led to emotion in adults, through its innocence and weakness. The picture of poverty was sure to triumph if its touching victims were children. They were touching because they needed protection. Private letters show the attention which was given to the health of children.[21] Collé's *Journal* brings us, on this subject, a private picture which was a full representation of the new feeling for childhood and family affections in noble circles. The children of the Duc d'Orléans had to be vaccinated against smallpox:

A few days before the inoculation the Duchesse d'Orléans wept in front of her husband who said to her, 'Madame, although I have taken my decision, if you do not wish for, or consent to this inoculation, it will not be done; they are your children as much as mine': 'Ah, Husband', she replied, 'Inoculate them, and leave me to weep'.[22]

The modern concern for the care of children's health was accompanied by a maternal sensitivity to their suffering, a constant solicitude for them. The tears which were shed over children were not reserved for an élite or those who escaped a precarious existence of perpetual dangers. On the occasion of the children's kidnappings which caused the riot of 1750, parents, (and not only the mothers) wept for their lost sons, once the moment of surprise had passed, and displayed the utmost sorrow.[23]

BRINGING UP A CHILD

Children could cause tears, but parents were also careful of their education. It was important that they should not weep wildly nor use their cries as a weapon against the will of adults. In *La Nouvelle Héloïse*, Saint-Preux had no particular feeling of tenderness towards the tears of children, and he praised Julie, who persuaded her little boy, who at first cried a lot, to be quiet so he could no longer be heard in the house. For a child must not grow used to pretence but should confine himself to the simple cries of Nature. Rousseau's *Emile* gave a full explanation of this schooling of the demonstrations of sorrow. His many directions for the education of tears showed their importance in his eyes. The young child would express his discomfort with signs, by a language which was unspoken but 'heightened by intelligible sounds'. He would cry frequently, 'this was as it should be' as natural language was the origin of spoken languages. And a child freed of his clothes which hampered him would cry less. The tears of the child, and his cries, were primitive displays of the use of signs but his tears constituted the first step towards his incorporation into the social order. The first tears of the child were prayers but if care was not taken they could become orders. The first years of childhood were the age of 'authority and servitude'. Before being able to speak, the child commanded through tears, before being able to act, he obeyed. To calm him, he would be flattered, he would be threatened or beaten to make him be quiet: he could only give orders or receive them. After fragility and dependency came the idea of authority and domination, he outgrew the age of nature. If the child became 'master' all was lost. Education took after socio-politics, it repeated the stages of the history of humanity. It was necessary to uncover the intentions of

the child, to know how to recognise why he cried, and to remain
unmoved by tears shed out of habit or obstinacy. Certain tears
should not be given in to, so that the child should not develop
the bad habit of allowing his whims free rein. One should simply
take account of signs of pain and be attentive to the necessity to
respond to them. Children were thus accustomed to crying only
for good reason, because they did not like to go to unnecessary
trouble. As soon as children began to speak, they would cry less
because they could give a verbal account of their suffering or
their needs.[24] The education of the ways of crying concerned
the learning of the rules of a language.

The gentle tears which were caused by emotion did not have
the same status. Rousseau in the *Confessions*, portrayed himself as
gifted from an early age with a precocious sensitivity. 'I may be
laughed at for presenting myself modestly as a prodigy. Be that as
it may: once you have laughed your fill, find me a child of six who
is attracted to novels, and who is interested to the point of crying
burning tears over them'.[25] With the help of the novel, Rousseau
demonstrated a maturity of mind and heart which raised emotion
to a moral and aesthetic level. These effects of reading, which
were exceptional for a child of that age, stood out; they were
the revelation of the imagination's awareness of itself. Nature was
already cultivated like Julie's orchard at Clarens. Sensibility was,
above all, the nurturing of subjectivity.

THE AGES OF LIFE

Rousseau recorded that, at a critical age, he had experienced
vague troubles which were the expression of dissatisfaction. 'I
thus reached my sixteenth year, disturbed, discontented with
everything and with myself, unaware of my state, devoured with
desires for an unknown object, weeping without reason, sighing
without knowing why'.[26] Was this the discovery of adolescence,
or the Iron Age of a tale of life which took the form of the four
Ages of humanity?[27] This feeling of a lack of achievement, these
unprovoked tears were evidence of a lack of balance, of an as yet
undetermined and painful sensibility but also of the sufferings of
a sensitive heart which endured loneliness. The moment of the
break with childhood was the departure of the young Rousseau
from Geneva. In *Emile* it corresponded with the beginning of

puberty. It was the moment at which Emile had to leave to discover the world before he married Sophie. At this time, he shed torrents of tears, while Sophie, his betrothed, adopted a discreet and modest demeanour which to the narrator at least appeared more touching 'than the troublesome complaints and the noisy regrets of her lover'.[28] This female discretion of which Rousseau was one of the most fervent partisans, this modesty which he would have liked to see adopted by women, should be developed through education. A certain restraint in the presentation of emotion was one of the precious qualities of the ideal young lady.

Diderot connected the state of sensibility with the ages of life: 'There comes a moment when almost all young ladies and gentlemen fall into a depression, they are tormented by a vague disquiet which envelops everything, and which finds no balm. They seek out solitude; they weep, the silence of the cloisters moves them'.[29] He set apart the languishings which belonged to this transitional period between childhood and adulthood, and maintained in parallel that an excessive sensibility could only be corrected by age which tended to dry out the fibres.[30]

FEMALE TEARS

Comments on women in general, and in particular on their capacity for tears, are found in a range of accounts. The faculty of concealment in women, the incomprehensible and double aspect of their behaviour formed part of a traditional discourse on the ambivalence of femininity. The heroes of the novels of Prévost, from Des Grieux to the protector of *Une grec que moderne*, spent their time in attempting to understand their fleeing lovers and questioning the tears that they shed; were they from love, pity, repentance, lies or perfidy? It was hard for them to determine the cause of the tears of the women they loved. The forces which animated and moved them remained plunged in shadow, and the male narrator remained perplexed. In worldly discourse the picture of these women in tears swayed between that of the actress and that of a fluctuating creature who could not be grasped. The Abbé Galiani interpreted men's attitude towards these female demonstrations thus: 'We care for them, we are moved with them. Their tears whether true or false tear at our hearts; we take an interest in them, we seek to distract them, to amuse them; then we leave them alone in their apartments'.[31] What did this compassion for women's tears matter if men continued to leave them to their unhappy fate in the solitude of their private world. We notice a certain lack of consistency on their part. In this matter the idea of true or false tears appears to have been of secondary consideration. Chamfort was severe on women when he painted the portrait of a woman who had some success in society in a little philosophical dialogue:

A: Would you believe that I saw Madame de . . . weep for her friend, in the presence of fifteen people?
B: But I told you that she was a woman who was successful at everything she undertook.[32]

To know how to cry in public was part of a woman's ambition. But society acting was not the only role which women played. The best knowledge one could gain of them was to detect which one they were playing to themselves. The honest woman, on falling in love, acted to herself a theatre of sensibility, of conscience, and of duty: 'She will tremble with elevation; the dignity of her remorse will console her for her fall; it is true that she is guilty; but she is at least so with decency, in consideration of the ceremonial of tears which she sheds'.[33] Thus Marivaux did not raise the question of the truth, of the sincerity of the tears of women, but of their place in the subjective spectacle which each of them offered herself. Through the voice of a female narrator, this complexity of attitudes and of states of mind was made clear without defining itself. Marivaux made the likeable Marianne say, on being asked the cause of her tears, which only led to more: 'We girls or women, we cry freely as soon as someone mentions that we have just been crying; it is a childlike trait, like an affectation, against which we cannot defend ourselves'.[34] The girl's affliction was a mixture of naivety and clarity of vision: she was constantly nourishing and embellishing it. She reminded herself of her problems to make herself cry and thought of her parents who had died when she was very young in order to hide from herself the cause of her unhappiness: that of returning a dress which she liked. For, according to her, this inclination to make her affliction more flattering was because 'being glorious in one's own eyes, one does cowardly things and chooses not to want to know about them, concealing them under other guises'.[35] Marivaux's touch was not harsh: his use of Marianne's tender and lucid internal monologue as she acted out the play to herself and described the masks which she chose for herself, left an impression of multiplicity without determination. There was no question of a defined female psychology, but of the observation of a mobility of thought, gestures and attitudes, which were acted out in different areas, led to satisfactions and questions, reproaches and complacency, and appeared to be particularly illustrated by women.

Tears were supposed to give a charming beauty to women; if they could not restrain them, they would still end up realising what a charming effect they could have on men in this state. Women learned, however unflirtatious they were, to present a face drowned in tears. Mme de Merteuil described the young Cécile Volanges in tears to Valmont thus:

> However little account she takes of flirtatiousness I guarantee you that she will often cry: on this occasion she cried without guile [. . .] Lord, how beautiful she was! Ah! if Mary Magdalene was thus, she must have been more dangerous for Christ in her repentance than as a sinner.[36]

The tears of women did not systematically fall in value. The text of the novel paid homage to their sensitivity. We cannot neglect those great female figures whose tears, far from being a sign of weakness, expressed a virtuous and sublime strength; examples abound with Clarissa Harlove, Richardson's Pamela and Rousseau's Julie. Also the various foregoing remarks should be weighed against the multitude of weeping female characters who shone in their sensibility and their sense of duty, to the point, sometimes, of somewhat eclipsing the male characters who accompanied them. The prospering of the literary theme of the misfortunes of virtue accorded a special place to female sensibility. It was true that sometimes this vertiginous ascent of the honest and touching woman would threaten her with such a fall as those of which the virtuous heroines of de Sade were the cruel victims. He defined thus the future wife of the debauched Franval:

> a lively imagination, but a little sad, a little of that sweet melancholy which leads to a love of books and solitude, attributes

which nature only seems to bestow on those individuals which her hand has destined for misfortunes, as though to make them less bitter than that dark and touching pleasure which they sample in experiencing them, and which leads them to prefer tears to the frivolous joy of happiness, which is far less active and far less penetrating.[37]

Such was the most choice prey, and the logic of sensibility, when pushed to its extreme, called on vice.

Baculard d'Arnaud, who made no use of irony, also exalted female lovers in tears; 'How ravishing and adorable are the eyes of a lover when they are filled with tears! The heart is completely submerged in them.'[38] The tears of women allowed some writers to honour the fair sex. Bernardin de Saint-Pierre, in *Paul et Virginie* waxed lyrical: 'Everywhere you were the first to honour the innocent victims of tyranny with your tears and to make a tyrant feel remorse [. . .] Your touching tears put out the torch of superstition, and your divine smiles dissipate the cold arguments of the materialists'.[39] This vision of universal redemption through the compassion and tears of women promised a long future. The woman in tears was destined to fight all ills by her moving presence, and her unmeasurable sensitivity soothed the unhappy.

Were female novelists different from their male counterparts? Some, such as Mme Riccoboni, insisted on the quality of the tears shed by their heroines. One of them found that tears gave 'the freedom to reflect on the secret cause of the feelings which made them flow'[40] and denied having ever shed tears of pride. One felt a will to portray women with worthy tears. Mme Roland, who did not hesitate either to honour female sensibility, took an eloquent tone:

Oh you, whose fate and privileges I share, who shine for a moment on the surface of the earth which you sprinkle with the tears of sensibility, join me in blessing the powerful hand which, in the sorrows to which it made us prey, placed in us the seed of the virtues to which the world owes its happiness![41]

Coquetry or faithlessness, strategy or weakness of organisation, the figure of a woman crying gave off many reflections. Women played a role in society, or played one to themselves, and men both mocked at them and treated them with levity. The exaltation of a Brutus-like heroism bestowed a superior merit on the tears of a man. But the loving tendernesses of the literature of sentiment ornamented their tears. The virtuous and sensitive female victims occupied the front of the stage, their modest attitude had a reputation for being moving. Discourses spread at the end of the century on the saving virtues of female tears which were shed over all the globe.

THE ART OF TEARS

Sensibility was not an unmastered expression of the body, it presented itself rather like an *art de vivre* which one should know how to follow while avoiding dangerous excesses and overly direct influences on the human 'machine'. On this condition, it could become a gentle and precious experience of self-enjoyment.

Its practice referred to a selective and nuanced use which enabled that emotion to participate in happiness and led to the establishment of hierarchies. Because of this, one can understand better why children, and sometimes women, did not generally attain these heights: the tears of sensibility referred to a refined culture of the self. A series of aesthetic, ethical and even medical stakes delineated the limits of this developed sensibility.

The fashion which was known as 'sentimentalist' rather jostled this balance and these delicate emotions, borrowing hyperbole to excess. One can detect in it the signs of the diffusion of a literary model among a broader public. If for Grimm, Baculard wrote for seamstresses and modistes, it was perhaps that they found in this sentimental literature, that which, until then, the bourgeoisie and the nobility of the *salons* had reserved for themselves: those sweet tears which sensitive souls love to shed.

4   Tears in the Theatre

SENSIBILITY IN THE THEATRE AND THE
THEATRE OF SENSIBILITY

In the eighteenth century tearful displays took place in public: the theatre could play the role of a microcosm of meaning on this count. Audiences cried a lot, and took pleasure above all in being seen to cry. A fundamental movement towards emotion began in the seventeenth century and then flourished in the 1730s. It retained all its magnitude until the period of the Directoire, holding itself above the aesthetic and ideological transformations which traversed the plays of that century.

The conduct of the theatre going public of the eighteenth century was a noisy marriage of the natural and the artificial, convention and sentiment, delicious tears and the 'animated moral lesson', as L.S. Mercier writes. The elegant beauties in their boxes would weep to the point of fainting over a virtuous son and his loving and understanding father. The theatre of sensibility took place as much on stage as in the auditorium. In observing what was likely to cause emotion, we encounter what at the time were called natural feelings, a seemingly rather vague notion, but which was, on the boards, related to repetitive and conventional scenes in which private relationships were played out. One was moved in public by private feelings and there was not the least paradox in this attitude of the audience, who liked the theatrical representation of intimacy, especially in its emotive aspects. The growth of family feeling which Philippe Ariès has taught us to detect was flaunted in a demonstrative way. This emotion, lived in an ostentatious way, was paradoxically a quest for the natural, unlike later concepts which associated nature with modesty, emotion with constrained charm and which accused all excessive demonstrations of sentimentality. 'There would be much to find', writes Michel Leiris, 'in the study of these ambiguous states where it is impossible to establish to what degree there is convention or sincerity in the behaviour of the actor'.[1] The attitude of the theatrical public fitted in with this type of situation where the code appears to have facilitated and even to have provoked

54

strange outbursts. These torrents of tears which were shed are witness to another age, where feelings were lived socially.

SPECTACLE AND THE PUBLIC

The theatrical public was reputed to be turbulent, noisy and active: it reacted to the performance with liveliness, but it also knew the rules of composition of a tragedy, of prosody, and sometimes even the text of the play being performed very well. An informed audience, true, but agitated. Its docility was far from being established, its attention was given to the boxes where visits were made as in a salon, where conversations were held as in a boudoir. For the aristocracy who subscribed to boxes made it its duty to maintain a constant performance. But as Grimm said, 'the boxes do not judge, or at least, their judgement has no influence, it is the pit which decides the fate of a play'.[2] Nothing could stop them when the play allowed room for allusions and jokes, the pit would throw out witticisms which, appreciated on their own merit, would make the rounds of Paris if they were considered good enough. This occurred to such a degree that in 1751 the French Guards were posted there in an attempt to moderate the critical ardour of the pit. This episode led to a strange incident: one of the adulated actresses of the time, La Gaussin, was so moving in the role of Bérénice that a sentry, 'dissolving into tears, let fall his rifle, more touched by the performance of the actress than occupied with his duty', while from the boxes and the pit, 'floods of tears flowed everywhere'.[3]

One can ask, what then was the function of tears for this rebellious public, so ready to interrupt the play, so concerned to appear and to be noticed? For, from the first half of the eighteenth century, there was no success without tears, to the point that the critics would make the passion of the public a criterion in the report of a performance. If the performance also took place in the audience it was because conditions allowed it. Lighting, in particular, was not focused on the stage, enabling the spectator to divert himself in the auditorium., which he did not tire of doing since he could successfully play his own role. It was not until 1759 that the little masters no longer paraded on the stage, and that their bench among the actors was suppressed. The stalls were seated only in 1782. A standing public was probably more mobile and critical than a seated public and for the time it continued to weep.

This encounter between dramatic content, the performance of actors and manifestations of the emotion of the public was transformed in the course of the seventeenth century to the end of the eighteenth century. It is in observing these modifications that one can grasp the issues of these tears which the public loved to shed.

EMERGENCE AND GROUND SWELL

In the course of the seventeenth century an entire strategy of tears in the theatre[4] was gradually established which replied to a pressing demand of the public. Emotion (admiration, pity, tenderness) was nevertheless restricted in a subtle way so as not to displease or dampen the enthusiasm of the spectators. For example, overly-guilty characters who did not deserve to arouse sympathy in the public were avoided, or too-innocent victims who would provoke too violent a reaction. It was accordingly necessary to avoid shocking the audience by rendering them indignant, saddening or overwhelming them to excess. The rules of verisimilitude and of taste guided those theatrical effects likely to provoke tears.

The successes of Racine were successes of tears. He felt himself to be amply honoured when the public wept at his play: 'I cannot believe that the public should wish me ill for having given it a tragedy which has been honoured by so many tears, and of which the thirtieth performance was as successful as the first'.[5] In replacing the sublime with the tender, he announced the taste for tears which took on a precise scale in the eighteenth century. Tears of admiration lost ground to the tender emotions of love and of the family. This tendency did not please everyone. Saint Evremond wished to reconcile the two types of emotion and did not like the excessive use of tears. At the end of the seventeenth century, accounts suggest that crying at the theatre was enjoyed, but that this phenomenon was the concern above all of women, and displayed the power which their taste exercised over dramatic art. 'What did it matter to ladies whether an actor wore buskin or boot providing that they might cry', writes the author of the 'Critique of Bérénice'.[6] He accuses women of setting the tone. At the end of the seventeenth century, it was 'the fine eyes' of women whose tears were vaunted. Actresses more than actors provoked feeling through the tears which they shed. For certain commentators, the values of heroism which theatre exalted did not appear compatible with the tears of male protagonists. It was of no use to refer to Classical times, to cite the tears of Alexander, of Caesar or of Ulysses, Achilles or Hercules, the presence on stage of actors in tears excited disputes. A good part of the male public remained reticent.

In *Judith*, the tragedy by the Abbé Boyer, dating from 1695, people went so far as to speak of the 'handkerchief scene' [translator's note: not to be confused with *Othello*]. The explanation given by La Porte is enlightening:

> The Abbé Boyer's Judith was performed throughout Lent. The *Cour* and the *Ville*, mainly the ladies, flocked to it in crowds. Every day there was such a great throng of all types and conditions that nobody knew where to put them. The men were obliged to give up the theatre to them and to stand in the wings. Imagine two hundred women seated on benches where normally only men are seen and holding handkerchiefs spread on their laps to wipe their tears in the emotional parts. I can remember above all that there was a scene in the fourth act where they burst into tears and which was called the handkerchief scene. The pit, where there are always jokers, made merry at their expense.[7]

The public here was not unanimous, the divide showed sexual and social oppositions. The women wept with great use of their handkerchiefs, they were on stage, close to the actors, and enriched the spectacle. The gentlemen, out of gallantry, gave up their places to them and took refuge in the wings. On the other hand, the stalls which were essentially masculine, more socially diverse and traditionally quick to jibe, mocked the weeping ladies. Laughter and tears would long continue to divide the theatrical public, through to the men of letters who discussed dramatic theory. But it was to become more and more difficult to be a mocker who laughed at the emotion of other spectators.

At this time La Bruyère in *Des Ouvrages de l'esprit* [on the works of the mind] was still surprised 'that we should laugh so easily at the theatre and that we should be ashamed of crying' and spoke of 'the extreme violence made by everyone to restrain his tears'. One can compare this remark with his observation on courtly behaviour: 'A man who knows the Court is master of his gestures,

of his eyes and of his face'.[8] One averts one's face to laugh and to
cry in the presence of the Great.' These tears, too often held back
in the theatre, at least by men, were an effect of curial logic and
of the development of self-control which it necessitated. But this
repression of the feelings seems to have been called into question
again and was relaxed to the benefit of an appreciation of tears
from the second half of the seventeenth century. Jean-Jacques
Roubine even thinks that this 'lachrymal claim' led to a progressive degradation of French classical tragedy in the eighteenth
century. At this period, any means was considered valid to obtain
a success of tears. This is why these plays appear nowadays to
be both mediocre and terribly out of date. This growth in tearful
performances did reveal, however, the rise of certain values.

IS IT FOOLISH TO CRY OVER THE CHILDREN OF INÈS?

Inès de Castro was a theatrical event which represented, through
the stir which it created, an important change in the attitude of
the public. In 1723, La Duclos, performing La Motte's tragedy
Inès de Castro had the idea of bringing her two small children on
stage with their nurse, so as to move King Alphonse of Portugal,
a character in the play. There was a stir in the audience, this was
the hour of innovation and the stalls were restless. As Diderot
wrote, 50 years later – for the incident was to remain famous –
they were immediately berated by the famous actress. Indignant,
she moved forward: 'Laugh then, foolish stalls, at the most beautiful moment in the play', the stalls heard her, contained themselves, the actress resumed her role, and her tears flowed with
those of the audience.[9] This relationship between the stage and
the audience describes the aesthetic issues in the event. La Duclos
achieved nothing less than a *tour de force* in reducing an audience
which was openly restless and deliberately mocking to silence.
This performance was to lead to a lively discussion: one can
enumerate a dozen pamphlets on the subject between 1723 and
1724. *Les Nouvelles Littéraires* of 15 January 1723 defended it thus:

> Some have dared to say that Paris has wept in foolishness at
> the representations of Inès. I wonder who is the fool, whether
> it is the man who allows himself to be gently moved by the
> feelings which he experiences, without questioning whether

he should be moved [. . .] or the man who calls him a fool
for being so moved, and for not looking deeply into whether
he should be so.

Feeling spirits gained ground and did not lay down their arms:
the fool was not the one we thought he was. There were some,
however, who laughed at a parody of the play, *Agnès de Chaillot*,
where the scene of the presentation of the children was derided.
The true 'Inès' was a success, despite the virulence of the formal
critics, and the public wept against all the rules. The Marquis of
Argenson cut thus through the debate:

> The success of this tragedy has been without equal, it was
> performed for a whole year in its novelty and it is often
> revived. The whole art of moving the emotions is driven
> to perfection, it could be read a hundred times and still
> be read with tearful effusion. We must therefore excuse a
> few poetic weaknesses in favour of so well treated a sub-
> ject: the success of plays does not come from versification
> alone.[10]

'The art of moving the emotions' here became an aesthetic
value, by the same right as versification. For, if one cried at
the hundredth reading – and this knowledge of dramatic texts
was appropriate to such an informed public – it was because the
emotions were not aroused by the surprise or daring of a scene.
The repetition of emotion conferred on it the status of an artistic
sign, and in this respect, the tears shed in the theatre seemed to be
a positive reply to a transformation of the dramatic codes. The play
was to be performed 107 times, and 70 000 people would watch it
in the eighteenth century.[11] The author of the *Critique des critiques*
wrote in 1723:

> I was taken to the performance of a tragedy. I found myself
> beside a gentleman who criticised it, while he wept in criti-
> cism; in such a way that his heart performed the critique
> of his mind. Two spiritual ladies replied with their lips: you
> are right, and with their weeping eyes told him: you are
> wrong [. . .] I believe that our minds are but poor dreamers
> whenever in such a case they are not of the opinion of our
> hearts.[12]

Strong minds are very poor dreamers, for, let us not fool ourselves, these gentle emotions were not raw feelings, but a reconciliation of heart and mind, of reason and feeling. Let us notice also that tears in the theatre were not the privilege of ladies. The border line was more a question of taste than of sex.

La Motte's tragedy represented a moment when norms were overturned which explained the hesitations of the public. The scene of the children, typical of family realism appeared to some to be a fault of taste, to others, the height of emotion. Montesquieu, who described contrasting reactions among the audience, saw in insensitivity one of the characteristics of the excessive refinement of manners, in which: 'Everything which concerns the education of children, the natural sentiments, appears to us to be something low, something of the people'. He was troubled by this 'too unhappy finesse' and remained convinced that this scene would have had an amazing effect on a less corrupt audience. Montesquieu therefore undertook to defend the play, because he saw in it one of the stages of the fight for the natural, and for a return to behaviour which was more careful than polished.[13] This was, no doubt, why the event had so much importance. This phenomenon was not to remain isolated and the contagion of tears when presented with scenes of childhood and the family was to gain ground, but in order to do so, it would be necessary to step outside the framework of classical tragedy which only allowed great figures onto the stage. From the end of the seventeenth century to the first third of the eighteenth century, one can point out a movement in favour of expressions of emotion which constantly overcame the reticence which it aroused: the extent of the argument was enough to make it felt, the aesthetic battle was also ethical.

TO CREATE IN ORDER TO CAUSE TEARS: THE COMEDY OF TEARS

Towards 1730 a new dramatic genre made its appearance. It was called, rather pejoratively, the comedy of tears. At the crossroads between tragedy and comedy, it had the peculiarity of bringing onto stage private characters in a serious plot which, according to Lanson's definition 'incites us to virtue in feeling for their misfortunes and in applauding their triumphs'.[14] If a few, such as Destouches or Voltaire, still mixed laughter and tears, the tone was set: comedies were, and had to be moving. The appearance of a theatrical genre can be of interest not only to the literary historian, but also the historian of social attitudes and imagination, for the public sought to weep together over the virtues of the private individuals whose touching figures left them in accord. Serious comedy became part of a new sentimental and moralising aesthetic whose premises we have seen in *Inès de Castro*. Domestic scenes were the framework for the triumph, after painful misfortunes, of love over prejudice, but did not, for all this, come up against morals.

Thus *Le Philosophe marié* by Destouches (1727), whose author wanted to 'show virtue in such a good light that it draws public veneration', brought on stage an understanding father and his son, who wept at his knee while confessing a secret marriage to him (Act IV, scene 1). The gentleness of the feelings of the father, took the edge off the traditional principle of authority, and this internal scene blended the tears of the public with those of the actors.[15] Tears remained nevertheless quite measured: Destouches did not abuse the pathetic. La Chaussée, on the other hand, resolutely forced the pace, and his deliberate will to cause tears, with neither economy of means, nor of effects, made of him, according to Lanson, the initiator of the genre.[16] In *Le préjugé à la mode* [fashionable prejudice] (1735), the sensitive Constance attempted to dissuade her husband from his fear of being ridiculed by society for conjugal love. The husband, moved to this delicious feeling, expressed himself thus at the feet of his tender wife:

I am at your feet
It is where I should die . . . Allow me through my tears
To expiate my excesses and avenge all your charms.

With the triumph of bourgeois conjugality, and despite a virtuous grandiloquence which could appear excessive, the public gave, according to Prévost 'extraordinary signs of approval for the new play. They laughed, they shed tears, they experienced all the passions which it pleased the author to arouse'.[17] With this quite soothing criticism of the traditional way of life of the courtiers, who mistrusted the affections in marriage, La Chaussée achieved a great public success: 17 000 people rushed to the 20 performances which were given. But the greatest triumph was known by La Chaussée with *Mélanide*, which introduced a theme which would become a raging success because of its concern with the misfortunes of virtue: from its creation in the year 1741 to 1786 it was to be performed 160 times. The success of his touching fables took on such proportions that many were the dramatic writers who followed in his footsteps. If La Chaussée is forgotten, authors who remain famous found themselves obliged to give themselves over to the new genre, such was the import- ance of the assent of the stalls in the indication of the summit of success of the time.

Marivaux consequently made use of intimacy and family feelings in *La Mère confidente*, an affectionate and understand- ing character who did not wish to force her daughter into a marriage against her will, and succeeded in making a friend of her. Angélique, her daughter confessed her loving feelings to her, speaking to her in these terms (Act I, scene 8):

> Come my mother, you charm me, I weep with the
>   tenderness of it,
> See the grace which you ask of me? I grant it to you.

Some, such as Collé, deplored the appearance of touching scenes on the stage, who saw in the success of the comedies of tears the influence of women who 'wish for a performance which makes them snivel'.[18] But the fashion for tears was such that Collé, far from opposing it in *La Partie de Chasse d'Henri IV* [Henri IV's hunt], made the good king cry, and the public with him. For this reason Choisel and Mme du Deffand shed tears over it.[19] If Collé attempted to dismiss the tears shed at the performance of comedies of tears, it was better to exalt those which were shed in the genre which he defended: the nationalist drama. He thus praised the 'Siege of Calais': 'There is nobody in France who, with a tender, honest soul, could restrain his tears, and whose sensibility and admiration would not make him shed them more than once in each act of this tragedy, even the weakest'.[20] The tears of the public thus constituted an issue in the aesthetic conflicts which divided the dramatists of the period. The genre of the national play appeared more worthy of men, like all plays which were propitious to political allusions, but they could still cry over it, while it seems to have been of little value to Collé to shed tears over family scenes. Such were the nuances which distinguished men and women, in his view, and not the signs of emotion which they displayed.

Voltaire, who criticised La Chaussée, would write a comedy of tears, so greedy was the public for them. In 1749, he presented *Nanine ou le préjugé vaincu* [Nanine, or prejudice defeated], a play about the triumph of virtuous love over birth. It is true that he thought to invent a mixed genre in which comic and pathetic met, which he defined in the preface to *L'Enfant prodigue* [the prodigal child] (1736).

We can see in it a mixture of the serious and the lighthearted, of the comic and the moving. It is thus that the life of men is variegated; often even a single event can present contrasts. Nothing is more common than a house in which the father scolds; the daughter, occupied with her feelings, weeps; the son laughs at both and several relatives take different parts in the scene. Very often in one room something is mocked which, in a different room can move to emotion; and the same person has sometimes laughed and wept over the same thing in the space of the same quarter of an hour.

To this mixture of laughter and tears was added the idea that the theatre must present the cross-section of a middle-class household. This desire to reveal the scenes of bourgeois intimacy was to be found in L.S. Mercier who would call for 'the portrait of our behaviour, the interior of our houses, that interior which is to an empire what the intestines are to the human body'.[21] The will to show these 'interiors' on stage illustrated a need for theatricalisation linked to the exaltation of the family sphere. To demonstrate its adherence to a certain code, the class of the theatrical public came to weep at the serious comedies, in a collective and spectacular fashion. It thus displayed its capacity to be moved and presented noisily its attachment to virtue and the family.

Voltaire knew well that it was absolutely necessary to make the audience cry and this was what controlled the choice of actresses for his plays:[22] they had to have the 'gift of tears', a theatrical term which meant, according to Littré 'to weep in such a way as to cause others to weep'. The technique of contagion from the stage to the audience which allowed for audience participation was in particular use at the time. Scenes likely to cause tears were extremely conventional, and the public of the 1720s to the 1750s made no mistake: they wished to shed gentle tears, and not to be at all shocked. But it was precisely this confidence in the limits of the acceptable, limits which, as we shall see, were to alter, which delineated the norms which the audiences imposed on the feelings which they loved to show. The actors spoke and behaved on stage with 'good manners' just like the public. The morals of the court were disapproved of (for example, arranged marriages, absence of family life) but their manner of conduct and decency were preserved, even if tears won over the impassiveness of the courtier.

A movement was nevertheless set in motion, and some such as Diderot encouraged it, for they found the public still too lukewarm and wanted to reform dramatic art:

It would be then that, in place of these petty transitory emotions, of these rare tears with which the poet contents himself, he would turn the mind upside down, he would distress the soul, and we would see those phenomena of ancient tragedy, so possible and so little believed in, reborn amongst us.[23]

MIDDLE CLASS DRAMA AND THE SEARCH FOR FEELING

In the second half of the century, bourgeois drama adopted prose, gave a larger place to show in the play of the actor, developed intrigue, the search for pathos and even the horrific, and attempted to transform the declamatory art. The desire to moralise became accentuated, and tender scenes multiplied in the name of the natural and of the exaltation of sensibility. This desire for renewal led to theoretical writings on drama, but also to moral evaluations of the effect produced by the theatre on the virtue of the spectator. On this account, the search for emotion and the way in which the public responded to it were thought of as moral evaluations, and this was probably the most innovative aspect.

Indeed, the dramatic processes themselves were not innovations without precedent: prose had already been used in *Cénie, pièce domestique* [Cénie, a household play] by Mme de Graffigny in 1741; the moralising and declamatory aspect and the development of complicated plots were already to be found in La Chaussée, whose tearful works were produced between 1733 and 1754. Finally the taste for the horrific[24] and realism in the scenery and the costumes were already at work in *Sylvie* by Landois (1741), a bourgeois tragedy according to the author. The new taste brought together all these elements. Good taste, polished style and delicate emotion lost their pre-eminence to the benefit of exclamations of distress and of pathos. The 'philosophical' aspect, which was still very measured and reconciliatory in the first comedies of tears, grew in magnitude: *L'Honnête criminel* [the honest villain] by Fernouillot de Falbaire (1767) protested against the oppression of Protestants with the help of the inevitable filial love element (the son was asked to take the place of his father who had been arrested at a forbidden meeting); the *Philosophe sans le savoir* [the unwitting philosopher] by Sedaine (1765), protested in the name of humanity against the barbarity of duelling.

As for comedy, it appeared to be definitively banished: 'It would be a great impertinence today to undertake to make the public laugh, when they claim that they only want comedies of tears', wrote Voltaire to the actor Lekain, on 25 April 1770. 'Metaphysics and tears have taken the place of comedy', he wrote on 24 November 1770 to d'Argental, whose taste he deplored: 'You have some inclination for that comedy of tears which shortens my days; I do not love you the less for it, but I weep in my retreat that you should enjoy weeping at comedy' (5 September 1772). Bachaumont also demonstrated this phenomenon: 'We cannot know, however, whether the present disposition of the spectators towards emotion and tears at our comic plays will long allow them to give themselves up to the frank laughter of this Molière farce'.[25] Molière's great plays appear little by little to have been abandoned by the public: in 1766, a fixed date for their performance could no longer appear on the playbill.[26] Even the plays of La Chaussée, which continued to be performed, appeared to D'Alembert, 'a strange mixture of laughter and tears' which gave a 'disturbed and undecided' pleasure, inferior to the pleasure of sentiment and tears.[27] The public wanted tears only.

In order to bring about the tears so desired by the public, dramatists used methods which we can attempt to pick out. It was acceptable to present touching scenes on stage, designed to shake the sensibility. One can perhaps understand better through this Diderot's taste for Greuze, his painting was theatrical but, with the same stroke, the drama created 'tableaux vivants', especially family interiors, which struck the visual sensibility of the spectators. The presence of children on the stage supplied a pretext: in *Le cri de la nature* [the cry of nature] by Armand there would even be a babe in arms on the stage of the Fontainebleau theatre. The author created the expected effect since, according to Bachaumont, the public shed floods of tears.[28] A series of extraordinary misfortunes which befell an innocent victim thus allowed L.S. Mercier in *L'Humanité ou les tableaux de l'indigence* [humanity, or scenes of poverty], to use the same visual methods. Realism took over the scenery: an attic, a poor man's room, an obscure cave, a cellar. The recognition scene, brought about with the help of secret marriages, shipwrecks and other improbabilities, provoked spectacular effects. These miraculously reconstituted families would embrace with many tears and the public would be moved. The method was used so much that the critics became used to evaluating its quality, as Grimm did in the *Correspondance littéraire*.

Elsewhere, emotion was caused by a recourse to a piecemeal style, to remarks interrupted by pain, to cries, to exclamations, considered to be natural signs which existed before language.[29] These means were used to translate the violent distress of the unfortunate or of the impassioned hero torn between virtue and love. Thus Diderot commented: 'but it is the cries, inarticulate words, broken voices, a few monosyllables which escape at intervals, some sort of murmur in the throat between the teeth which are always moving'.[30] The mime also had to interpret the movements of the heart, contrary to the strict symmetry of the classical formation on stage where each actor in turn would come forward towards the stalls to speak his lines. Rather than preserve these weighty, polished and cold gestures, it was necessary, according to Diderot in the *Entretiens sur le fils naturel* [conversations on the natural son], that the body should display the passions and distress. Concerning the fourth scene of Act II, where Clarville and Dorval threw themselves into each other's arms, one exhaling cries, the other shedding tears over him, he wrote:

Is it possible that we should not feel that the effect of misfortune is to draw men together; and that it is ridiculous, especially in moments of turmoil, when feelings are carried to excess, and the action is at its most agitated, to remain in a circle, separated at a certain distance from each other and in a symmetrical order.[31]

Certainly, it was a concern for the 'natural' which presided over the development of display but there was also a new cult of the body opposed to the aristocratic manner in which the posture of the 'fine air' was controlled. It is also interesting to note concerning this that the deportment training of the 'honnête homme' and the work of the actor each led to the other. The educational techniques of the Jesuits gave a large place to stage practice, for the theatre could both instruct and moralise. But most important, the young learned to hold themselves well in the theatre, Vigarello tells us,[32] and actors took the nobility as their example in their stances.[33] The important role of this renewal of dramatic play sprang from this, which broke with a certain habit of behaviour.

OF THE MORAL EFFECTS OF THE THEATRE

However much the public gathered in the theatres might cry, they were nevertheless sharing a model of euphoria. Observers confirmed this, and their accounts, in their optimistic grandiloquence, were part of this same movement. Grimm's *Correspondance littéraire* described it:

> Men are all friends when leaving a play. They have hated vice, loved virtue, cried together, developed the good and just elements of the human heart side by side. They have found themselves to be far better than they thought, they would willingly embrace each other [. . .] one does not come away from a sermon feeling better disposed. To read in silence and in secret does not produce the same effect. One is alone, there is nobody to witness one's honesty, one's taste, one's sensibility and one's tears.[34]

The theatre as a setting for tears shared in mutual recognition, allowed everyone to prove his natural bounty through tenderness, and all to prove the excellence of their relationships which pushed them to fling themselves into each other's arms. If theatre was worth more than solitary reading, non-religious effusion went so far as to compete with the church, since the love of virtue was combined in it with a delicious collective emotion. The observation and the participation of others multiplied the moral effects. The tears which were shed revived the sensibility and were a commitment to virtue.

Mercier, who wanted to give drama a social function thought that the spectator passed judgement as a public man and not according to his private interests.[35] Theatre as an antechamber to public activity? It would be tempting to believe:

> no passions are portrayed which do not move the assembly; who will shed gentle tears, and tears shed in unity are all the more gentle, no one could shy away from the rays of a sympathy so superior to the shrunken views of self-love and personal interest.[36]

Tears shed in company sealed a kind of social pact of sensibility which turned the theatre into a sort of political assembly. The poor man himself was invited there as 'he more than any other had need to weep and be moved' and would be tolerant of his ills on seeing that 'the assembled nation' did not close its ears to 'the accents of the unfortunate'.[37] Commiseration through tears was hence a gauge of social peace. In this unanimous assembly of tears, the man whose eye remained dry was in a dangerous position; he was either far above or far below humanity. Scoundrel or genius, he would hold himself outside not only the rules of society but those of humanity. Despite the soothing aspect of the proposition, Mercier was a reformer who would open the doors of the theatre more widely, in order to make of it a means for the moral education of the people while still portraying bourgeois life on stage in all its facets. The pleasure attached to tears had direct moral effects for him, if it was caused by the misfortunes which affect the lives of everyone, and not simply the lives of the great: 'What a mistake to forget that man is made of a wax which can be moulded by the hand which shapes it', he cried. Thus emotion was a means capable of transforming moral attitudes and the mission of the theatre therefore took on strange proportions because it could change men through tender emotions.

Mistelet shared the same bourgeois optimism but for him the goal was already partly achieved. The taste which the public had developed for serious comedy in which reason and sentiment were a matter of honour was the evidence that the Nation 'becomes enlightened, attains perfection and carries itself towards virtue'. The only unconquerables who remained restive under such treatment were 'our elegant youths, our little mistresses' who laughed to the point of indecency at the emotional points of the play whereas sensitive souls shed tears while sharing the trials of the unfortunates.[38] For, unlike those giddy young spirits who experienced nothing, they were ruled by humanity and they 'held their peers in some esteem'. To discount the behaviour of those who laughed, Mistelet constructed a theory of human nature which considered tears to be a more noble manifestation than laughter:

> All men seek pleasure, the bad with the good, and all express their feelings through signs and sounds. The pleasures which only touch our organs superficially are made known by laughter; but those which truly affect us and fill our souls, in other words the great pleasures remain concentrated in our hearts or are expressed only through tears.[39]

Tears of sensibility were at the summit of the hierarchy of the signs of pleasure given off by the body. In addition, the artist who followed the tearful genre must not only be sensitive but also must have a deep knowledge of the human heart in order to provoke tears. In order to provoke laughter, some small thing was enough, a well-placed word, a witticism. It was much harder to cause tears than laughter.

The desire to demote those who laughed, along with those whose eyes remained dry, in the virtuous evening assembly which confirmed its unity through the tears shed together, indicated new social conventions of the theatre. Those who faced up to them were rare, as an anecdote of Chamfort tells us.

> The Maréchal de Noailles spoke considerable ill of a new tragedy. He was told: 'But Monsieur d'Aumont in whose box you heard it, alleges that it made you cry. 'I?', said the Maréchal, 'not in the least, but as he himself wept from the first scene I considered it right to share in his pain'.[40]

Tears were here more the evidence of an obligatory participation in the emotion of one's neighbour than of an aesthetic or moral adhesion to the contents of the play. If one gave off the signals of sensibility they were no longer a homage paid to certain values, but simply a gesture of good taste and good neighbourliness or a simple phenomenon of contagion which led La Fontaine to say that the theatre made up a 'chain of people who weep'. Between the emphatic declarations of sensitive men of letters and the severe eye of the moralist, there was an interplay of the images of sociability. If appearances were to be believed, the former like the latter indicated the social usage of tears which were broadly shared by both the men and women of the eighteenth century. The conventional, agreed, often stereotyped aspect of the scenes which made the public cry, were, to them, neither boring nor embarrassing, quite the contrary. It allowed for a play between life and the theatre which followed an ethical and aesthetic code. The disappearance of delicate character studies in the style of Racine, which were deplored by certain theatrical historians, to the benefit of a dramatology which was 'all in the appearance', 'without psychological undercurrents or intimate emotions to analyse',[41] demonstrated a transformation in the purpose of performances. Far from being simply inadequate, these uses of grand gestures, of tears and of declarations of intent which made the characters transparent, adapted themselves to the questions which the members of the public were asking on self-presentation, and in particular the way of showing one's emotions. They were looking for a typology, a conventional expressive palette which could be used in the town, and which was different from the attitudes of the court. To cry together at a play also allowed them to be reassured and to demonstrate to each other the goodness of the human heart, their capacity to live with their peers – it was a pleasant sort of philosophical experience. The social aspect of the establishment of the value of sensitivity belonged to the century of Enlightenment, which, far from seeking the specific nature of individual emotion at the theatre, sought, on the contrary, those elements which brought men closer together. If to cry at a performance was a social code, a phenomenon of group involvement, even a function of nature, it was also a way of testing out a theory of social ties, which was proposed by the plethora of speeches given by the actors on humanity, virtue, charity, the excellence of nature, and which was made triumphantly explicit by the playwrights.

But in this concert of tender satisfaction a voice was raised, which even as it spoke, warned that it would not make itself heard. Rousseau, effectively, discounted theatrical emotion:

> We believe that we are drawn together at a performance, when it is there that each of us becomes isolated, it is there that we will forget our friends, our neighbours, our dear ones, and direct our interest towards fables, weep over the misfortunes of the dead or laugh at the expense of the living. But I feel that this language is no longer in season in our century.[42]

The spectator, alone in the crowd, escaped into the imaginary to the point of neglecting the circle of his intimates.

Rousseau did not believe in the moralising value of the theatre; the love of (moral) beauty was natural to the human heart, and it was not from 'an arrangement of scenes' that it was born. The gentle tears which the author caused to flow came from the way he flattered this sentiment, not because he had created it. But furthermore, this passing emotion was nothing but sterile sympathy 'which feeds on a few tears' and did not produce the least act of humanity. 'The beautiful weeping ladies of the boxes' so proud of their tears, reminded him of cruel Messalina, who wept for the eloquent defence of Valerius Asiaticus, but who nevertheless continued to demand that Vitellus should not allow him to escape.

He set himself to analyse why it was easier to be moved in the theatre than in real life. The classic argument, that of the Abbé du Bos, distinguished only a difference in intensity between the emotions. Audiences would weep at the theatre because their emotions were less painful and because they wished to experience affliction. However, for Rousseau, tears were not voluntary: 'Many choose not to go to tragedies because they are moved to the point of being overcome by emotion, others, ashamed of weeping at the performance cry despite themselves'.[43] But he distinguished above all a difference in the nature of the two emotions. Theatrical emotion was free 'of concern for ourselves': it made it easy to satisfy the right of humanity, whereas the presence of the unfortunate demanded help which necessitated efforts which one would wish to avoid: 'It would appear that we harden our hearts for fear that they should be softened to our detriment'. In Rousseau's view, the practice of virtue was not as simple as the conciliating themes of the century might lead one to imagine. This distinction had serious consequences because the man who had just 'wept over imaginary ills' was well satisfied with himself, he had just paid homage to virtue while applauding his own 'fine spirit': 'What more could be required of him? That he should practise it himself? He had no role to play, he was not an actor'. The spectator who was accustomed to seeing virtue at work on stage became passive and lost the movement of charity in the streets. His self-esteem was flattered by the sensitivity which he had displayed at the theatre, he had none left to give to his daily actions.

For Rousseau, pity was a natural feeling which had its place in the most corrupt of societies, in which one's tribute of tears was paid to good account in going to the theatre. Far from leading to a virtuous act, this passive pity reassured and satisfied men once and for all, thus dispensing with active and charitable sympathy, and isolated them even further from one another while flattering their self-esteem. He therefore did not wish for a theatre in Geneva, which was society of mutual knowledge where pity and compassion had preserved their freshness, and where the citizens gathered in pleasant and good-natured celebrations. In Paris where the evil was already done, he distinguished a few serious plays in which morals and virtue were respected, such as Mme de Graffigny's *Cénie*, which was worth more than 'certain other plays whose moral effects are disastrous'.

Diderot was less severe on tears shed in the theatre and believed in its moral value. 'The stalls of the theatre are the only place where the tears of the good and the bad are mingled.'[44] The good man, living amongst a corrupt people, reconciled himself with the human race and found, on stage, those with whom he would like to live. The bad man was indignant over actions which he could have caused: the impression he had received remained and 'he leaves his theatre box, less disposed to do ill than if he had been berated by a severe and harsh orator'. Certainly, the evils were imaginary, but they softened him, and, entering his heart in an indirect fashion, they would strike his soul which 'offered itself up to the blow' all the more forcefully. In addition, it was necessary for the reform of the theatre to provide a goal to make virtue loved and vice hated, by making impressions on the spectator and by disturbing him. He would then come out of his peaceful state to concern himself with the misfortunes which tried the constancy of the good man, and the performance would excite in him an impulse of interest for the troubles of virtue which 'cost him tears'. Diderot accordingly believed in the beneficial effects of the theatre.

It was the status of sensibility which was to change in the development of his thought. But the problem here became less moral than psycho-physiological: 'Sensibility is not without weakness of organisation. The tear which escapes the man who is a true man touches us more than all the tears of a woman'.[45] Sensibility had its hierarchies: there must be a distinction between that which came only from the body, connected to the extreme 'mobility of the diaphragm', and the enthusiasm in feeling and the mind which were married. He thus distinguished tears associated with a tragic accident from those shed over a moving tale:

We hear a fine thing described: little by little the mind is troubled, the entrails are moved, and tears flow. On the other hand, at the sight of a tragic accident, object, sensation and effect meet; in an instant the entrails are moved, we cry out, we lose our heads, and tears flow; these come suddenly; the former are brought about by a progression.[46]

The mediation of the mind, whether artistic or moral, was to be distinguished from a passive emotion connected to the disorder of the organs, for it allowed the agreement of the feelings and of virtuous reason: it was from this that the difference was born between 'natural man' and 'poetic man'.[47]

But it was necessary to leave these weepers in the stalls and to place the greatest of them all on stage, that is, 'dramatic man'. He had all the attributes of genius and his tears 'fell from his mind': his power was not to be found in his sensibility, as was too often believed, in his sensibility, which produced only mediocre actors, but in his capacity to produce the exterior signs of feeling perfectly and with sang-froid. He knew exactly when he would get out his handkerchief and when tears would flow, and his emotion was more touching than a genuine pain which was 'almost always subject to grimaces'.[48] The mission of the theatre was to embellish nature and not to copy it slavishly, artifice could be more moving than natural feeling. Thus spoke the 'Paradoxical man' who, following the success of the *Philosophe sans le savoir* [the unwitting philosopher] by Sedaine, encountered the author in this fashion:

I go up to him, I fling my arms around his neck, I lose
my voice, and the tears flow down my cheeks. This is the
sensitive and mediocre man. Sedaine, stiff and cold looks at
me and says: 'Ah! Monsieur Diderot, how fine you are'. This
is the observer and the man of genius.[49]

For the admiration which Diderot expressed for Sedaine
was also the declaration of his own dramatic failure, and
of the success which he generously attributed to his friend.
The latter had been mixing plaster while Voltaire and Diderot
who could not hear a pitiful line without weeping, were being
fed on classical texts. Sedaine was all the more able to create
the impression that the audience were truly witnessing the life
of a family: this was the bourgeois theatre of which Diderot
dreamed. His theoretical texts on the theatre, were in the form
of lively dialogues, but have nevertheless retained a singular
acuteness. Indeed Diderot and Rousseau display the magnitude
of the problem of emotion experienced in the theatre through
their thoughts. Writing in the form of a euphoric and conciliatory discourse, they did not devote any fewer criticisms
to such a subject. For the theatre and the status of sensibility
provided the measurement of the importance of such conduct
for society itself.

Rousseau deliberately placed himself in moral ground in
criticising the urban ways of life. He knew that he was speaking
into the desert, but for him there was nothing worse than the
sterile sympathy which could easily be assuaged with a few
tears and which allowed self-esteem to become more proud of
itself, while the audience neglected to concern itself with its
nearest and dearest. For pity, which was of such importance
in the state of Nature because it 'takes the place of laws, morals,
and virtue, with the advantage that none is tempted to disobey
its gentle voice,'[50] had only the status of a relic in the theatre,
even worse, artifice replaced a true commiseration. Rousseau's
debate was established between the moralising tendency of the
theatre-going public which loved to cry, and the real practices
of the same people in the street or in the home. In this, it can
support the questions of the historians who attempt to interpret
the types of thoughts and actions of a period with the help of a
theatre which it created and applauded . . . and where people
went to weep. The difficulty which we have in grasping the

how and why of this taste for tears in the theatre comes from a strange meeting of the prizing of 'natural feelings' with a society of public appearances which displeased Rousseau.

Diderot's point of view, when it was not moral, was an attempt at the definition of public man but he defined him as a great man and a genius (artist, actor, man of state) who was in any case not generally a good and virtuous family man, as he reminded us of the 'neveu de Rameau's' famous uncle. The actor, a cold observer, was the prototype of the great man since he was capable of giving, all the appearances of sensibility through his capacity for self-mastery. Was this not, as Diderot himself wrote, the very ability of the unbelieving priest, of the seducer, of the beggar, and of the courtier who thus manipulated the art of tears and its conventional truths? The insensitive man could be great, he was not so from the moral point of view, but through his creative capacity. But for Diderot, not everyone was Lekain: the stage and the audience had never been more separated. Although emotion was marvellously acted out on stage, the audience came to the theatre to weep tears which were not of the same type as those of the actor. The 'guts' were involved, whether immediately in the constitutions of the feeble, or in a mediated fashion for the others. This distress called for the moral feelings of the spectator and could have beneficial effects.

THE FEMALE PUBLIC AND TEARS IN THE THEATRE

This exceptional propensity to weep which was characteristic of the eighteenth-century public has been interpreted as one of the consequences of the large presence of women in the audience and of their preponderant role in social life. Already Paul Hazard saw, in the appearance of the tide of emotion, the sign of the transformation of the position of women. Henri Lagrave even suggests that this taste for tears betrayed 'the feminine character of the emotions of the time', which stemmed, according to him, from the sociability of the salon, where women exercised a power over men (it was still necessary to define which power). Women, it would appear, thus fashioned an 'effeminate' public.[51] Furthermore, as the heart, according to him, was possessed of no class barriers, the success of the comedy of tears was a result of the subjective alliance between society ladies and bourgeoises. It is

hard to judge this sort of phenomenon in retrospect, especially
when it concerns the symbolic divide which distinguishes men
and women in a society.

Though the taste for sensibility was particularly developed in
women, it was also present in the eighteenth century man: one
should remember the tears of the man who was truly a man of
whom Diderot spoke, and of the weakness of the organisation of
women. For misogynist comments were not lacking at the time;
these ladies who wept at the death of a canary were constantly
laughed at. The tears of men were even more esteemed because
they wept only at strong emotions, and because compassion for
the misfortunes of others was a homage paid to the whole of
humanity. Voltaire, who could not hear a sad tale without
dissolving into tears, found that effeminacy came from too great
a desire for love in a tragedy. At the time subtle distinctions were
established, since tears were a language which was related to the
situations in which they were produced and in this respect were
far from being associated only with the feminine. We have seen
this concerning Collé who thought that La Chaussée's theatrical
success was due to women, thanks to his exaltation of the virtue
of a sensitive heroine, but who was himself very proud to cause
tears over a more virile, political subject.[52] Diderot thought
accordingly that if it should happen that on watching a tragedy
a great figure of the Republic should shed a tear; 'what an effect,
you may believe, his grief would have on the rest of the audience?
Is there nothing more moving than the unhappiness of a venerable
man?'[53] The taste for an assuredly virile Roman heroism in no way
contradicted the tears which fell: those of a great man had moral
effects on the people who surrounded him. It was considered to
be more dignified for a man to weep with admiration than with
the tender emotions of love. The argument often used to criticise
a play was that it was too pleasing to women who loved to weep.
Sensitivity had its hierarchies, its grandeurs and its pettinesses
which all had a highly skilful power of discernment and which
should not be measured against the yardstick of contemporary
sexual identity.

5 Tears during the Revolution (1789–94)

The revolutionary days led to collective expressions of emotion in public places which the conquest of political space enlivened and broadened. According to contemporary accounts, tears often fell in an astonishing climate of emotional intensity. The revolutionary period allowed a formula which until then had grown up mainly in literature, in the theatre, in letters and memoirs, to be enacted in the streets.

It is not original to remark upon the amazing emotional atmosphere of the first years of the Revolution. But it is common to see in it the effect of the disappearance of fixed social, political and ideological environments – the excess of tears was a result of the sudden disappearance of traditional rules of behaviour. The men of the eighteenth century had not waited for the Revolution, however, to develop the habit of tears. In exceptional circumstances, the intensity of demonstrations of emotion only appears to have been possible if people had a language in which to share them, available to them. The model of the communication of the emotions, defined with the help of literary texts, can on this point shed light on the attitudes of the revolutionary crowds.

The accounts collected together which dealt with tears generally made use of written language (correspondence, memoirs, periodicals, petitions, addresses, proceedings) in a narrative fashion which in no way excluded lyricism. Some accounts were descended more from the harangue, or from speech, in short, from the art of oratory. Perusal of these texts recalls de Tocqueville's note on the literary spirit of the French Revolution, but one thinks more frequently of Louis Sébastian Mercier than of the Rousseau of the *Contrat Social*. In commenting on these texts I do not intend to interpret the revolutionary process from 1789 to Thermidor. It is more a question of examining the recording of tears, scene by scene in order to try to define an imaginary space or to detect a field of thought.

We are approaching a moment of change of attitudes. These tearful scenes present the final moments of an old order of behaviour like a sort of paroxysm, even an apotheosis of the taste for tears and of the communication of the emotions. The expression of the feelings took on at this time a socio-political meaning, interwoven with the issues of the hour. This exaltation of communal fallen tears should also be born in mind in order to understand the phenomenon of rejection which followed the Revolution.

FROM JUNE TO OCTOBER 1789, THE TEARFUL WEEKS

From the States General to the installation of the King in Paris, there was hardly an event which did not end in collective tears and embraces. There was no lack of witnesses to exalt these delicious tears, shed in the flow of the political transformations.

Nicolas de Bonneville wrote in *Le tribun du peuple* of 19 June 1789, after the announcement of the creation of the National Assembly: 'It was on the 19th of June that I sprinkled my patriotic tears over the Deliberation of the National Assembly which places the creditors of the State under the safeguard of French honour and loyalty. Oh happy month of June!'.[1] Such loyalty, sealed by an outburst of emotion over legal political papers was common practice. Pleasure was taken in bathing the work of the Assembly with tears. This surprising mixture of precision and emotion, of moral abstractions and precise solutions which juggled with the opposing power relationships, demonstrates that the good nature of the time was not naive.

On 27 June 1789, when Louis XVI was persuaded to invite the representatives of the three Estates to join together to form a National Assembly, in order to sanction a move to gather which had already been vigorously initiated, he appeared on the balcony of his apartments. This is how Marmontel described the scene: 'The queen is with him, and both hear their names echo to the skies. Gentle tears fall in their embraces, and, with a gesture which melts hearts, the Queen clasps in her arms the object of their gratitude'.[2] This tender conjugal scene of royalty might appear surprising at the height of a political upheaval which put an end to absolute monarchy, but this royal couple, acting out happiness and marital love, resembled a moral tale of Marmontel, characteristic of the sensibility of the eighteenth century: it was good to see private emotions presented in public. The figure of a sentimental monarch indicated the transformation of his status.

But the king did not have the privilege of tears. Dissatisfaction could also make itself known through tears. Thus, at the moment of Necker's disgrace, one could read in the *Journal de l'Assemblée Nationale* of 12 July 1789: 'Consternation has become general at Versailles, people encounter each other everywhere in tears. In Paris, consternation is rapidly changing to fury'.[3] This was the veiled menace: if the representatives were weeping sadly, the people were growling.

Following people's disquiet, there came enthusiasm: at the session of 15 July, on the retreat of the troops which the King had massed around the town, the Assembly and numerous spectators were in tears. According to a witness, Delaville le Roulx, M. le Breton, the Deputy from Besançon was overcome with joy, several representatives were taken ill, and the Marquis de Brezé fainted.[4] That same day was rich in emotion, it moved next from the Assembly to the city. Sylvain Bailly's memoirs report the scene of the delegation to the Hotel de Ville. The people crowded into the path of the Deputies: 'Everywhere there were exclamations, blessings and tears [. . .] cockades were distributed to them [. . .] their hands were clasped, they were embraced'.[5] His description which was focused on the representatives did not have the power of that which an anonymous countryman produced the next day, on 16 July:

> Yesterday, at five in the evening, when I was in the Place Louis XV, I saw an unbelievable crowd in the Tuileries, who were clapping their hands: 'Long live the King and the Nation!' I ran and I saw forty deputies of the States General who had said that they were bringing the olive branch. France will never have a finer moment than that. Everyone wept with joy and I cannot write of the event without thinking of it, without shedding tears. That wonderful moment cannot be described, enthusiasm suffocated our voices, tears prevented us from saying whatever we wished to. We ran, we pushed forward, we embraced without knowing each other, without speaking.[6]

Collective emotion at its zenith encountered the model of sociability through tears, a language between strangers, supplied by literature. This effusion which appeared to be produced in an undescribable turmoil and which caused its actors to lose the use of speech, explained a concept of social ties which was situated in the unforgettable immediacy of a 'wonderful moment'. It set the seal on a new pact, in a moment out of time which would remain in the memory of those present. The Revolution might, at its birth, have been a festival of the public word but it also found in these tearful celebrations the means for informal and unorganised ceremonies which were born of the event, and which were only possible because of social codes, linked to imaginary performances, of the interchanges between men.

One can of course laugh at the President of the Assembly, Lally-Tollendal[7] weeping for joy under the crown of parsley with which he was crowned after the taking of the Bastille. But to do so would be to misunderstand at a fundamental level the expressive signs which allowed these group events to happen. His emotion did not spring from a weakness of organisation, but bore witness to a participation in general scenes of sociability which suspended the course of time, above (or beyond) obstacles and violence, but here and now. It should be noticed in any case that there was little symbolic splendour in these assemblies; an olive branch, a parsley crown and cockades were enough to celebrate the rediscovered accord, tears made up the rest.

The king who agreed to come to Paris and to appear at the Hôtel de Ville on 17 July 1789 was also the cause of scenes of exquisite tears. According to Bailly, Mayor of Paris, a witness and a participant at his side in the events, who did not hesitate to bestow a fine role upon himself, the eyes of the king 'were filled with tears' and he could hardly utter the words: 'My people can always count on my love', his voice strangled with emotion. The crowd pressed round, replying to him in the same register: His Majesty 'wore on his august features the expression of sensibility and happiness, while around him nothing but exclamations of joy could be heard, and nothing but tears of tenderness and joy could be seen'.[8] There is no doubt that the author was elaborating, but that Bailly should have magnified the royal sensibility and the reply of the French people in tears, is appropriate to the imagination of the times. While this type of small happening has led to ramblings on the weakness of Louis XVI, it appears that at the time and outside any individual psychology, the blending of tears was the best shared thing in the world. In place of the blinding monarchy of the sun there was the sensitive monarchy: 'All eyes, filled with tears,

were turned towards him', wrote Bailly. But the king probably did
not show his delicious emotion sufficiently.

Rétif de la Bretonne also described the scene, but remained
unconvinced: 'I was moved, touched. I think that the unfortunate
Louis was also: I thought I perceived tears in his eyes. Were they
tears of tenderness?'[9] The quality of the tears of Louis XVI was not
the same as that of his people.

Some, such as Rivarol, did not at all appreciate the arrival
of the king in Paris. With a change of scenery: he evoked a
different scene of tears, those of the brave partisans of absolute
royalty who attended the royal departure:

> Versailles will never forget that day and that departure: the
> king's old retainers could not watch the French Monarch set
> out without pomp and without defence in the middle of the
> populace, towards a frenzied capital in order to approve an
> armed insurrection without shedding tears.[10]

The counter-revolutionaries already wept tears of pain, while a
crowd in tears received a king whom they wished to believe to
be sensitive and loving: the demarcation lines were already being
drawn.

Michelet, who grasped the importance of these expressions
of emotion and these 'eyes filled with tears', thought that on 17
July the king had replied badly to the crowd which 'appeared
to need to give vent to suppressed feelings'. 'The slightest kind
word, uttered at that moment, would have been repeated with
enormous effect' but the king gave 'not a word, not a sign'.
Worse, when he returned to the palace in the evening, he took
part in the following scene: 'On the staircase he found the Queen
and her children in tears who came to fling themselves into his
arms [. . .] The King had therefore run a great risk in visiting his
people! Was this people the enemy?'[11] This final manifestation of
tears was harmful, in Michelet's view, to the royal image, beside
a people which only asked to express its tender emotion and its
friendship and for whom it would have been enough to have given
the happy occasion for it to do so. Thus the political ramifications
of an event may be measured against the yardstick of the tears
which are shed: shared with the public they would have been
gentle. The bitter tears shed at Versailles buried the hope of a
meeting between the king and the Parisians.

On the same balcony of the Hôtel de Ville, Necker would, on 31 July 1789, make a fine figure in his turn, after having brought about numerous tears with a 'true, sublime and moving' speech and persuaded the electoral Assembly to vote for a general amnesty. Michelet described it to us thus: 'He showed himself at the window, his wife on his right, his daughter on his left, weeping and kissing his hands. His daughter, Mme de Staël fainted with happiness'.[12] Here was a successful sentimental scene: one can imagine the Parisian men of means, supporters of Necker, going into transports over that touching scene of a wife and daughter charmed by public success and the goodness of the heart of their husband and father. It was such a pleasure to weep over loving families!

The night of 4 August and its results were also rich with emotions. Beyond those directly concerned in events, an anonymous writer wished to recount his emotion. Proposing, on 19 August to the Assembly, a design for a commemorative medal according to its decree of 6 August: 'The reading of your orders of the 5th of August current, and of the days which followed, exalted in me a patriotic enthusiasm, my poor mind was electrified, and I shed delicious tears. How much I now love my country!'[13] The engraver, agreeably disturbed, became fired with enthusiasm and shed tender tears. This electric imagination, often developed by the contemporaries of the Revolution should be studied. The works of Mesmer seem to provide pictures which are appropriate to these movements of collective enthusiasm,[14] just as the liquid state of tears could lead to the merging of beings who, until that point, did not know each other. L.S. Mercier, who, in *Le Nouveau Paris* described the celebration of the Federation, expressed it thus: 'It was like an electrical experience. Everyone who touched the current must have felt this turmoil'.[15] It was a question, as we have commented concerning the circulation of tears, of a model of direct communication. If the current flowed, then people embraced and wept, as on 6 October, when the people of Paris celebrated the installation of the king in the capital, and he appeared, flanked by the tricolour cockade. Michelet again spoke of a crowd in tears, of its cry of love and gratitude.

These emotions demonstrated a large participation in the model of the emotions. Literary rhetoric was then to be measured against the curious events which proved that its imaginary figures were imprinted on behaviour to the point of permitting new practices of conduct. The French Revolution was thus the theatre – and the image is appropriate – for moving shared experiences of tears which also had a political significance. The patriots wept at the announcement of the works of the Assembly, they thus signed their delicious consent to and participation in the movement to which they were witnesses. Emotion would sometimes be collective, and this sharing of tears showed a use of the public space which confirmed the enthusiasm of opinion for the train of events, just as it placed the seal on a sort of social undertaking. Another type of collective demonstration of emotion was born of the image of the family (conjugal or filial love) which several public figures presented, and which made all those who attended, melt into tears: it was related to a sort of comedy of tears.

Loustalot, in *Les Révolutions de Paris* from 3 to 10 October 1789, took part in this reconciliatory and familial emotion, but already operated dividing lines: the presence of death transformed the terms of the expression of emotion. He wrote, in fact, in this newspaper, a sort of address to a father whose son, an eighteen-year-old bodyguard, was killed in revenge for the murder of a member of the national guard when a section of the crowd penetrated the palace of Versailles on the morning of 6 October:

Ah, please permit us, unfortunate father, to mingle our tears with yours, that the blood of your son should not be held against us, but against the instigators of the conspiracy, that the sight of your pain should always be in their minds, that it should feed eternally their remorse, that they should be punished by their children, by all that which is dear to them, and that death itself should not provide them with an escape from pain and despair.

In blending their tears with those of the father, in participating in his suffering, the revolutionaries cleansed themselves of a crime, in throwing their curses at the invisible and unnamed enemy who was the true agent of his son's death. The theme of blood and tears, on which I shall place some emphasis, was here expressed through shared tears which deflected the direction of the vengeance bound to the blood which was spilled. As one might ward off ill fortune, the author attempted to transfer the ill to those who should rightly ward it off, and with such violence!

Punished by their own children, pursued even in death, the guilty parties were vowed to eternal remorse. The division between blood and tears in the language of invective and of curses, would define the divisions between revolutionaries and counter-revolutionaries, then between the poor and the exploiters, between sans culottes and moderantists, between Thermidorians and Jacobins.

FROM THE FEDERATION MOVEMENT TO THE TERROR, OR CONCILIATORY EXPRESSIONS OF EMOTION

Michelet has passionately disinterred the Federation Movement which assembled men all over the country through the taking of an oath in an attempt to make it live again. And he did not forget the tears which fell, nor those of the women:

> In some village, the men were assembled alone in a vast building to make an address together to the National Assembly. The women approached, they listened, they entered with tears in their eyes, they too wished to take part. Then the address was read again and they joined in with all their hearts.[16]

Michelet certainly transposed his visions, but he probably did not invent the anecdote. The participation, however ephemeral, of emotional women in a public space which had already been reserved for men, was definitely connected to the ideal of sharing which was presented in scenes of tears. These federative expressions of euphoria could not manage without either women or children.

> There was another sign which was no less deep which also appeared in these celebrations. Sometimes, a small child would be placed on the altar, who was adopted by everyone; and who, endowed with the gifts, the avowals and the tears of all, belonged to all.[17]

Rather than concentrate on the emblems and symbols of the celebration of the Federations, Michelet lingered over the signs: the women, the children, the old. The fortunes of these moving literary scenes of the eighteenth century, for which we have seen so many tears shed, knew some fine hours once again, in the revolutionary festivities. We understand that the presence of women and children pleased Michelet. But above all, as his conception of historical labours engaged him to, he revived shared tears to weep for and commemorate the dead.[18] The outbursts and the vows were not lacking from the first celebration of the Revolution of 1789 (the conclusion of a movement which had begun at Valence in November of the same year) although unfortunately on the day of the festival of the Federation, at the champ de Mars, it rained. In January 1792, Louvet, the author of *Faublas*, was deeply moved by the modesty of attire of the women at national feastdays. 'I cried with joy and I said to myself: the revolution which is to regenerate our morals has already strongly influenced those of our companions.' This tender moralism was the bearer of hope.

Another sign of the times was the swearing of allegiance to the Constitution by the members of the Legislative Assembly which had just been formed in October 1791 and which was also a moving ceremony. After the most senior members had carried the constitutional text in procession, the representatives, placing their hands on it, swore the oath of allegiance. According to Robespierre, many of them wept tears over it and covered it with kisses.[19] The gravity of the ceremony was combined well with the expression of sensibility.

We know about the famous scene of Lamourette's kiss, at the Legislative Assembly of 7 July 1792, an intensely emotional reconciliation, and a sentimental joining of previously opposing sides. The representatives wished to abolish the divisions which separated them in an ostentatious fashion. The right and the left, from the Feuillants to the Montagnards, and the King himself, were invited to this demonstration of affection. The will for unity which obsessed the men of the Revolution found in the expression of emotion a way of dissolving differences of opinion.

Reinhard gave another example of this state of tearful sensibility, under conditions which appeared to him to be completely unexpected. On 8 July 1792, a deputation from Gravilliers' Ward came to the Jacobin club to bring a petition in favour of Pétion, the mayor of Paris, whom Louis XVI wished to remove. The petition began thus: 'A weeping family comes to ask you for the return of its father'. It appears that these words were enough, according to the proceedings, to bring about a scene of 'sensibility which no words could express' and that they caused many tears to fall. These moments of sentiment which were centred on an imaginary family were not a simple relief of tension. They were part of a secular movement of contagion through tears based on a model of reference which allowed for emotion between strangers, especially concerning family feeling.

On 30 July 1792, Santerre, who advocated insurrection, turned up at the head of the people of Marseille, with two hundred men of the National and Federal Guard. The encounter took place at the entrance to the Faubourg Saint-Antoine. From there, the procession went to the Bastille, with drums and flags, singing the Marseillaise. In the square, a thousand Jacobins were waiting for them, and considered them to be so dashing that they shed tears at the sight of them.[20] It may be surprising that this demonstration of revolutionary force, which made use of such patriotic and military trappings, should have caused tears in such a way. Along with the bloody scuffles, the participants of 30 July knew tears. On the moral level, we should notice that the assuredly virile stance of the people of Marseilles and the admiration caused by revolutionary heroism were well-suited to expressions of emotion. Tears of admiration were indeed part of the same level of feeling as the exaltation of a Brutus-like heroism, and they equally made up the appropriate reply to a touching scene. The association of emotion with the deployment of the apparatus of the military was in any case destined for a sure future.

These impulses of a generosity which was nothing less than spectacular were to be observed by Michelet on the evening of 10 August and they were for him the proof that the revolt had 'in no way quenched the feelings of humanity in the hearts of the attackers'. The scene took place at the Assembly where a group of victors burst in, pell-mell, with members of the Swiss Guard. One of them then spoke up:

'We have made prisoners of these unfortunate instruments of treason, many have thrown down their arms; we will employ against them only the weapons of generosity. We will treat them like brothers' (he threw himself into the arms of a Swiss guard and in the excess of emotion, he fainted; the representatives came to his aid). Then, resuming his speech: 'I must have vengeance. I beg the Assembly to allow me to take this unfortunate with me, to lodge and feed him.'

And everyone wept before such a grand gesture. His feeling of reconciliation was translated into the public undertaking to take the stranger who had made the mistake of selling himself to despotism into his own domestic sphere. The demonstrations of generosity and of sensibility were sympathetically joined together in this.

At Le Mans in July 1793, Philippeaux re-established agreement in a town which was divided after 40 hours of conflict. The Girondins and the Montagnards all embraced each other. According to the *Gazette Nationale*: 'It happened in the square, in front of 20 000 men who were moved to tears'.[21] Michelet was amazed by this reaction of emotion which led men to embrace and weep who had previously been prepared to kill each other. These paroxysmal movements of reconciliation which followed the conflicts can indeed appear strange. We have seen this scenario repeat itself under different conditions. This recurrence proves a community imagination which was instantly recreated through tears and accolades. In that moment of conquest of the public space which saw the birth of discord among men in 1789, there were still those delicious moments when words were lacking, where the discussion was halted, only to find a sort of euphoric expression of emotion which proved to all the excellence of their hearts, and the stupidity of dispute.

These sudden reversals, where group opinions gave way to common unity and those collective emotional enthusiasms, could be described as a general sensibility in the manner of Rousseau's general will, which aimed to 'blend people who think of themselves as individuals into the social or political body'.[22] This comparison seems to me to come close to Durkheim's interpretation of this concept of Rousseau. 'In order to understand it well, we have to go down below to the less conscious levels, and to reach habits, tendencies, and moral tenets.'[23] Let us then judge that these tears which were so often shed, were the demonstration, perhaps as much as the speeches, of the concept of a social bond which drove these conscious men to formulate the premises of a society which had no precedent. Strangely, when presented with the experience of individualism, men mingled their tears, not so much to ward off misfortune, as by a moral habit which demanded that one should weep with one's neighbour. From this comes the paradox that while they were founding a society they collapsed in tears.

TIME SUSPENDED

Gusdorf sets apart the act of the oath which he esteems from the manifestations of sensibility at the time of the Revolution, which made up a mass phenomenon, a moment of communion manifesting the relief of tension, and which, for him had little sense:

> While sensibility dissolves with time, and allows itself to be dragged from one extreme to another, from jubilation to tears, the oath forces time and space to bend to the decree of a personality which binds itself according to its most difficult demands.[24]

Now the oath and the expression of emotion happened simultaneously, for instance in the Federation movement, in a moment suspended in time which we find hard to conceive, but which we are told of in the accounts of these fallen tears.[25] The oath was not so much the decree of a personality which binds itself, as an act of association beyond the dead, the living and the unborn. And tears were not just excess, but a movement of enthusiasm which literally transported entire assemblies in the sharing of a delectable social moment.

Kant attempted to define the extent of the French Revolution by asking the following question: 'Is there in the world around us an event which could be described as memorable, demonstrative and a prognostic of a permanent progress which carries with it the whole of humankind?' According to Michel Foucault,[26] he was looking for a sign which would show that this had always been the case, that things were happening like this at that time, and that everything would continue to occur in this way: a moment of suspension, where past, present and future clasped hands. The French Revolution constituted this key event for Kant, but it was not the revolutionary drama itself, its numerous setbacks and its great figures which would confer this status on it. It was rather the spectacle of the Revolution for those who took part but were not the major actors in it, while demonstrating 'a sympathy of aspiration which was on the verge of enthusiasm'. This moral disposition of humanity demonstrated the people's right to give themselves a political constitution.

This was a striking formulation of the state of mind of these crowds which shed delicious tears: these great scenes of collective tears came from admiration, from benevolence, from sympathy. Occasional assemblies showed a new wave of it.'It is in the nature of enthusiasm to communicate itself and to grow through the number of enthusiasts', Diderot had written in the *Lettre sur les sourds et les muets* [letter on the deaf and dumb]. The propensity to bathe the constitutional text with tears seems to have played a good part in this movement. The tears of sociability, produced by the Enlightenment, took on a political sense which there was no question of making into a lost paradise but which undertook to refine observation. It suggests a different reading of collective movements, against the tradition begun by Gustave Lebon who interpreted the demonstrations of the crowd as a surge of irrationality, a revenge of raw emotion over Reason, in the absence of an instituted ceremony. These lachrymal practices, at once both spontaneous and codified by a model of communication of the emotions, forged a social bond around the Constitution.

The Constitutionals, the Conventionals, and the Jacobins, wept with tenderness and admiration in the Assembly, in the clubs, and in the streets. The representatives and the Jacobins were no doubt acquainted with the comedies of tears, and sentimental novels. But the Parisian crowds, or those of the anonymous Federations who loved to shed tears together testify a broader spread of the taste for tears. André Monglond thinks that if the Revolution was an explosion of feeling, it was because, through Rétif, and the plays of L.S. Mercier, it flowed like a flood through the people of Paris. He notes that in 1789 almanacs with significant titles appeared: *Le Joujou des coeurs sensibles, le Jardin des âmes sensibles, l'Apologie de la tendresse*, [The plaything of sensitive hearts, the garden of sensitive spirits, and the apology for tenderness].

The passage of the literary or para-literary model in these amazing ceremonies of tears remains, however, a mystery, unless political invention was mingled with the imaginary universe to elaborate on ways of co-existence which were appropriate to the event.

SPECULATORS IN TEARS AND DRINKERS OF BLOOD

Following the euphoric scenes of tears, the use in oratory of the image of blood and tears had an assured success during the Revolution, a success which was connected to its capacity to arouse indignation. On 12 July 1789, Rétif de la Bretonne used a high-flown metaphor to speak of the Bastille 'whose towers rested on their deep foundations watered with the tears of so many unfortunates'. He also attacked the abuses of the *Ancien Régime* when he denounced the magistrates as 'greedy for blood, for tears, and above all for money'.[27]

A more socio-economic argument followed the denunciations of the arbitrary nature of revolutionary zeal. During the sugar crisis in January 1792, Hébert in *Le Père Duchesne* made use of such rhetoric against the speculators and monopolists whose magnificent mansions were 'cemented with the tears of the unfortunate'.[28] Jacques Roux went further with this written image of those who stockpile basic commodities and 'who submit the tears and poverty of the people to usurious calculations'.[29] They did not only cost the people tears, but based their speculations on suffering itself. On 25 June 1793, at the Convention, he used four times over the image of tears, and did not fear convoluted metaphors to support his economic demands: 'Must the widows of those who died in the cause of liberty pay a ransom even for the cotton which they need to wipe away their tears?'[30] The increase in price of the fabric for handkerchiefs stole their mourning from the widows of the soldiers who died for the Revolution. He questioned the new debt which the grocer and the banker would 'collect in the blood and tears of the sorrowing' and accused the royalists and moderates of vampirism who would 'drink in golden goblets the blood and tears of the citizens, under the protection of the law'. These speculators and tear-drinkers exhibited the barbarity which sentimental novels denounced in seducers. And the metaphors of the cost of tears which were part of literary rhetoric here took on a heightened contour since they were aimed at the denunciation of the profiteers of the high cost of living. We can see clearly here how an available language could become part of the play of the revolutionaries.

The extremists also benefited from the horror story, well-suited to support their political battles. Jacques Roux exhorted the left wing of the Assembly thus: 'Deputies of the Montagne, if you would climb from the third to the ninth floor of this revolutionary city, you would be moved by the tears and the trembling of an immense people without bread and without clothes'. While the counter-revolutionaries lapped up the blood of the poor, the Montagnards were called on to climb up to the attics, there to experience compassion and pity. The sequence was worthy of a play by L.S. Mercier, in particular *L'Humanité ou les tableaux de l'indigence* [humanity or scenes of poverty] whose title alone was evocative, but it had an element of attack, because it implied that the representatives did not know about the life of the people.

Beside the denunciation of barbarity there was the call to tender charity: the administrators of the Haute-Marne wrote to the proprietors of their area on 31 May 1793: 'Ban the barbarous usage of paying the labourers with merchandise which they are obliged to resell because you might as well tear the morsel of bread which they bathe with their tears from them'.[31] The picture developed by Rétif, which described a mother neglected by her children, was here to be found generalised for paid workers in order to arouse the pity of their employers. Chaumette also used this image of bread softened by tears, and summed up the life of the poor man as follows: 'Always bent under the weight of an exhausting and difficult task (he is destined to) live out his days in difficulties, in order to eat in the evening in a hovel, a piece of bread which he often waters with his tears'.[32]

These conventional pictures of the poverty which exacted so many tears obliged the revolutionaries to punish those who fed on the tears of the people. The sensitive man who comforted the unfortunate became the good Jacobin who must protect the populace with decrees, without sympathy for the tight-fisted employers because their cruelty came from barbarity. The conciliatory speech on the pleasures of doing good was transformed into a far more combative plea when it was transposed into the conflict between the moderates and the extremists. The pictures were all the more accusing, the metaphors all the more extreme because the audience had to be moved and dividing lines created between those who wept and the guilty parties who caused the tears.

THAT ON CERTAIN OCCASIONS THERE SHOULD
NOT BE TEARS

Saint-Just, in his speech of 13 November 1792 to the Convention concerning royal inviolability used an expression which made Michelet tremble: 'They seek to stir our pity, soon we will be purchasing tears as is done at funerals in Rome'. To Michelet, this phrase indicated a stage which he feared in the history of the Revolution: 'The day when pity became mockery began an age of barbarity'.[33] Beginning with a memory of his classical upbringing, Saint-Just called to account a pity which had been manipulated by corruption. He also took up again on his own account the argument which the Catholic Church had used since the earliest times to denounce the presence of professional mourners at Roman funerals.[34] But above all, he overturned the dream of a generalised compassion which was part of the model of the emotions. The idea of a counter-revolutionary conspiracy threw this attitude into doubt. If tears could be bought, a concept could founder. The act of weeping over the king or queen became ideological. To cry over their execution was to reveal royalist opinions. The confusion of the public and the private which Mona Ozouf perceives in the *Institutions Républicaines* of Saint-Just, the will to alter morality and to live in glass-houses, were to be found among the chief accusers. The legal archives are evidence of this. Thus Joseph Duhamel was incarcerated after being denounced for having wept at the death of the queen and having said that the revolutionary tribunal was a tribunal of blood. A statement accompanied a petition signed in his favour, and sheds light on the difficulty of accusing a man because of human sympathy. It was probably written by an advocate or by a public scribe:

> Even if the fact were as true as it is false, this act of weakness would only have been the effect of Nature, or of sensibility of which no man is master. There are a number of examples in which many people have burst into tears at the news of the death of a dog or of a cat which they had the greatest interest in seeing destroyed.[35]

The philosophical and literary formulations on the emotions acted as an argument in defence of Duhamel. Occasionally a weakness of organisation, emotion cannot always be mastered even when it contradicts reason. It seemed absurd to accuse the manifestations of Nature. The example given was not chosen at random: we may weep over the death of an animal nevertheless pronounced dangerous, therefore we may over that of a queen, even if she was harmful. A good republican could not so easily hold back tears which should not be shed over the enemies of liberty, and it was hard to judge natural behaviour which did not necessarily show an opinion.

The revolutionary tribunal would have much to do with this sensibility which was so widespread among the people of Paris. In the following example it found itself confronted with the emotion of some denouncers, who retracted their accusations after a most intensely tearful scene, and who from then on, did not stop 'making mistakes in their declarations'. This change of direction had occurred several hours previously: before going to give evidence at the tribunal, the four men were convinced by the wife of one of them that they were conducting those accused to a certain death;

> they were so moved by this fate and were even so horrified that one and all began to weep, which led to the most noisy of scenes, and they were sorry to become the involuntary instruments of the death of their neighbours.

After these loud and painful tears caused by pity, the informers refused to accuse the couple whom they had frequented every day. The revolutionary tribunal had much difficulty in seeing the case clearly, and the denouncers then found themselves in the dock of the accused.

We can then see contrary demands in conflict: the habit of pity for the fate of others, sustained by a whole discourse from the Enlightenment was set against the image of the hardened and pure revolutionary who fought the enemies of liberty without mercy. It reveals to what extent the irruption of politics in daily life, confused the reading of the signs of emotion.

But it was not a matter of combining the intensity of sensibility which the actors of the Revolution showed with the 'excesses of the Terror'. There was in fact, a whole tradition which associated tears and bloodshed. From the time of the Directory onwards, witnesses denounced the climate of optimism, the ability to be moved and to dream of a new society which had presided over the Revolution and which would have led to worse terrors. Bitterness was mixed with a new realism, and called back into question the utopias and delights of the emotions. The theorists of the counter-revolution would build a whole system of them. Closer to us, Lenoble resumed their analysis in the name of his religious convictions:

'Natural freedom' produced the Revolutionary Tribunal and the Committee of Public Safety; the Supreme Being and natural religion supplied the guillotine, and all this in floods of tears, tears of tenderness, because pity, like goodness, was natural to man and because Virtue must triumph. Nothing demonstrates better how the sentimentalism and religiosity of Rousseau only served to charge the acidity of Voltaire with explosives.[36]

This reading of the Enlightenment and of its tears, measured against the blood which was shed during the Terror, which here becomes a combination, even a tissue of stupidities, deserves to be refuted, so popular has it been. Although the men of the Revolution might have followed the emotional model to different degrees, with the delicious sharing of deistic agitations, while passing through general pity, this type of feeling was sometimes in contradiction with the necessities of the hour and the pictures of inflexibility which were exalted by some. Monglond speaks of the false sensibility of the representatives on assignments and the members of the Committee for Public Safety who could massacre while shedding floods of tears. He criticises in particular Lequinio who 'wept crocodile tears' before killing his prisoners.

This infamous Lequinio wrote, on 12 brumaire an II, a curious text entitled 'Of happiness' which joined a long line of eighteenth century treatises on the subject, but which is to be distinguished on other points. This text gives a good account of the contradictions which filled these revolutionaries, steeped in Rousseauist sensibilities who felt their actions criticised. He exalted in it the pleasure which was to be felt in soothing misfortune, while adding a bitter observation: 'delicious tears always come to sprinkle the good acts which he has done and to avenge in secret the injustices of evil men and the mistake of the public who are fooled by them'. In the face of the incomprehension with which the virtuous Jacobin was surrounded, Lequinio proposed a solution, he should, according to him, seek happiness within himself, in 'the abnegation of the self', the love of others. This new system led him to describe some strange states of the soul. He could thus be a witness to the misfortune of another and suffer from being unable to act, but in the pain itself a gentle impression was formed:

> the man who abnegates himself [. . .] almost enjoys his desires and his regrets, his eyes fill with tears and the tears which he sheds over public calamities become a happiness for him, because he finds that he is satisfied with feeling that he wishes seriously for the happiness of others, even when he can do nothing for them.

These contradictory comments demonstrate an attempt to save something which could still be good at the moment when he perceived that 'a society can be good without each individual finding happiness therein'. What one might call Lequinio's 'pleasurable, self-abnegation' felt the haunting of intrigue and the certainty of the philanthropist, a tragic phase in the final hours of a firmly embedded taste for tears.

On the matter of democratic revolution and 'the uncertainty concerning others' which might have resulted from it, Marcel Gauchet and Gladys Swain write thus:

> It would be a study in itself to follow and to analyse at the turn-ing point between the eighteenth and nineteenth centuries, the series of crucial transformations through which this dissolution of the preregulated ties between men was translated, with what it signified in terms of the liberation of a partially savage space in the area of interpersonal relationships.[37]

Between the eighteenth century and the nineteenth century, it seems that, where tears were concerned, a redistribution was in operation. An absence or mutation of the norms of communica-tion, tearful dreams were mocked, and sensibility and the value of tears were reinterpreted in literature and private writings. This transformation was for some a deliberate break with the model of the Enlightenment and its revolutionary consequences. The discontinuity could also be seen in a less deliberate but broader fashion, through the disappearance of delicious expressions of emotion, of shared tears, and a re-evaluation of solitary emotion and loving expressions which came up against the unsolvable separation of beings.

The revolutionary episode figures as the changing-point of many modes of thought, of many ways of behaviour, which then had to be evaluated. Beyond the trauma which it sometimes caused and on which certain men of letters based their denunciation of the tearful outbursts of the eighteenth century, there was a new concept of the intimate, of individual truth, of the representation of the self which was at work. It seems to have been connected to the democratic revolution and the formulation of individualism. This phenomenon widely exceeded ideological distinctions, and represented an anthropological change.

Part II
From Modesty to Aridity

6 Towards a New Sensitivity

To leave the streets and the revolutionary crowds and return to literature is to change universes. We cannot, however, study the new forms of sensitivity advocated by men of letters at the beginning of the nineteenth century without referring to the Revolution and through it to the Enlightenment. In the solitude of their studies, they attempted to think the unthinkable, to feel anew and they weighed their heritage. The practice of writing was an issue on the same basis as political opinions. A new literary subjectivity was born of these wanderings and with it different ways of perceiving tears on the horizon of Romanticism.

SENANCOUR'S JUDGEMENTS

In 1799 Sénancour published *les Rêveries sur la nature primitive de l'homme* [Reflections on the primitive nature of man]. Until then he had led a wandering and solitary existence. For this isolated writer, born in 1770, the Revolution was a break, but he did not re-immerse himself in Christian tradition in order to condemn it as the neo-Catholics did. His world was disenchanted, with no sense of the beyond and no transcendence; he wished to meditate about mankind and wandered the Alps alone in order to discover a new use of the senses which required a quite original relationship within the self which consisted above all of 'self containment'.

Sénancour, a pivotal figure, was connected to the eighteenth century through his philosophical demands and his dreams which brought him close to Rousseau and appears as a precursor of Romanticism through his description of states of the soul. Close to the Ideologists, he was one of those writers who attempted to rethink the status of man after the revolutionary experience. But above all Sénancour wanted to break deliberately with the traditional concept of sensitivity, and to formulate a new one which he considered in *les Rêveries*. Sensibility had, from his point of view,

been the object of a traditional contradiction which assimilated it
into sentiment: 'the sentimental affection which is called feeling
because in fact it replaces it, but it is better called sentimania'.[1]
In severely censuring this mania for sentiment, the semi-illness of
the end of the eighteenth century, he clearly placed himself on
different ground. He distinguished what had often been confused,
for example by Diderot: the ability to be moved, and the ability to
experience sensations. For Sénancour, sensibility was produced
by sensualism, by the development of the capacity to feel:[2]

> Sensibility is not only a tender and painful emotion, but the
> faculty given to the perfectly organised man of experiencing
> profound impressions of everything which can affect the
> human organs. The truly sensitive man is not the one who
> is moved, who weeps, but who experiences sensations where
> others only find indifferent perceptions.[3]

The sensitive man did not allow himself to be moved but had
a superior perceptive acuteness and organised his perceptions.
Sensibility was no longer a model for communication but was
part of a science of man. On this matter, Sénancour's thought
joined that of the contemporary Ideologists who, taking perception as a starting point, invented an educational system which
first concerned itself with observation through the senses, and
ended with the formulation of ideas. For Destutt de Tracy, 'to
think is always to feel and is nothing but feeling': from this
idea we can more easily understand the issue in Sénancour's
definition and his desire to break with sentiment. To feel was
an act of recognition and necessitated an organisation of the
perceptions which emotion would render impossible. To feel
was therefore not to be sensitive. Also, Sénancour preferred
a cold attitude without tender goodwill to the taste for tears:
'The sensitive man should prefer the indifferent and wild man to
the sentimental man'.[4] This praise of indifference made a clean
break with previous conceptions, which based sensibility on the
possibility of being moved to tears by the sight of misfortune,
or by shared affection. Here the moral and social viewpoint
was deliberately put to one side to the benefit of a 'superior'
understanding.

In *Obermann*, an intimate novel published in 1803, he definitively
dismissed this curious sentimania:

We have collectively too narrow an idea of the sensitive man; we make a ridiculous character out of him. I have seen a woman made ridiculous, one of those women who weep over the indisposition of their bird, who faint at the blood of a bird's scratch, and who tremble at the sound of certain syllables, such as serpent, spider, grave digger, smallpox, tomb, and old age.[5]

Sensitive men bore too close a resemblance to such affected women who were moved by the slightest thing, frightened by the least factual term, preferring illusion to truth, fine expressions to practical words, preciousness to virile firmness. For this new sensibility was also a reform of language where a series of worn expressions which had come from the pastoral mode were abandoned. In the 'Observations' which preceded *Obermann*, Sénancour proclaimed loudly that his style did not make use of those 'hackneyed expressions, of which the least bearable, in my opinion are the figures which are used several million times'. As an example he gave: 'the enamel of the meadows, the azure of the skies and the crystal of the waters' but also 'floods of tears escaped his eyes, he melted into tears and drowned those who watched him'.[6] Thus the old rhetoric of tears in its use of hyperbole and the sharing aspect of its nature, along with the sentimentality which accompanied it, was made redundant. Sénancour's sensitive man wanted nothing of these worn expressions and following Rousseau and with the Ideologists, looked for a new way of writing: his sensitivity was also a matter of style.

It also formed a different vision of life and unhappiness. When one of his friends came to die, Obermann could not weep for the death of this virtuous man, for whom life had only reserved torments:

> I have not said that it was a weakness to shed a tear for evils which are not our own, for an unhappy stranger who is nevertheless known to us. He is dead: it does not mean much, who does not die? But he was always unhappy and sad, existence was never good for him, he has suffered only sorrows so far, and now he is nothing.[7]

The traditional motif of compassion and tears for the death of a human being whatever he may be, could not resist the vision of the absurdity of an individual life, which here only contained sadness and pain. And this sentiment of suffering which was inherent to life itself completely rearranged the relationship between Sénancour and the signs of emotion. Human existence was bathed in illusion and poverty:

> I admire this Providence which makes everything large; but how man is thrown down among the clippings! Gods in our thought, insects in our happiness, we are the Jupiter whose temple is among the smaller houses; he takes the wooden bowl of steaming soup which is brought to him in his hut for a jar of incense; he reigns on Mount Olympus until the most vile of gaolers gives him a slap in the face which brings him back to reality, so he can kiss his hand, and soak his mouldy bread with tears.[8]

Sénancour's line of thought was established on the ruins of a certain concept of happiness which had existed in the finest days of the eighteenth century and the Revolution. The sensitive man had overcome these human vanities and could better perceive the truth. For this, a superior understanding was required which was not given to all. To attain happiness, it was necessary to succeed in ridding oneself of the mirages of the imagination, and to seek to 'restrict one's soul in order to be in full possession of it', to mark out one's own limits and to remain within them, not to open oneself up; a concentration not an expansion of the spirit.

To arrive at such a position, Sénancour believed that it was necessary to discipline oneself; to learn to master the impulses which led to excess and which were harmful to the perception of the relationships between things. The new sensibility should create a sort of new man:

> I conceive a certain *moderation* in all which moves us, a sudden combination of contrary feelings, a habit of dominance over the very affection which commands us; a gravity of the soul, and a depth of thought, an expansion which calls to the secret perception in us with which nature wishes to counter visible sensation; a moderation of the heart in its perpetual agitation; and finally, a mixture, a harmony, which only belongs to the man of great sensibility; in his strength he has already experienced all which is destined for man; in his moderation, he

alone has known the melancholy of pleasure, and the mercies of suffering.[9]

It was not a question, as in the eighteenth-century treatises on happiness, of not allowing an excess of passions and emotions in order to live properly, but also of the development of a knowledge of what was appropriate to man. This labour of moderation on the self allowed one to liberate oneself from emotional shocks in order to deepen the secret relations which were not at first evident, by adapting oneself to the movement of the soul through the agency of a certain self-mastery.

We can better understand now why Sénancour chose the form of the personal novel, the novel of a character's development, to follow Obermann's itinerary; the sensitive man who went through the torments, dissatisfaction, and absurdity which are linked to existence itself, in a search for the depths which were so hard to reach, allied with an interior equilibrium which allowed him to broaden his field of understanding. His knowledge of human destiny in its darkest misery was the price paid for superiority by this still-young man. Furthermore, it was with bitterness that he told of the states of his soul at a certain period in his life:

The night was already dark. I slowly withdrew into myself: I walked at random, I was filled with dissatisfaction. I needed tears but I could only shudder. The early days are over: I have the torments of youth and none of the consolations. My heart, still weary with the fire of a useless youth, is withered and dried as though it were in the state of exhaustion of cold old-age. My fire is quenched without being calmed. There are those who rejoice in their ills; but for me all things have passed: I have no joy, no hope, no rest: nothing is left to me, I have no more tears.[10]

We will often encounter from this time on the description of a state of unease which was manifested by the inability to shed tears which were nevertheless wished for. Pain itself could not be magnified, and dissatisfaction crushed everything, without being able to achieve indifference through this. To be at once too old and too young, to feel too much and not to feel enough, to be threatened by aridity, such were the new torments of the children of the century when they set themselves to write.

Sénancour took us towards a new sensibility which broke
with previous definitions, and did so with a full knowledge of
its cause. Sentiment was out of fashion: tearful outbursts, shared
tears, delicious feelings of tenderness were all the weakness of
ridiculous women. The compassion which caused tears to be
shed over a stranger's misfortune was no longer to be defended,
because on earth below life was worth little more than death and
all was illusion and the vanity of vanities. Also, the far-seeing,
tormented sensitive soul no longer had the consolation of tears.

Only a constant labour of moderation of the self could
bring the élite soul to taste refined emotions: 'the melancholy
of pleasure and the mercies of sorrow' which were in opposition
to a too easy sentimentality. Emotions in half-tones were the sign
of true sensibility without excess in a solitude which was not
contaminated by the reign of appearances, and which did not
seek to be shared.

That a man born in the eighteenth century should have
rewritten the elements of sensibility which no longer existed
following the French Revolution and which denied even that
of the Enlightenment cannot leave us unmoved. He was not
the only one to do so. Ballanche, Joseph de Maistre and
Chateaubriand whose starting point was religion, but also Mme
de Staël, Benjamin Constant and to a certain extent Stendhal,
all demonstrated a renewal of ideas and behaviour. A new
reading of the gestures of emotion, and a different concept
of sensibility were born, illustrating a concept of the self and
others which was fundamentally reworked: a more discreet but
lasting change, an anthropological transformation which called
public and private relationships into play, and the masculine and
feminine roles.

Sénancour's work remained one of the major expressions
of the process of modification of the status of tears through
the extent of his transformation and through his proximity to
the Enlightenment (he is often considered to be a disciple of
Jean-Jacques because of his love of the Alps and his high retreats).
His ability to put a new concept of sensibility into words, with
his description of the states of the soul in which dissatisfaction
and absurdity transformed private emotions, sufficed to make
of him an author of show-texts which invited reflection on
the part of the reader, even if he was little read by his
contemporaries.

THE AFFIRMATION OF CHRISTIAN DOLORISM AND
THE LESSONS OF THE REVOLUTION

A questioning of the philosophy of the Enlightenment led to a neo-Catholic movement to repopulate the heavens, to give a meaning to unhappiness, to the duality of body and soul: tears rediscovered a religious meaning which broke radically with the conceptual field that had been explored until then. The ability to cry was spiritualised: an important tendency which would be found in Romanticism.

Joseph de Maistre, the theoretician of the ultras, participated in a positive way in this rejection of the French Revolution. He altered the value placed on sensibility in a singular way, by reintroducing divine will. The texts which reaffirmed it were completely caustic even provocative. He took over the discourse on natural goodness in order to take it to its extreme and to draw from it a paradoxical lesson:

> It is man who is ordered to destroy man. But how can he fulfil the law? He, who is a moral and pitying being, he who is born to love, he who weeps over others as though for himself, who finds pleasure in weeping, and who ends up inventing fictions to make himself weep, he, finally, to whom it has been declared that every last drop of blood which he may have shed unjustly will be reclaimed from him: it is war which will fulfil the decree.

'War is therefore divine in itself, since it is the law of the world', he concluded in the seventh interview of the *Soirées de Saint-Pétersbourg* (1821). The pleasures of weeping through virtue, compassion and pity, literary and philosophical themes of the eighteenth century, were struck with inanity in the face of the violence of war, the sign of the reign of evil over the earth. This fatalism rendered obsolete all human striving for a happiness on earth: including those longed-for tears, cultivated with so much care, on which the relationship between men was founded. To explain the traumatism of the fall of the monarchy some saw in it the sign of a divine testing. The necessary expiation of faults and original sin which was made mystical by the men of the Revolution would finally be revived. The renewal of sensibility was a historical vision.

An entire movement of thought would attempt to bring the heritage of the Enlightenment and the Revolution into question by reintroducing the Christian theory of suffering. For the counter-revolution loved to dress up in mourning and suffering in order to affirm a new sensibility. The death of the king remained a loss and a sacrilege which was still wept for, along with the victims of the guillotine.

For Ballanche in 1808, 'there is no reality other than tears'. He can be included in the movement of rehabilitation for redeeming and expiating suffering, which came from an updated Christian tradition which was opposed to the mirages of the Enlightenment which had optimistically appealed for happiness. His writings develop the logic of the transformation of the status of tears.

> We lack a form of measurement to appreciate the sum of happiness and sadness which is reserved for each man. Destitution and poverty live in the rich man's home, and the happy men of the century are prey to poignant sorrows which are unknown to the poor. We only see external appearances, the secret and private things escape us. Laughter often conceals sorrows, and happiness is sometimes austere and serious, the *lacryma-christi* grapes ripen on Vesuvius's flank.
>
> We would be far less surprised at our suffering, if we knew how much better life is adapted to sorrow than to pleasure. Man, within whom everything passes in succession according to his wishes forgets to live. Only sorrow matters in life, and there is no reality beyond tears.[11]

On the ruins of a philosophy which relied on thoughts of happiness, and with it society, a concept was defined in which each individual had a mysterious and impenetrable fate whose outer appearance (that of riches for instance) did not correspond to its inner reality and was generally misleading.

Human knowledge was strictly limited to external matters and was proof of our inadequacy. All was contained in those intimate and secret things which escape us. Here, privacy, and secrecy led to a religious experience, but equally to the realisation that man, who could only refer to the appearances of emotion, profoundly misunderstood the feelings of his neighbour: laughter was sometimes only the mask of unhappiness. Happiness itself was not necessarily characterised by expansion and movement:

it could be austere, hidden, serious, and conscious of the role of sorrow which was most natural to us. For private experience found its truth, and even its life in suffering; beyond the illusions and mirages of human perception, the awareness of sorrow was at once the most real and the most intimate.

We can understand how the message of redemptive suffering, which we shall call dolorism, found here a new beginning: when all points of reference were shifting with the condemnation of comprehension through external things, tears were the only intimate truths and the only effects of reality which could prove to each individual his existence in suffering.

Chateaubriand also wept for the death of the queen: 'memories for which we will never have enough tears'[12] and which the French people have not finished expiating. Christian rhetoric often flowed from his pen, and he constantly remembered the weight of sorrow which lay on the world and the omnipresence of death, which made all individual pleasure absurd: 'At each minute of our existence, of our smiles, of our joys, sixty men are dying, sixty families groan and weep'.[13] In addition, the Christian faith was the only comfort since it 'always presents to us the picture of man here below in a valley of tears, who only finds rest in the tomb'.[14] Chateaubriand displayed a particular predilection for the biblical image of the valley of tears (Job), a desolate landscape where men would not stop weeping until their deliverance. But, if the earthly condition condemned men to tears, society demonstrated that condition: 'Alas! each hour in society opens a tomb and causes tears to be shed' exclaimed René in narrating his youth.[15] A sign of the times, it was not only worldly prejudice which harmed happiness but the whole of society which was responsible for the many sufferings of particular individuals.

The experience of true suffering was close to the 'there is no reality but tears' of Ballanche, which was accompanied by an intimate and secret perception of a personal experience of truth which belonged to neo-Catholic dolorism. Thus, René experienced the ambiguous pleasure of shedding tears which were all the more true, when Amélie, on taking the veil, placed herself out of his reach for ever:

Oh my friends, I knew then what it was to shed tears over an evil which was not in the least imaginary! [. . .] I even discovered a sort of unexpected satisfaction in the fullness of my grief, and I perceived, with a secret rush of joy, that sorrow is not a feeling which runs out like pleasure.

For the anguish of the imagination filled the void with bitter tears, true sorrow had greater meaning, it allowed a certain fullness and more gentle tears.

In his novels he developed fully these tragic metaphors by emphasising the situations. In *Atala* the blind Chactas would weep unto the tomb despite his infirmity: 'Men may already be unable to see but they can still weep'.[16] Also, the account of his life was punctuated with tears, at the picture of the sufferings he had endured: 'At this point, for the second time since the beginning of his tale, Chactas was obliged to interrupt himself. He was drowned in tears, and he could only utter broken words.'[17] Chateaubriand did not fear worn metaphors and weeping hyperboles as Sénancour did; his use of tears did, however, remain connected with the sorrow which was our lot on this lowly earth. The image of the Cross gave meaning to this suffering:

'Here it is, Atala's crucifix,' he cried, 'this proof of adversity. Oh René, oh my son, you can see it; and I can see it no longer! Tell me, after so many years, is the gold not spoiled? Can you not see the trace of my tears on it?'.[18]

Religious dolorism became the only area in which tears had significance. The Abbé Lesage, a critic of *Atala*, nevertheless found that the Père Aubry was a 'lachrymophile'[19] and the employment of tears in Chateaubriand already appeared excessive to his readers who were tired of the torrents of tears which were connected to the literature of the eighteenth century.

AESTHETIC EMOTION

Although Chateaubriand's characters wept frequently, he did not wish to arouse an excess of emotion in his readers. Indeed, in the preface to *Atala*, he even went so far as to revolt against the literary practice of aiming to cause tears of emotion and tenderness:

I would say further that my aim has not been to exact many tears; it seems to me that this is a dangerous error, put forward, like many others, by M. de Voltaire, that good writings are those which cause the most tears [. . .] To torture the soul is not to be a great writer. True tears are those which fine poetry cause to be shed; there should be as much tenderness mixed into them as sadness.[20]

Aesthetic emotion gained in dignity, and the tears which the cult of the Beautiful would cause to be shed were not those which were the sign of the agreement of the stalls, or the bestselling successes which formed the relationship between the man of letters and his public in the eighteenth century. Elevated taste was distinguished from sentimentality and led to the demand for tears. Sainte-Beuve wrote that Chateaubriand would say when the fancy took him that, despite his reputation, he had never wept from anything other than admiration.[21] Here is a more likely proposal: 'These are the only tears which should dampen the strings of the lyre and sweeten its tone. The Muses are celestial ladies who never mar their features with grimaces; when they weep, it is with the secret aim of beautifying themselves.'[22] Chateaubriand was not the first to celebrate tears of admiration. They were very well adapted in the men of the eighteenth century to the exaltation of a Brutus-like heroism. The value of a moving tale was then measured by the tears shed in a salon and that of a tragedy by those which it provoked in the theatres. However, in the provocation of emotion, the art of the teller was not distinguished from that of the tale, that of the dramatist from that of the virtues which he portrayed. But the fact that the highest admiration should have been reserved for the art in itself and not for the heroes who were represented in it, that the most esteemed tears were those which were brought about by the worship of the Muses, is evidence of a new trend which established itself in the nineteenth century: to weep with admiration for the love of art.

The fact that Chateaubriand should have allied this movement to the sanctification of the individual destiny of the Artist, a tendency which was exaggerated in him to the point of affectation, distinguished him from the very discreet Ballanche. We know to what extent in his *Mémoires d'Outre-Tombe* [memoirs from beyond the tomb] Chateaubriand loved to reproduce his solitary feelings.[23] He had here taken up his position on the Saint-Malo rock: 'In the midst of this reverie, if the wind bore to me the sound of the canon of a vessel which was putting out to sea, I shuddered and tears come to my eyes'.[24] If, on occasion, he experienced an excess of theatricality in the language of tears, his effusions, which were always dignified, spoke of glory. This was in order to enlarge the emotional scope of the Genius, which was related to his own individual journey which he retraced stage by stage. As with Sénancour, this sensibility was not given to all, even though Chateaubriand's distinction came of a total lack of moderation.

The exaltation of impassioned emotions, providing that they came from the soul of an artist, could coexist, even if they were expressed through a break with the behaviourial model, with the advocation of moderation and restraint. The furies of the romantic passions, the floods of tears shed in corners, the anguished sobs shed alone, of a disturbed nature, could only be understood against the background of self-control, which according to Elias was more interiorised in the bourgeois model of conduct. Without this precise definition, the study of literary sources would be the foreground of the analysis of a pattern whose significance is perceptible only if the two propositions are considered together although they appear paradoxical. For the exaltation which led to the shedding of tears, and the moderation which withheld them, were both curiously part of the same movement, of the same economy of the imagination, which redefined the intimate, and with it the public.

Literary activity, in the first half of the nineteenth century, may appear in certain respects to have been a rejection of the middle-class way of life, occasionally adorned by frankly 'bourgeoisophobic' declarations. But this reaction to the model of self-constraint and of encompassed privacy was accompanied by an affirmation of the personality. These private tears, these personal torments which were advertised in the full light of day, these loving passions which were widely discussed in the coteries, salons, cafes and theatres, and which were peddled in books with cries of indignation and disapproving commentaries in country towns and middle-class families, were a part of this movement of the affirmation of personal emotion.

The worries and crises of the artist which passed over the 'wall of private life' (the expression was coined by Talleyrand according to Stendhal) by the publication route were, in their way, a quest for a personal intimacy, although it was still necessary that the person should be exceptional, or that he should wish to manifest his subjectivity through a private diary, the fashion for which took off at the beginning of the nineteenth century. By sometimes declaring his conflict with the world in which he lived, the writer made a major issue out of the relationship between the individual and society, following the new terms of conflict. And the readers were party to this exaltation of the individual without necessarily living the lives of romantics. Between a private life which was unknown to others, and the internal and the secret, contained in the heart of a being, a relationship developed which was further promoted by the publicity given to the author. Hidden things were constantly revealed for some, as though it was necessary to write about this new problem for it to exist.

DREAMS OF GENTLE TEARS AND THE REMAINS OF THE CIRCULATION OF THE SENTIMENTS

It is curious to observe to what extent the model of the communication of the emotions whose eighteenth-century contours we have outlined led to a parallel and quasi-underground life in the nineteenth century. Outside the circles of writers who broke deliberately with the style of the Enlightenment, writers who have remained unknown appeared to find in it an appropriate tone for the expression of their dreams and the state of their souls.

The *Mémoires* of Agricol Perdiguier thus revealed the persistence of Rousseau's example among the artisans of the beginning of the industrial age. Alone before the vision of the ocean, Agricol experienced a delicious wave of subjectivity:

> I was absorbed! [. . .] I was no longer substance but entirely thought, entirely feeling, my heart was moved, my soul floated through space, the tears ran from my eyes, I wept. And why? I was sad, but I was happy, I experienced suffering, but this suffering was joy, a voluptuousness, a celestial sweetness, I was ravished. My happiness was without measure and no words can describe it.[25]

When the words were lacking to describe this flight of the spirit, only tears, which mingled sadness with the pleasure of the experience of existence, the enjoyment of the self and the fading away of the worker's body, could express a moment, the memory of which renewed Perdiguier's emotion. Fluctuating between sadness and happiness, effusion was an expansion, a discovery of the

self which recalled the weeping ecstasies of Rousseau or of the
Prince de Ligne. To this solitary emotion, there was sometimes
added the evidence of human goodness which made gentle tears
fall. Perdiguier thus described a touching scene in which charity
and generosity were displayed. On the occasion of one of his
voyages on board a boat, a taylor announced himself unable to pay
for his passage. In the face of the inflexibility of the transporter, an
orange-seller gave the unfortunate the money which he needed:

> The owner of the boat himself felt his heart soften, rise up,
> become more noble, and replied to the young man who offered
> to pay: 'Keep your money, you do not have too much'. I was
> moved by it! Gentle tears began to flow from my eyes. An air
> of contentment reigned in the boat. All the souls drew close,
> communed together . . . See! If we wished for it, how happy
> the earth could be![26]

The characteristic of humanity which affected all the spectators
present, and caused such delicious tears to fall, this moving
communion reminds us of the eighteenth-century scenes of
charity, and led Perdiguier to dream of a better world, freed from
selfishness. He wished for universal reconciliation, but above all,
he wrote in the cause of that of members of a brotherhood who
were divided by a fratricidal struggle, for he had known painful
tears. He had kept a burning memory of the death of Beauceron
in a fight which occurred between the independent journeymen
and the Companions of Duty.

> There was Beauceron, who just a moment before had been
> thinking of his mother, and dreaming of such a fine future.
> The blood was still dribbling from his wounds . . . I cannot
> say how deeply I was struck, moved by such a sight . . . I
> had tears in my eyes and in my heart; and the corpse and the
> drops of blood remained imprinted on my imagination.[27]

Deeply affected by this meaningless death, which he wept
for with his eyes and with his heart, he vowed himself to
the reconciliation of quarrelling brothers.

Another notable characteristic was the political emotion which
he shared with an innkeeper to whom he offered a willow leaf
which had shaded the tomb of the Emperor on St Helena: 'the

innkeeper was delighted! He kissed the incomparable relic a hundred times! He wept with tenderness and joy! He was no longer in possession of himself . . . I joined in his emotion.'[28] Under the Restoration, it seemed that the Napoleonic cult, in popular circles, led to the shedding of delicious tears: in this case the sharing of emotion was political. Perdiguier liked to reveal his capacity for emotion: his tears were movements of the heart. Telling, at the end of his work, of his return to the village of his birth, a major scene for this itinerant journeyman, he even wrote a defence of tears: 'It was a fine day! . . . There were tears of joy . . . Tears return to my eyes at so fine a memory, they fall and dampen my paper. Great sadness, and the deepest joys are expressed in the same way, have the same language; tears! tears!'[29] It was even these tears born of the memory of great pains and great joys which soaked the paper on which he wrote his memoirs.

The dreaming workers, who are revealed to us by Jacques Rancière, often appeared to evoke the young Genevan apprentice who became a man of letters. We can also find Fénelon there, the model of tearful sensibility of the seventeenth century who seems to have retained his acuteness. Joseph Jaccotot, inventor of the system of 'intellectual emancipation' suggested that all workers: 'who were conscious of the dignity of their being should learn from the book of *Télémaque*, lying open at the chapter of Calypso's lamentations, the secret of learning all and expressing all'.[30]

For, to regain possession of one's own existence it was necessary to find out how to speak and write, and to be set free by learning about oneself. The worker could tell of his sufferings, but could also hope for the sharing of gentle tears. Tears of suffering, tears of pleasure: the cabinet maker Boissy invited his brothers to move on from 'tears extracted by unhappiness and suffering' to 'tears which we love to shed', a promise of the future happiness of a loving humanity.[31] The confessions and the letters of the workers of the first half of the century, drawn by the followers of Saint-Simon, gave a place to tears born of a sadness which resulted from their condition. 'You ask me how my present life is, here it is as usual. I am weeping at present from a cruel soul-searching. Pardon my childish vanity, it seems to me that I am not following my vocation by hammering iron',[32] wrote Gilland. For soul-searching was not the repentance of the romantic, but the realisation of dispossession in the work of the craftsman, which it was not always easy to express without being vain.

The same Gilland revealed to us, in a tale entitled *L'Incompris*, the sadness of the young child with poetic feelings, when confronted with the hard life of the workshop: 'during the night, when I was too tired to sleep, I wept for my lost illusions as the exile weeps for the sun of his country'.[33] The writer-locksmith wept for his worker's exile chained to the workbench, dreaming of a life of the mind and soul. This was true suffering, wrote Gauny, 'that of the worker at the mercy of the terrible scenes of the workshop, that financial necessity which gnaws at the spirit and the body through the dissatisfaction and madness of his long labour'. And Gauny did not believe much in tears of the romantics, their cries were too fine and made haloes around their souls: 'Child Harold, Obermann, René, declare the perfume of your anguish frankly. Answer me. Were you not happy in your fine melancholies?'[34] Though the intimate sufferings of these family sons, who lived the life of their souls freely, without suffering from the separation of the productive body, might attain the status of art, it did not always get across to the audience, for those who knew of the most terrible exile. And we can understand better why these craftsmen revived the model of Rousseau, connected with an experience of uprooting and retreat from culture, rather than the sorrows of the romantics who were nevertheless their contemporaries.

The answer to the suffering of these lives cut off from their goals, was the emotional encounter with the Saint-Simonian creed. Bazin, who first came to listen with a mocking curiosity was 'amazed to surprise a tear dampening his eyelid'. He defended himself by criticising his 'emotion of cowardice', and thinking of the orators: 'they are scholars but they are tricksters',[35] only to rally to them in the end and to come to know fine emotions.[36] For these workers who dreamed of gentle tears were afraid of being taken in, before they gained confidence in these men of science who preached socialism together with a new art of living together. The philanthropist expressed in fact a desire to move the emotions, and to exchange tears and knowledge. Raspail defined the militant activity of the doctor who approached the people, adding that it led to 'tears of sympathy which were far finer than those of joy'[37] among those for whose benefit he was communicating his knowledge. The encounter of the workers and the bourgeoisie was bonded by expressions of sociability.

Should we perceive 'a popular physics of humanitarian currents and fluids' in these exchanges of love and blurred gazes of Saint-Simonian communion, as Jacques Rancière suggests?[38]

In the first half of the nineteenth century, these workers spoke of another suffering, that of self-exile in work, dreaming of tearful exchanges, which were the promise of a future happiness, of an ideal of liquid circulation among men. The notion of humanity and natural sympathy which affected them, was part of the heritage of the Enlightenment (coming in particular from the mesmerism of tears during the French Revolution, a popular science of communicating sensibilities) which made a clean break with the romantic developments of personal suffering.

MEN AND WOMEN: A NEW INTIMACY

Stendhal, Benjamin Constant and Germaine de Staël were writing at the same period as the authors of neo-Catholic dolorism. However they did not take part in this strong reaction to the philosophy of the Enlightenment, even if, in their own ways, they learned from it by reviewing it. Germaine de Staël wept in public beside her father during the Revolution. Stendhal as a child and precocious republican intoxicated himself to the point of tears with certain formulae like 'Long live freedom or death'. In their novels and private diaries they hardly ever criticised the sensibility of the eighteenth century, and its tearful procession of happiness and emotion. These were a far cry from the forcefulness of the preceding declarations and more prudence is required in unravelling the diverse signs of a transformation of emotional manifestations: this was the time of microscopic modifications. It is therefore necessary to go to autobiographical or novelistic accounts in order to see singular events in play, and most of all to see new methods of presenting tears, starting with the questions of the intimate and the public, from the male and female roles. What, in my view, sets this writing of tears apart is less the deliberate break with old models of sensibility than the introduction of new nuances in its description. The deciphering of tears became a central consideration as though access to them was no longer assured but was subjected to several interpretations. In this tears were not to be shared in the immediacy of a delicious moment but were observed, and decoded in a constant fluctuation of meaning. And, through these developments of the behaviour of others, through the demands of restraint and modesty which were revealed.

The development of new literary genres and of new practices, like the personal diary, redoubled the questions. Recourse to a diary was characteristic of the post-revolutionary period: it revealed, through descriptions of different ways of crying, an observation of the self and of others which was thoroughly replenished. The written analysis of one's tears or those of the people one mixed with, as a sort of private moment of the day, or as the deciphering of the emotional states of others, led to a particular meaning. The keeping of a private diary could shed light especially on the link between private life, personal privacy and self-expression in writing, as it was elaborated and transformed in the nineteenth century. But it also observed others and was the vehicle for an awareness of the observation of others.[39]

As for autobiographical writing, it had the benefit of a series of filters through which it was sometimes hard to perceive oneself. For example: when Stendhal (delighted at having heard Milanese spoken for an entire summer in a salon because he breathed 'the idea of Métilde' in it) went up to his charming room, as he called it, to correct 'the proofs of *De l'Amour* [on love] with tears in his eyes', we can question this on different levels. He spoke of the sweetness of his tears shed in a studious solitude, which were caused by the aching of his heart, but also by the correction of his work *De l'Amour*. Why then did he describe this scene in his *Souvenirs d'égotisme* [memories of selfishness]? The moist eye of the writer blended different writing activities (essay, autobiography) with memory and with life itself in an amazing palimpsest where the different layers bespoke each other without surrendering the meaning of the fallen tears. These games of hide and seek with texts led to the proliferation of points of view.

READING THE SIGNS AND SELF-OBSERVATION

'Stendhalian love is among other things a system and an exchange of signs [. . .] feeling tends naturally, so to speak, towards cryptography, as though through a deep superstition', writes Gérard Genette concerning the telegraphic codes which the lovers used in the novels of Stendhal in order to communicate among them-selves.[40] In his diary, Stendhal was constantly writing, day after day, about the slightest amount of moisture discerned in the eyes of the women he was in love with. A tear concealed with the help of a discreet movement, furtively wiped away, or red eyes, or even 'the look of having cried'[41] on her face, could indicate that his love was returned. But these fragile and complex signs did not give him the assurance that he was loved. This was perhaps one of the reasons which moved him to write of these scenes in detail, for example the following one: 'At the moment of departure, she appeared to soften towards me. She even had tears in her eyes, but I am far from believing first that they were sincere, and second that they were shed for me'.[42] These traces of tears led to two questions; that of the genuineness of the emotion, and that of its destination. He did not know what to think and these various interpretations fed his private writing; Mme Palfy, as he called her in his diary, would have reddened eyes on other days when with him: she would hide herself behind her work, or would withdraw for a moment to cry. What Stendhal passionately looked out for as the sign of love, but with great discretion and deception, playing with the children so that he could watch her, were 'tears of happiness'.[43] He was watching for tears of a particular quality which would be evidence in his favour and which would be the infallible sign of love.

But women played with tears through coquetry, their tears were not always true and Stendhal did not neglect to recognise this. Thus, Mélanie, the young actress he was in love with when he was about 20, would sometimes display emotion out of coquetry. 'She was certainly impressed by my tender soul; but I do have a small fault to reproach her with, although what woman is not a little flirtatious? She was really moved; when she spoke of her father she dabbed at her tearless eyes'.[44] This gesture of pretence could not please Stendhal, and cancelled out the signifying effect which tears could have. Not that Stendhal doubted Mélanie's emotion, but to display it through artifice, to fall short of natural expression was, to all intents, to reduce it to generality. What was this feminine coquetry if it was not the use of the agreed signs of seduction? One day, however, she shed delicious tears, when Stendhal announced to her that he was giving up everything for her:

She turned her head towards the window for a while so that I should not see her cry, then she asked me for her handkerchief. It was not in the bedroom, I went to look for it in the salon where people were returning. I did not dare to wipe away these charming tears myself, at first sight I was wrong, but perhaps I was right in the eyes of those who know mercy.[45]

This amazing bedroom scenography exercised such a spell over Stendhal that he restrained himself from wiping away her tears for fear of breaking it. In this he described himself as different from the man of a forward nature who would not let an opportunity to draw close to a woman pass. He knew well what the male account was of women in tears who were ripe for the plucking. He himself preferred to take pleasure in his own sensibility, he delighted in feminine charm and in the mercy of love which were both born of these ballets of tears. Mélanie's emotion, which he reflected on, took on an infinite value in the remainder of this page of his diary:

She wept a lot. These were obviously tears which resulted from her smiles following the sight of happiness, she found me to be so good that she wept. After she had turned her head away, I spoke to her for a while longer before she asked me for her handkerchief. Her soul was experiencing a movement similar to liquefication, to the rift in the soul experienced by the Chevalier des Grieux when Manon spoke to him of her cabin in New Orleans.

And it is amazing to read to what point Stendhal immersed himself in Mélanie's soul through these tears; they were the liquefication of the being. Only literary memory could account for it: Prévost's novel, the model of a sensibility admired by Stendhal, was the means of understanding the beauty and mercy in the life of a soul. The reference to an eighteenth-century text was the very element which allowed him to give its proper value to this fascination for female liquidity.

The ardently awaited sign, which was so disturbing and marvellous, came then from the tears caused by a smile, when happiness allowed itself to be glimpsed unawares; as Stendhal said in *De l'Amour* 'tears are extreme smiles'.[46] The very concept of crystallisation was connected to it:

the sight of anything of great beauty in nature and the arts, can recall in a flash the memory of one's beloved. This is because, through the agency of the Salzburg mine, all beautiful and sublime things become part of the beauty of the object of our love, and this unforeseen view of happiness immediately fills our eyes with tears. It is thus that the love of beauty and love give reciprocal life to each other.[47]

In this way, the deciphering of the signs of love led to the search for an aesthetic.

If Stendhal shared a love of beauty with his contemporaries he was nevertheless a special case. He did not magnify pain and its tears, he sought tears of happiness, and the works of eighteenth century men of letters would belong to his ideal library; in them he found models for the expression of emotion. But he reinterpreted two concepts from the Enlightenment for his own use: happiness and nature, which then became the quest for happiness, and the search for the natural. Tears of happiness came from surprise, a fragile moment in the encounter between the love of beauty and love, and his rejection of affectation made him exacting in his painstaking search for the true sign.

Educated in the central school of the Ideologists, he developed the acuteness of his perception and studied Destutt de Tracy, Pinel and Cabanis as he noted in his diary. He conceived of the idea of describing the passions which he observed with the help of their writings. The regard which he turned on women then became quite different. After having spent his day in a salon he noted: 'As for me, I always return to the physical laws. The nervous fluid runs through the brains of men and the hearts of women, this is why the latter are more sensitive.'[48] Aggravated by women's ability to be moved, he called on medical theories to reduce it to a natural phenomenon. It was by transposing the discoveries about electricity into the human body that doctors adopted this idea of a nervous fluid which sometimes came close to magnetism. Cabanis thus thought that sensitivity behaved like a fluid of invariable quantity but which ebbed and flowed in channels and was reduced in the centre of the body.[49] For specialists in mental illness, the brain was considered to be the seat of intelligence and the centre of the emotions, but the digestive system regulated the humours. They were in fact

opposed to the principles of organicism which considered madness to be the result of a lesion on the brain. Thus the madman
who was deranged in his emotions and not in his reason was often
indifferent to those who should have been dear to him. He would
signal a return to normal by being moved to tears at the sight of
them.[50] This is why, by taking action over moral matters, physical problems could be resolved: 'joy, sorrow, the emotions of the
heart excite the outburst of tears which is often critical in nervous
disorders', wrote Esquirol. But Stendhal added to these famous
physical laws a sexual differentiation of the male brain and the
female heart, while psychiatric doctors used the term epigastrial
to define the centre of the passions. Stendhal distinguished himself from women, through an imaginary geography of the sexual
body. He turned the heart into the place where feminine feelings
flowed through a metaphoric shift which transformed the theory
on which he based his ideas.

This explorer of feminine liquids, observing women in the
salons, was also amazed by their strength of judgement, their per-
tinent ability to seize on certain significant details, thus displaying
qualities of the head, but he deplored that at the next moment;
'they allowed themselves to be moved to tears by a platitude'.[51]
The easy tears of the heart left to one side women's discernment
and good taste which could nevertheless sometimes be so assured.
The lover of beauty made more subtle distinctions in living out his
sensibility. Women's coquetry and their sentimentality made their
tears, which could be so charming, banal and reduced them to
organic determinations. One could thus describe women as mental doctors described madmen: they reasoned but they remained
ruled by their sentimentality, as the madman was by his passions.
We can thus see Stendhal develop many arguments in his diary,
and these different systems of references defined an original
approach to emotion. Concerning women, he moved from the
observation of the lover to that of the doctor when he did not
plunge himself completely into the eyes of a female lover in tears.
From proximity to distance, from marvelling to condescension, a
plurality of images were born. 'A thing to note well', he wrote in
his diary, 'the soul can only offer states of being, not qualities.
Where is the joy of the man who weeps? Nowhere. It is a state'.[52]
These discoveries of the state of the soul, sampled at leisure, most
often alone, were proof neither of goodness, nor virtue, unlike the
descriptions of tears of the eighteenth century. These subjective

moments, the promise of happiness or of gentle sorrow, could only be fleeting moments and could not demonstrate any qualities of the soul. The pleasure of tears did not lead to moral reform, but a living sensation of a present which left no trace. However, and perhaps because of this, Stendhal, in his diary observed and described himself, relating his states of mind, as though to attempt to retain the marks of their passage, with those women who had loved him. Thus the changing nature of the soul, the tenuousness of the signs which it gave out, such as rare tears of happiness, were the motivation for the keeping of a personal diary, in order to decipher them ceaselessly, to discover what was natural amidst the multiplicity of worldly or conventional attitudes and physiological determinations. Remarkably, in the opinion of Stendhal who wished to encounter them in art and in life, happiness and nature called for an attentive reading of the signs of communication and a self-observation, which were developed by keeping his diary.

THE WORRIES OF BENJAMIN CONSTANT

Benjamin Constant, in his autobiographical writings and his personal diary, brings an interesting light to his concept of the tears of the women with whom he had love affairs. Charlotte, whom he called Cécile in the autobiographical work which he devoted especially to her, was divorced because her husband 'a private and hard man', found himself pained and wearied by 'the sight of a young woman often in tears'.[53] Once remarried, she became Benjamin Constant's lover, for he had deliberated too long to be able to marry her in time. He arranged an impossible meeting at Besançon with her, during which they both found themselves to be very distraught.

> Our situation was terrible, and while speaking of unrelated things, we felt the tears which we both sought to hide from each other fall from our eyes. Suddenly, Cécile fell in to such a profound faint that all my attempts to revive her were useless.[54]

These troubles, born of misunderstanding, these concealed tears accompanied by bland remarks, were so unbearable that Cécile fainted. This fragility appeared very touching to Benjamin

Constant. For the whole duration of this love story, poor Cécile (or Charlotte) did not stop weeping: because of her new husband, because of her mistake, because of Constant's permanent indecision. The latter also praised the discretion of this unhappy lady: 'She never complained. I have seen her tears, without ever hearing a reproach. She always agreed to my smallest wishes, and in her lengthy sacrifice she became twice as tender, patient and resigned.'[55] Charlotte cried but soundlessly and without complaint. This silent submissiveness accompanied by discreet tears made of the consenting Charlotte a very different woman from Benjamin Constant's other lover, Germaine de Staël. We thus find in his diary on 8 March 1803: 'Scene after scene, and torment after torment. For three days, Germaine has been furious and pursues me with so many invectives, tears and reproaches that I myself am moved from indifference to fury, and from fury to indifference.'[56] Constant criticised women who made scenes, who were impatient, who cried out and who in addition shed noisy tears filled with reproach. His policy consisted of avoiding these tests which made him angry as much as possible; thus on 3 August 1804:

> I supped tête-a-tête with Biondetta [one of the nicknames of Mme de Staël, in reference to the *Diable amoureux* (the devil in love) by Cazotte]. I was happy, she was sad. She scolded me, I at first became impatient, but then I considered, I was evasive, the moment passed and we separated without tears or cries. At present this is the greatest degree of intimacy between us.[57]

In order to escape these tears, Constant obtained a truce through a clever tactic but the result was no less disappointing for their relationship.

Between these two female figures; Charlotte submissive and constantly choked with silent tears, and Germaine, who combined arguments and sobs, Benjamin Constant was very far removed from the loving fusion of shared tears. These encounters were conducted on the level of incomprehension, both tragic and ordinary, even banal, which the passing of time and the circumstances dictated to the lovers. The ideal figure of the woman who suffered without complaint was nevertheless distinguished from the one who exploited tears in domestic rows, exciting the anguish which haunted the male imagination. His love for Charlotte, he wrote in his diary in October 1806, was different from that which he felt for Mme de Staël:

> the contrast between her impetuousness, her selfishness, her constant concern for herself, and the gentleness, the peace, Charlotte's humble and modest way of being, makes the latter a thousand times more dear to me. I am weary of the man-woman whose iron hand has chained me for ten years, and a truly womanly woman intoxicates and enchants me.

These two portraits define the feminine tears which fitted into Benjamin Constant's dream. He was not one of those men who was irritated by the sight of a woman in tears, but he could not bear the noisy tears which indicated a desire for power. The esteem in which tears were held was illustrated by counter-examples which demonstrated how much was bearable.

Constant preferred to weep over the books of Mme de Staël, as they could sometimes show a true sensitivity. He noted thus in his diary on 5 October 1804: 'Read a part of Minette's book on her father. I could not prevent myself from weeping. There is a sensitivity which is all the more genuine for being completely lacking in affectations.'[58] His truest of tears, if not the most gentle were shed in solitude, and over the writings which were intended to celebrate the memory of the dead father of a woman, who was nevertheless such a burden that he could not leave her, despite his vague desire to do so. For in the work of Mme de Staël, he discovered a sensibility which was all the more true because it did not make use of artifice and did not have pretentions, because it was true and natural. As for Stendhal, only the absence of affectation could make an expression touching. In this work, written in mourning, she revealed a truth of feeling which carried her away from her usual theatricality which was so deplored by Constant. In weeping over this book, Benjamin Constant was moved by the death of M. de Necker, and by the grieving memories of his daughter, a Mme de Staël whose art of writing developed a hidden truth of her person: true sensibility.

This death of Necker was, for Constant, a revelation of the profound sensibility of those who surrounded him. Thus on 26 April 1804, on the occasion of the visit of condolence of the Duke to Mme de Staël: 'Said goodbye yesterday to the Duke at Minette's house. He was touched to the point of tears by her sorrow, and

he is one of those men who are called hard.' He explained this
in his diary:

> Visit to the Duke. Men who are called callous are in fact far
> more sensitive than those whose expansive sensitivity is boasted
> of. They harden themselves because their sensibility, being real,
> makes them suffer. The others do not have any need to harden
> themselves; what sensibility they have is easy to bear.[59]

What was most visible, most on the surface, was only proof
of a minor, inconsequential sensitivity. Under his shell, the profoundly sensitive man whose appearance was considered harsh,
was protecting such a suffering intimacy, that it only appeared
on rare occasions: a death was one of them.

Benjamin Constant in love was taken with violent fits of
despair: he wept. We will recall here his heartbreaks with
Juliette Récamier with whom he was in love and in front of
whom he could not hold back his tears. He wrote thus on 17
September 1814: 'I could not restrain myself with Juliette. I went
outside. Convulsions of pain and tears. What a scourge is my own
character! How will it end! Finally it must end.'[60] These surges of
pain overwhelmed him, took on an almost pathological aspect: he
cried to the point of convulsions. In addition, he was disgusted
with himself, with his natural emotion, although he had avoided
the worst in leaving suddenly. On the following days, he wrote,
he cried constantly, spending 'delirious' nights and days alone.
On 27 September he obtained an interview with Juliette: 'I melted
into tears in front of her. She was touched with pity'.[61] But he
could feel that she was mainly 'embarrassed by our encounters'
while as for him 'he lost his head all the time'. He continued to
spend his mornings in tears.

Women were not the only ones to develop a strategy of tears.
Benjamin meditated on the best behaviour to adopt with Mme
Récamier for whom he sighed. In his diary he planned clever
tactics, all the more because he had a rival:

> Monsieur de Forbin is wounded by the progress which I
> appear to make. I expect a withdrawal on Juliette's part,
> because he wept at her feet. I must support her gently, making
> it easy for her not to become upset, unless there is the need for
> her to be moved to great sorrows. But I must not forget that grief

is for her only a passing instrument, sometimes necessary, but always leading to unfortunate consequences.

That a man should weep at a woman's knee was accepted, but he must not abuse the privilege for fear of tiring her. Constant attempted to master his emotions, in order to make use of them at the opportune moment and without excess, adapting himself to Juliette's humours. On 4 October, he decided to find a way of calming down: 'I must try to get a grip on myself. I have prayed. I have wept. Prayers can sooth. O merciful God! I thank you. If the terrible pain returns I shall pray and weep until it has passed.'[62] It was thus in prayer that Benjamin Constant found a palliative for those painful sensations which overwhelmed him. The tears which accompanied it took, through it, the role of an outlet, as though they did not have the same properties as those shed before. The quietist spiritualism of Benjamin Constant here encountered the pronouncements of a neo-Catholic kind. Prayer brought a more gentle pain and gave him: 'the ability to resign myself, to weep'.[63] He even went so far as to write a prayer, which made him collapse into tears. The practice of religion in his room softened the tears, and made him accept pain, Constant observed the healing effect of this. This private prayer permitted him to take hold of himself.

In their originality, the autobiographical writings and the personal diary of Benjamin Constant are the scene of a transformation of the position of tears, in which the male and female roles, truth and strategy, self-expression and privacy dictate the pattern of fine conduct and affirmed reticence. This constellation is, at its most extreme, no more than a personal case which teaches us more about Benjamin Constant's uncertainties, but which concern shared concepts. The interpretation of gestures and the search for truth and for a profound sensibility, as well as the modesties and the excesses which surpassed them, appear to me, however, to have expressed new questions which were entering personal worlds because they provided them with a more general application. Benjamin Constant, the liberal thinker, and writer on the consequences of a democratic revolution, kept his diary. He can also be considered to have been the initiator of the modern novel in *Adolphe,* in which the bonds of passion fought with the desire for liberty in whirlpools of uncertainties and internal conflicts.

THE MISUNDERSTANDINGS OF ADOLPHE

Unlike the diary, the novel developed a narrative logic in which the prevarications of the author were accompanied by an increase of dramatic intensity. Adolphe, the narrator of Benjamin Constant's novel, feared the influence which women could exercise over men, and tended to rebuff Ellénore, who loved him and who had sacrificed everything for him, only to suffer in return for the pain which he had caused. In the preface to the second edition, writing in reply to a criticism of the work, he presented this behaviour as typically masculine. Men made themselves appear worse, and less serious than they were:

A doctrine of fatuity, a sorry tradition which is bequeathed to us by the vanity of the older generation an irony which has become trivial, but which seduces the spirit with titillating reactions, as though reactions could alter the depth of things. In a word, everything they hear and everything they say appears to arm them against tears which have not yet fallen.[64]

What men said to each other when discussing women, what they communicated to each other as the older ones told of their amorous conquests, gave them advance warning against the tears of women, even before they had caused any. The pain which they could cause, seen from afar, seemed to have no substance. 'But when these tears are shed, nature returns to them despite the artificial atmosphere which surrounds them. They feel that someone who suffers for love is a sacred being.' This sanctification of the suffering of women in love would lead to a reasonable return to nature. But it would perhaps come too late. In breaking off with the woman who had believed in him, part of a man's soul was stricken to the point of death. Thus Adolphe, who was naturally sensitive, was so wary of the power of those beings who attempted to cut off his freedom through their tears that he became hardened by it. This is how he lamented the ruin of his life with Ellénore:

I displayed the harshest of principles, and the same man who could not resist a tear, who gave way to dumb sadness, who was pursued even when absent by the picture of the suffering which he had caused, showed himself in all his utterances to be untrusting and devoid of pity.[65]

Manly speech and a sensibility touched by the vision of the pain which he caused, led to contradictory impulses in the narrator's inner soul. Ellénore, irreproachable and resigned, did not seek to restrain him, but he, in causing her suffering only found distress, disquiet and discontent. The liberty which he attempted to regain at the price of this woman's tears was useless to him.

These masculine remarks, which constantly reappeared in Adolphe's mouth, always more hurtful than before, made Ellénore weep after moments of calm and regret. He accepted her tears like 'a burning lava'.[66] They fell drop by drop on his heart, making him cry out in pain. In front of Ellénore he suffered but he did not weep. It was only when alone that he began, while walking, to shed tears of regret. The tears associated with solitary retrospection, when memories crowded in, appeared to occur in men, who feared the presence of women in tears, but who shed just as many in remembering them. This absence of communication through tears was the degree to which Adolphe suffered from interior conflict. The tears of Ellénore touched him, part of him was moved and suffered, but another voice within him was immune to them and led to intransigent expressions. This voice was ironic, mistrustful, filled with all the male vanities.

Between the man of feeling, and the libertine of evil counsel, the roles were no longer divided between two people, as they had been in the novels of the eighteenth century. It was the same individual who conquered women and left them to weep when he abandoned them, and who was deeply tormented by the tears which he cost and the feelings which he experienced. Adolphe was sorry for Ellénore in tears, but this emotion which limited his sensibility was more cruel than indifference itself. Ellénore ended by dying while weeping on Adolphe's shoulder.

This absence of a common language between men and women, this discordancy in the manifestation of emotions and in the timing of the feelings, which made tears so painful, were here connected to the avowed mistrust of men for the power which women could exercise over them, but also of the heartbreak which was the result of it and which brought many levels of language into play even in a male narrator.

RESTRAINT AND MODESTY

It is appropriate to turn towards the writing of women to see whether the position of the female novelist implied a different treatment of the manifestations of emotion. The great figure of the beginning of the nineteenth century was assuredly Germaine de Staël. An examination of her work is also a means of redressing the balance, because Benjamin Constant's portrait of her was exceptionally severe, even repulsive. The texts echo each other in a certain way. She kept a diary only in her early youth, in 1785, and it is therefore through her fictional writings that we can hope to understand the status which this woman gave to sensibility. In her novel: *Corinne ou l'Italie*, the lovers would sometimes weep together, but the delicacy of their feelings demanded a restraint in the expression of love which led to many hidden or contained tears. In men, a discreet sensibility, behind a dignified exterior, was particularly well considered. This was Corinne's taste at least on meeting Lord Nevil:

> she was accustomed to the lively and flattering compliments of the Italians: but the dignity of Oswald's manners, his apparent coldness, and his sensibility, which he betrayed despite himself, exercised a far greater power over her imagination. He never told of a generous action, he never spoke of a sorrow, without his eyes filling with tears, and he always sought to hide his emotion.[67]

The British charm, in all its restrained sensibility, its modest concealment, moved and intimidated Corinne who only knew the grandiose gestures of the Italians. If the circumstances which led to the shedding of tears of compassion and admiration were close to the eighteenth-century themes, these attitudes had lost their demonstrative strength and their touching beauty came instead from the will to conceal them. The few tears shed by Oswald marked an event in the life of his affections. He cried little, but always 'sincerely'. In love with Corinne he allowed himself thus to weep in private: 'tears escaped his eyes: they were the first since the death of his father which had been drawn from him by a different pain'.[68] In a man, the act of weeping was all the more valued because it was involuntary, because it was rare and because it reached deep layers of sensibility. The counting of emotional outbursts became one of the measures of male character and this economy of tears made the moment of virile sensibility all the more valid.

If in Mme de Staël's novel, the Englishman appeared to triumph over the too expansive Italians, it is hard to tell which attitudes were most favourable to female sensibility. French women had a reputation for being light, frivolous, unfaithful. Considered to be coquettes, they 'had recourse to art to inspire emotion'. Of Mme d'Aubigny, Oswald's deserted mistress, a Frenchman who knew her and her kind well declared: 'She will weep because she loves you, but she will console herself, because she is a woman who is reasonable enough not to wish to be unhappy and above all not to appear to be so'.[69] The opinion of the salons controlled the length of sorrows. The French society woman might be sensitive but the vanity of appearing attractive was more important to her than the pain of losing a lover. In a more general way, the tears of these women were purely strategic, but their extent was limited:

> Perhaps women are wrong to command in the name of tears, and to subjugate strength to their weakness in this way; but when they do not fear to use this means, it is almost always successful, at least for a time. Feeling is probably weakened by the very power which is exercised over it, and the power of tears, too often used, cools the imagination.[70]

This weapon of weak women over the strength of men eventually evaporated, suffering from the ravages of time and habit. Women did not hold on to power for long with the strategy of tears: to see them weep too much was wearing for men. This typically female usage was indeed a contrast to the rarity of male outbursts. Tears were used too much, lost their value, the effect of tears on others called for a strict economy, in which female inflationary practices led to a loss of power.

Corinne did not use these methods and ruses, she did not number among those who abuse tears. But she would suffer from her passionate and impulsive character which did not fit in with the ideal of femininity. Artistic and enthusiastic in temperament, she attempted to dam her vitality so as not to lose merit in Oswald's eyes.

She recognised him, cried out, flung herself quickly towards him, and seized his arm, as though she feared that he would escape again, but hardly had she committed herself to this impetuous movement than she blushed, remembering again Lord Nevil's character, for having shown so vividly what she was feeling, and letting fall the hand which grasped Oswald, she covered her face with the other to hide her tears.[71]

Since Oswald was so modest as to wish to conceal his tears, Corinne sought to arrest a movement which betrayed her. She moderated her impulses and shed modest tears of sadness in vain, for Oswald was to follow his father's advice; he married an English girl, Lucile, who matched his temperament. He was attracted by her modesty and her discretion. Thus the tears which she shed while reading a prayer and which she attempted to conceal, did not escape Oswald, an attentive observer: he 'had seen them fall; and a tenderness mixed with respect filled his heart'.[72] The modesty of young English girls imposed respect while influencing gentle feelings. Lucile's conduct could therefore be considered ideal, but this was not the case because a restraint which was taken too far could harm communication between husband and wife. Later, when Oswald spoke of Corinne to Lucile, she was strongly moved but she did not show it: 'Tears were ready to suffocate her, and if she had abandoned herself to this emotion, perhaps it would have been the most touching moment of her life; but she contained herself, and the trouble which existed between the couple only became more painful'.[73] Between the excesses of fallen tears, and these emotions which were too restrained, the balance appeared to be hard for a woman to find. Tears should not always be held back, they were a delicate but necessary communication between those who loved each other. Strategic tears, like over-impetuous movements did not suit men. French vanity was assuredly lacking in the natural, but the Victorian model had its inconveniences, and Mediterranean vivacity was displeasing.

For those with a powerful imagination like Corinne, it was better to revive the same painful memory in solitude to 'wear out the soul with tears' than it was to oblige it to 'concentrate on itself'.[74] The need to sooth an excess of tension with tears is a familiar concept to us, but its formulation here was new. This sort of mechanics of liquids, an internal economy which connected feelings and physical reactions, and which made it necessary for an over-full heart to overflow with tears one day, was associated with a new face of sensibility, which made restraint and modesty into the fragile and tenuous ideals of relations between intimates. Emotion should be expressed, especially in women, but communication through tears was no longer to be found in the immediacy of a delicious impulse: it had to show itself to be sensitive without any shocking display, to be touched without ill-controlled gestures, without strong impulses and to seek to conceal its tears to make them more moving. Solitude was the remedy for these over-constrained hearts; there, there was no question of moderation.

These few personal and novelistic texts, written during the first 20 years of the nineteenth century reveal fragile and uncertain nuances: do we not still weep a lot? the voice of common sense would say. However, the attention paid to the anatomy of a gesture like the practices of observation which it required indicate a transformation of the status of tears. A discussion developed around tears which illustrated the difficulty in reaching the truth within a soul, the deepest feelings, beyond the appearances of sensibility, which were often only illusions. This quest for personal truth which did not make tearful expressions easy, turned on the distribution of male and female roles. For women, coquetry was to modesty what artifice was to truth. On the male side the defiance which was born of this coquetry and the distrust of the rule of weakness over strength, led to a distance which sometimes led to rupture. Women undertook to discipline their emotions, while respecting the modesty which became them so well, to suit men who were sensitive under their cold manner. It seems that, for women as well as men, restraint and modesty transformed attitudes, as though the feelings presented were all the more true for being suppressed. Finally, for all of them, from jubilation to anguish, the profound sensibility of a person was only revealed on rare occasions, which one had to know how to grasp hold of, without ceasing to observe others and to observe oneself. From appearance to truth, from coquetry to modesty, from weakness to strength, from the visibility of behaviour to the depths of the soul which conducted it, the holes which had been created continued to be dug. These opposing pairs were also formed by the relations which existed between the terms. Thus modesty, as restrained truth was part of the question of true feeling. The elaboration of a measured attitude required work on the self; the interiorisation of this constraint was then accompanied by a knowledge of one's own nature. This vision, which looked beyond appearances, encountered the difficulty of communicating such deep intimacies. And this difficulty provoked solitary expressions of emotion, from pain to a state of ecstasy, which soothed and revealed the soul. These processes became involved in relationships of love. The search for truth in feeling, associated with the difference in attitudes and sensibility of women and men, saw the horizon of the encounter between two separate private entities move further away. One could not speak of a model of behaviour based on these networks of feelings because a true impulse could harm modesty, just as excessive modesty could harm communication, when the absence of affectation demanded a constant elaboration of nature. It was around this paradox that the question of tears was raised, which would trace the fragile boundaries of doubt, rejection, respect or fascination.

7 The Discreet Charms of Suffering

THE GENERATION OF LAUGHTER AND OF TEARS

When, after Chateaubriand, the Romantics exalted their intimate torments with tears, in the same gesture, they often declared their position in a generation of men and women. And from the time of that generation a constant comparison was being made between past and present: what had been possible and what was no longer possible. Between Musset's childhood dreams of his future in the noise of the cannons of Napoleonic conquest, and what was available to him as a young man, there was a deep pit which his tears could not fill. Faced with an insipid present, he chose between two possible options:

> From then on two camps were formed, on one side the exalted, suffering spirits, all those who expansive souls who had a need of the infinite bowed their heads while weeping; they surrounded themselves with unhealthy dreams, and one could only see frail reeds on an ocean of bitterness. On the other side, men of the flesh remained upright, inflexible, surrounded by positive joys, and they had no other care than to count their money. There was nothing but a sob and a gust of laughter, one coming from the soul and the other from the body.[1]

These frail bodies, these sagging heads filled with sickly dreams, possessed a supplement of the soul in their pain, their bitterness and their tears, whereas the revellers, bourgeois men of flesh and money solidly planted on the ground, hard and inflexible, allowed the noisy laughter of the body to be heard. The spirit of the times, or rather its background noise was made up of superimposed tears and laughter. The present study leads us to hear more of the tears, but often with relapses into mockery, irony and cynicism, for which Musset's *Confessions* supplied many examples. This ambivalence indicated the complexities of romantic expression.

The borderline between the man who laughed and the one

who cried was not so watertight. The sceptic could thus experience delicate tears. This was supported in the following review by Sainte-Beuve, published in 1840 in the *Revue des deux mondes* on the novels of Eugène Sue (while the author was in his first period, writing maritime novels, which contrasted with the sentimentality of his popular novels, written later).

> The spiritual, ambitious, unbelieving, blasé generation which has occupied modish society for ten years is wonderfully painted, that is to say, frighteningly so, in the collection of novels by M. Eugène Sue. The systematic disillusionment, the absolute pessimism, the jargon of the rake, of socialism, of religious feeling, the aristocratic pretentions natural to young democrats and to the *nouveau riche*, the mania of the Regency and of spontaneous orgies, the brutality which was soon close to the most exquisite tears, he has expressed all this with verve in his characters.[2]

Musset created extremes which in Sainte-Beuve's work were more mixed, in the definition of a generation. Bourgeois materialism, full bodied and positive, seeking pleasure and shaken with laughter, materialism which revelled in the accumulation of riches, contrasted with romantic spiritualism which associated tears with suffering, with the thirst for the absolute, with the exaltation of pain, illness, and unachieved dreams. But there was a curious hybrid in fashion between 1830 and 1840, ambitious, rakish, seeking his fortune, who had seen it all before (disabused, pessimistic, blasé, unbelieving) playing the aristocrat but preaching democracy, idealism, socialism or leaning towards religion. A practitioner of spontaneous debauchery, all his indifference could be overturned in 'the most exquisite of tears'. Whether it was a question of politics, religion or sensibility, young men passed from one extreme to the other.

These tears which were shed should not make us forget another aspect of romantic sensibility which manifested itself through the description of a particular state which prevented tears from being shed. The experience of aridity was not conceivable except after a journey through life. The ability to weep was already expended, the male character remained dry in the face of something which could have moved him to tears earlier. Mlle Maupin's narrator thus declared:

Nothing touches me, nothing moves me; I no longer feel those sublime tremblings which used to go through me from head to foot when I heard of heroic deeds – all of it seems rather stupid to me – no accent is deep enough to bite at the stretched fibres of my heart and to make them vibrate: I see the tears of my peers fall through the same eyes which I see the rain with, unless they should happen to be made of beautiful water in which the light is reflected in a picturesque manner or they happen to flow down a beautiful cheek.[3]

A heart which was too worn and a sceptical mind which feared ridicule could no longer experience emotion except on a distant and aestheticising plane. There was no longer a taste for pity, compassion or feeling, only the picturesque or plastic beauty of tears could distract the indifferent observer. The narrator said elsewhere that he mocked the finest heart for its sentimentality, and laughed that he could no longer weep. This absence of tears was coloured with regret: 'Ah! who could cultivate a tear in my dried-up eyes?'[4] For his encounter with Rosanette, although pleasant, could not bring him out of his inability to be moved: 'Sensual pleasure itself, that diamond chain which joins all beings, that devouring fire which melts the rocks and metals of the soul and makes them fall in tears, as real fire can melt iron and granite, powerful though it is, has never tamed me or moved me'.[5] This aspect of a lack of sensibility leads us to study these metaphors of impossible fusion. Incapable of melting into tears, and through this of attaining liquefication of the soul through physical pleasures, always aloof, he chose the path of nonchalance and witty words. Thus when Rosanette complained of his coldness, while she wept, he joked:

Rosanette: 'Ah! heart of stone, water can wear stone away and my tears cannot penetrate you' (she weeps)
Me: 'If you weep like that, you will certainly turn our bed into a bath! an ocean. Do you know how to swim Rosanette?'.[6]

In this caustic mode which rejected any sentimentality, there remained nevertheless, a vague regret for absent tears, in particular those which were shed for love.

The mutual distinction of the romantic and the bourgeois was to be found in the sceptic's work. His mocking laughter did not have the strength of the carnivalesque laugh, it was traced with the pain of no longer being able to feel or the fear of too much suffering. A transformation of comic culture, this laughter revealed the 'infinite internal character of the individual' and illustrated interior contradictions.[7] Thus, the painful experience of an expansive soul could sometimes be transformed into cynical and heartrending laughter. Individual progress alone, made up of excess and disillusion, could explain these seeming contradictions. The suffering which was encountered became a personal truth which was kept a secret for tears, which were produced by the spirit, could only lead to pain, even if they had a discreet charm. On the other hand these true tears were all the more rare and precious for being spiritualised. This was translated into an inability to feel, to weep, for tears were not always available to soothe the anguished hearts. Finally, the succession of the states of laughter and tears in the same person, provoked disquieting crises, which were caused by illness. Thus dolorism, scepticism, incapacity to weep, a state of crisis and instability of mood, formed the horizon of the romantic conception of tears.

Pain was refined by fits of irony which split the male character with troubling ambivalences. Bursts of laughter, refined by pain, bitter-sweet tears, divided attitudes towards a woman's tears: passing from compassion and even the regarding of feminine suffering as sacred, to the most devastating cynicism, the romantic hero had an infinite capacity to suffer and to cause suffering, to repent and to retract, to believe and to mistrust.

SUBLIMATED PAIN AND THE THREATS OF DROUGHT

The experience of tears had a privileged status: Octave, the narrator of the *Confessions d'un enfant du siècle* [confessions of a child of the era], who led the life of a libertine in the daytime, would shut himself in his room in the evening and find himself alone: 'then I pushed the bolt on the door, I fell to my knees and I wept. It was my evening prayer'.[8] Addressed to God, tears also had the power to purify, even to lead the way to virtue. These spiritualised tears referred essentially to a solitary retrospection. After cruel deceptions in which his emotions were toyed with, he thus encountered the truth which was harboured by pain: 'In the midst of all this, tears came to my aid and I perceived that there was no truth but my pain'.[9] This private crisis, in which the soul was comforted by tears, suggests that it is only in the depths of oneself and through suffering that it is possible to escape illusion. Octave described this solitary experience in more detail: 'I knelt beside my bed, and my poor heart was comforted. What tears! What vows! What prayers! Galileo struck the earth crying out: "But it moves!" Thus I struck my heart.'[10] This astronomy of the bedroom was proof of existence through penitence. Nothing could silence these movements of a heart in tears, which were witness to a discovery of the self.

But it could be dangerous to revel thus in one's own tears. Desgenais, Octave's friend, deliberately chose to harden himself: 'An early experience had made him bald before his time; he knew life and had wept in his time, but his pain bore a shield, he was materialistic and awaited death'.[11] Prematurely aged, he had passed beyond the time of tears shed by an inexperienced heart which suffered without knowing how to defend itself. The absence of visible sensibility was then the result of a painful experience, and of work on the self to reduce one's emotional receptiveness, which could not happen without renunciation. What was sensitive and painful in him was protected by a shield which he had created himself. He also counselled his friend to do the same, unless he wished to surrender himself to his 'crippled nature' and to see all the sap of his life escape.[12] To weep was also to weaken oneself.

When Octave later fell in love with Mme Pierson, he rediscovered redeeming tears: he saw in his lover's tears a heavenly blessing: God blessed his tears, and pain taught him virtue.[13] The conversion through tears was filled with a suffering religious feeling which broke with the Rousseauist jubilations. Furthermore, weeping allowed the purification of physical love: 'I protested my respect for her on both knees as far as the foot of the bed, I entered it as though entering a sanctuary; I held out my arms to her while shedding tears'.[14] But the mercy of tears was not given to him for long, he was soon repossessed by a ravaging scepticism. Indeed, Octave was subject to spectacular changes of humour and emotion:

A quarter of an hour after insulting her, I was on my knees, no sooner had I ceased to accuse her than I asked for pardon; no sooner did I cease to scoff than I wept. These movements of the heart lasted for entire nights, during which I did not cease to speak, weep and roll at Brigitte's feet.

Alternately the accuser or the penitent, defiant or in tears, mocking or filled with sad humility, Octave tested his lover severely. From cruel irony to tearful repentance, his instability was almost an illness and added to his unhappiness. It was no longer the laws of society which prevented the lovers from weeping together, but a complexity of mood and states of mind which made the encounter between them particularly difficult.

As a result of passing from supplications to insults, and from laughter to tears, Octave took stock of himself. After having inflicted a thousand torments on his lover, he questioned the limits of the redeeming power of tears: 'You do evil and you repent? Nero did too when he killed his mother. Who then told you that tears could cleanse us?' For there was a moment for repentance, and tears which came too late could not erase the fault and suppress the wrong: 'You who begin to weep too late, take care for one day you will no longer weep'. By putting it off for too long we risk losing ourselves, and being deprived of the ability to weep which purifies and blesses. Tears, a spiritual experience of truth, threatened to be withdrawn from one who only knew how to feel regret for the sufferings which he caused in his fits of aridity. The passage from the destructive laugh to tears of regret contained within itself all the tragedies to come.

The narrator of Sainte-Beuve's *Volupté* also explored his destiny in 'wounding himself' with injuries and in drinking in tears 'as in pleasure'.[15] We find a similar importance in this novel placed on private suffering in religious expressions of emotion and also the threat of the loss of the ability to be moved. Indeed the ability to weep was not always granted, the experience of dryness was mingled with that of effusion. Amaury, having barely left a state of charitable purity through the mercy of tears shed beside his love, found himself carried away by a feeling of coldness: 'Often, at the moments of her greatest goodness, when I had just shed tears over her hands, and when I had considered myself fortunate, I found myself suddenly dry, arid'.[16] Thus the happiness glimpsed in respectful tenderness, was wiped out by returns of aridity, which drew Amaury into guilty excesses. Further on, he blamed for it the harmful influence of urban concentration which crushed all the seeds of goodness and excellence with the coming of the night:

Who can say how much, in a large town, at certain hours of the evening and the night, treasures of genius, fine and charitable works, tears of tenderness, vague fruitful impulses, are periodically dried up before being born, murdered in essence, thrown to the wind of a senseless prodigality?.[17]

The individual in the city lost his ability to be moved. Here a state of sensibility which was invisible because it was still latent, was swept away by the general state of corruption, and by a strongly parching movement, which was part of urban life: this was a collective drama and Amaury was a part of it.

We find, in Sainte-Beuve's *Volupté*, in a style filled with affected charm, the association of tears with repentance and purification: 'Serious repentance should then blend its intercession and its tears with the involuntary sighs which are drawn out by our weakness; prayer should shed on it its purifying dew; at this price only, is the Christian permitted to remember himself'.[18] The necessary mediation of tears can also be achieved through saintly souls:

There are nevertheless some fine spirits, so tenderly gifted, so strongly fed that they are the constant receptacles of strong and unchangeable divine Love, through the thousands of rays of great charity, and surrender it to their fellow-men through a thousand loving deeds, through abundant tears shed over all wounds and through sublime devotions.[19]

This charity spread by saintly spirits in a shower of tears over poor sinners had the merit of being exemplary. The young Amaury, the narrator of the novel, encountered these charitable tears in the person of the Abbé Caron, at the head of his flock of the sick and the poor. From that day, he broke with his experiments of the senses and shed abundant tears, this was a conversion through virtue:

The precious gift of tears returned to me. I had lost it, my friend, during that preceding year of dissipation, of frivolous ploys, of obstinate pursuits and conflicts. According to a Saint, this sort of disturbance makes the inestimable gift disappear as easily as the fire melts wax. But three or four days after the break with Madame R., while walking alone in an interior fog which was

fairly dense, I suddenly felt a sort of deep spring unfurl itself
and well up in me; my eyes poured out in streams.[20]

This stage was, according to the narrator, the foretaste of
happiness and the eternal youth of the spirit in the Lord.
This reactivation of a Christian theme which made of the gift of
tears a mark of sanctity (one could cite Saint Louis, who aspired
to the gift of tears without having it, and above all, Saint Francis
of Assisi, who was singularly gifted with it) here indicated the
return to virtue. Disquiet and heartbreak on the other hand were
factors of aridity.

At once an internal spring and divine mercy, these tears
alone could be shed without constraint and in abundance, even
with a saintly jubilation, for they came from the world of the
divine and from the depths, unlike those which were shed by
incontinent and voluptuous people who only had: 'a semblance
of compassion, a surface of tears'.[21] These tears, given by God
and highly spiritualised, appeared to break with all links with
the body, unlike the model of the Enlightenment. And although
they might flow in streams in a sort of mystical experience, they
gained from being held back: people vowed to chastity were not
so inclined to tears as the men of the flesh who appeared to love
everything. Also, Amaury invoked Christ who 'felt on his feet the
flowing stream of the tears and perfumes of Mary Magdalene': 'I
prayed to him that he should make me serious without constraint,
sober without dryness, suddenly hardened, gifted with clarity and
unknown accents, master of my tears'.[22]

Religious feeling, beyond the mystical experience of the gift of
tears, also led to an ideal of restraint. Still, though, in becoming
master of oneself thanks to divine intercession, one must not fall
into aridity. The charm of tears was reserved at this cost.

The association which was so frequent between tears and
Christian rhetoric, was active on many levels. In isolation,
in the solitude of a carefully locked room, tears were bound
to prayer as though the address to God was born of painful
emotion experienced alone. Tears of repentance were purifying,
the return to virtue led to the rediscovery of the gift for tears.
This profound and purifying spring followed the experience
of debauchery and of the pain which was caused by lack
of understanding between people, the poverty of the human
condition in modern societies. Self-examination, the intimate

withdrawal appeared to be in agreement with the Christian message.

In its dolorist version, this phenomenon was applied to a humanity which was suffering in its entirety and in tears. The mediation of Christ or of saintly spirits who received and shed tears, established a sort of vertical communication between men and God. Virtue, compassion and charity no longer led to a circulation of tears among men, but were conceived in relation to religion. This would imply that this private quest for truth and the depths of the soul, which was often accompanied by disillusion concerning others, and by a renewed questioning of communication between individuals, encountered images in Christian rhetoric which rearranged the concept of tears.

Dryness threatened tormented souls, who had grown old prematurely, and they began to bemoan constantly the loss of this ability to weep, which was on the scale of an impossibility: that of melting into another being. Norbert Elias underlines the aspect of reaction against the armour of self-restraint in romantic love. The intensity of the desire for fusion, the frenzy and the tears which accompanied it, could not be conceived except with regard to an interiorisation of the boundary which the Romantics believed tragically separated people. They constantly encountered this obstacle while seeking to abolish it, each one shutting himself off into a private world, to the extent that the body refused to produce tears. Life, or rather, the experience acquired during youth, could make the capacity for tears disappear for ever. A deep wound made a shell grow up against anything coming from outside. Privacy was protected but it was by a radical pessimism. The only alternative, on a lighter note, was to laugh while regretting the tears which could not be shed: in this the fear of ridicule played a not inconsiderable role for men. A too easy sentimentality could effectively only attract smiles and sometimes one had to defend oneself from great sorrows. The most tragic heartbreaks could sometimes no longer find the solace of tears. Insensitivity was not an ideal state, it was often a palliative for the excess of suffering, or the result of an individual development which could only be recognised. Tears still had many charms but they were not given so easily.

In *Lélia* by George Sand, a female character was at the centre of a personal novel. We find in it the same diffuse religious feeling, the enhancement of the dolorist experience, combined with human destiny. The reference to the valley of tears, to the 'great abyss of fury into which the tears of men fall without ful-filment', like the figure of the priest charged with 'collecting in a vase without blemish the tears shed at the feet of Christ' in order to present them to God, illustrated the same romantic conception of tears which did not hesitate to spin out the religious metaphor which gave meaning to suffering and associated it with sacrifice, with purification and with expiation. But the novel was also the story of a sensibility and of an impossible love. Lélia, in tears in front of the poet Sténio, expressed her bitter regret that she could no longer weep: 'You weep! . . . You can weep, then? Happy are those who weep! My tears are more dry than the sandy deserts where the dew never falls and my heart is more barren than my eyes.'[23] Sténio did not cease to suffer from Lélia's inability to shed tears on his bosom, for if their tears were to mingle he would finally be able to 'live within her'. Perhaps the fusion was all the more sought-after because it represented an extreme ideal, too great a demand for these separate souls. But in this case, it was a woman who suffered from aridity, whereas the young poet had easy tears: the sexual roles which were currently allowed were thus brought into question.

Lélia explained her apparent insensitivity by a tragic experience, that of pain which must be concealed:

> that which must be shut off, a pain of infamy and curses, that which must be hidden in the depths of your entrails like a bitter treasure, that which does not burn you, but freezes you, which has no tears, no prayers, no dreams, which constantly watches, cold, pale and paralysing, in the depths of the heart.[24]

This deeply embedded internal wound, this pain which was close to illness, could offer no tears, and prevented any from ever being shed.

This troubled sensibility was connected to her own experience of life and of the lack of understanding which surrounded her. The young Lélia suffered from the conduct of her lover:

> he laughed harshly at my tears. Sometimes his infamous egotism revelled in them with pride; and when he had broken me with ferocious embraces, he would fall asleep at my side, careless and harsh, while I swallowed back my

tears in order not to wake him. Oh unhappiness and servitude of woman![25]

The reply of male laughter to the tears of women did not lead to any revolt; these suffocated tears which they forbade themselves to utter indicated their daily servitude. Lélia, refusing this submission, learned to harden herself, and not to show her feelings.

Lélia was stronger in appearance than any other creature of her sex. Never, since she had been Lélia, had anyone surprised the secrets of her soul in her impassive face, never had anyone seen a tear of emotion on her smooth colourless cheek.[26]

This impassiveness which denoted a strength of character superior to her sex, came from that mastery of the self which prevented others from decoding a physiognomy, from reading emotions in a face. This coldness was closer to the male character which had to give way to the demands of a public life while avoiding giving indication to others of his private self or his weaknesses, whereas women tended to abandon themselves to suffering, to emotion and to their deeper nature.

She despised the pity of others, and, in her greatest moments of distress, she retained the instinct for concealment. She therefore hid her head in her velvet coat; and, far from the world, far from the light, huddled in the long grass of an abandoned corner, she shed her pain in vain and cowardly tears.

This concealed pain, withheld for too long, which feared pity as the image of its own weakness, could know only valueless tears. Even in the absence of a witness, painful emotion represented for Lélia a lack of courage which confined her to the point of absurdity. Her virile strength rejected any outburst of tears, although she could not prevent herself from shedding them. On hearing someone arrive, she was mostly ashamed, irritated at being surprised in a weakness which nobody had ever seen in her, 'she leapt to her feet in a sudden courageous reaction, and stood up before the foolhardy intruder'. This daring leap further accentuated the virility of Lélia's character, who could pass rapidly from tears to an almost menacing attitude. Lélia remained separate, for her female nature never appeared to return, and she wept like a man, that is in shame.

Lélia's sister who saw a form of life in suffering and tears, compared this tragic state of insensitivity to death. Beyond dolorism, this silent misfortune which gnawed at Lélia led to nothingness. Such was the abyss of suffering without tears. George Sand created a female character who resembled the male romantic heroes. Her apparent insensitivity corresponded to a will to protect herself from emotion in order not to be weak, but, committed to the inability to feel and to love, the strong Lélia suffered tragically from being different from other women.

A TEARFUL RELIGIOUS FEELING

This diffuse religious feeling, these relapses into dryness, and these troubling states were transposed into letters and private diaries. In the first half of the nineteenth century, religious practice led to expressions of emotion, or at least appeared to be accepted by the writer of the diary or memoirs. Vigny thus preserved a tender memory of his first communion: 'the sensation of my weakness and the infinite generosity of the divine which were so directly and so intimately combined in a feeble creature covered my childish cheeks with tears'.[27] This rather saintly description sought to represent the depths of a child's faith. We know of its developments at Saint-Sulpice which promised it a long future. Maine de Biran, attending the ecumenical marriage of his son, wrote in his diary:

> I was preoccupied with family affections and with the wedding of my son which took place on 3 April before the protestant minister and the Catholic priest at Saint-Sauveur. The sermon of the first, filled with unction, moved me to the point of tears and there was an emotional scene for the whole family.[28]

Marriage, the first communion, religious and family ceremonies were probably all special occasions for emotion. Religious tenderness appears to have been particularly well regarded in the first half of the nineteenth century. We thus witness a passion for figures of saintly men in tears such as the Curé of Ars, whose amazing prestige with the crowds who came on pilgrimage to see him has been evoked by Alain Corbin, and who shed floods of tears.[29] The image of a secularised century, accumulating goods and producing scientific texts in profusion sometimes makes us forget that romantic religious spirit which made so many tears flow.

But the exaltation of private suffering was then coloured by personal exaltation which was not given to all. Religion also involved the abnegation of the self and written instructions for the attention of nuns revealed the limits of the admissible. The Sisters of the Nativity were asked in 1820 to avoid 'precious, tender and weeping devotion', and to weep 'for reason and not for a whim'. The expression of emotion was 'reserved for the happy moment when mercy would move them to tears of compunction and of devotion'.[30] Without a doubt it was a question in the convents of funnelling the taste for a spectacular sanctity, for mystical scenes which almost verged on heresy, or even simple self-esteem and typically female emotions. This was a more obscure side of the history of tears than limits and silences, the fear of excess, denied pride and sorrow, the admitted humiliations.

From romantic tears to religious effusion, from the cult of the woman to humanitarian faith, the manifestation of emotions was often reserved for exceptional figures who expressed in full daylight, or delivered in the secret of private writings, the complexities of their subjectivity. The act of crying, if it was sometimes given value, appeared to stem from a personal quest which moved away from dreams of tearful communication and necessitated the mediation of prayer.

FECUNDITY OR ARIDITY

Michelet had a taste for tears and associated it with femininity and with humanitarian faith; his original concept of the emotions was exercised both in his private life and in a historic vision of humanity. He in no way participated in the Catholic orthodoxy but in seeking for a new faith he made use in his own way of its language in his diary. His political aspirations transformed the religion of suffering into participation and universal commiseration faced with the pains of the oppression of peoples and nationalities. To his wife who asked him what to say on

All Souls day of 1849, he replied: 'I said to her. Everything that
dies, everything that cries, the psalms of the Jews, of the Irish,
the Polish, of all the nations who die and who weep, if they have
created songs.'[31] More widely, the figure of woman, baptising
and regenerating humanity through her tears, animated certain
humanitarian theologies.[32]

Michelet furnishes us also with a direct account of the pernicious effect of the imperial period on the sensibilities. He felt this
climate, associated with material poverty and the militarisation of
society, penetrate him in his childhood if only through breathing
the air which surrounded him: 'These words will appear strange
in the mouth of a child, I felt parched. It was a dry and sad
aridity with no need for tears, that guilt of the heavens which
I know today.'[33] This wind of aridity, which blew on the men
of the eighteenth century defined the new generations from the
Empire to the Louis-Philippe monarchy. The feminine continent
was an obligatory destination for any who wished to know the gift
of tears. His love letters to Athénaïs revealed a vision of woman
which was Michelet's own. He thus exclaimed in a letter dated
3 January 1849: 'Death or life, what does it matter! I shall always
thank God for having known you one day, for having revived my
heart, for having given me pain itself through you and the gift of
tears which I had lost for so long.'[34] For him, womankind was
the mediator between man and God. His humanitarian faith was
a call to women who sided with humidity, sensibility, fecundity
and fertility against dryness, rationality, sterility, and the cerebral
which characterised male values. The tears of Athénaïs refreshed
him, made him younger, quenched his thirst, revived him. Thanks
to her, he could finally weep and the places where they wept
together were sacred.[35] If the tears of the woman appeared
sublimated by the images which were dear to Michelet, we also
know through his diary that he was fascinated by all the feminine
secretions of the pure Athénaïs in a sort of cult of the woman.
This indiscreet spectator of the menstruation of his young wife
which he described as the 'crisis of love', the 'divine rhythm
which month by month measures time for her', associated all
the humours of her body with a dialogue with Nature.[36]

A surprising passage in the diary of Michelet, who did not
cease to write of the ups and downs of his loving relationship
with Athénaïs, revealed that he was not exempt either from these
returns to dryness. He declared on 5 March 1849:

I threw myself into her arms, I crushed her, my dear child, against my panting chest and flooded her with the most pure and burning tears which had ever, I believe, been shed in this world. A little more and I would have fainted, oppressed at once by so many different feelings. The impossibility of expressing them wore out my strength and dried my tears, leaving me sad for a moment. Oh barrier of the hearts, how can we surmount you?[37]

For, beyond restraint and modesty, in unparalleled effusion and exceptional tears, Michelet tells us, that incurable separation of beings was revealed, that impossibility of expressing all the feelings which move one's most intimate being. The encounter with this limit dried his tears: Oh barrier of the hearts.

THE HEART AND THE NERVES

The storms of passion between George Sand and Alfred de Musset were accompanied by calm periods in which delicate intentions joined religious reference. Sand wrote on 15 April 1834 to Musset, after their break-up in Venice: 'When you are alone, when you need to pray and to weep you will think of your George, of your true friend'.[38] And Musset declared on 23 August of the same year: 'Our friendship is consecrated my child. It received, before God, the saintly baptism of our tears'.[39] The theme of the religious harvest and of the sacrament through tears was thus transposed into this love correspondence. Parallel to these moments of friendly reconciliation, the high degrees of emotional intensity of this love story produced some strange states. The diary of George Sand, during the year 1834, suggested a description of Musset which demonstrated some worrying changes of attitude:

He obsesses me with caresses, with tears, he seeks to surprise his senses through a mixture of audacity and humility. Why this crescendo of displeasure, of disgust, of aversion of fury, of cold and mistrustful mockery, and then suddenly, these tears, this gentleness, this ineffable love which returns?

The passage from harshness to effusion, from anger to repentance made his attitude unbearable: the dreams of romantic love turned to drama. This ambivalence was all the more troubling for being divided, he would pass from the most touching tears of humility to the most devastating cynicism. He suffered from it himself: in his correspondence with Sand, he blamed his fatal childhood for having painted on his countenance 'a convulsive laugh'[40] which prevented him from crying with Sand. His laugh was a sculptured mask which hid a desire for tears. It was in solitude that he shed a thousand heart-rending sobs, although this did not prevent him from mocking himself, declaring that he wept like a calf. Romantic dolorism was often shaded by irony, by a distancing from the self. Musset also described himself as particularly subject to nervous attacks and gave a pathological aspect to these movements from laughter to tears which were the signs of madness. The questioning of the integrity of the individual, the experience of a multiple 'I' thus transformed the status of tears.

A fashionable illness from the first decades of the nineteenth century onwards, nerves won a victory over the vapours of the previous century. But whereas the vapours, at least in literature and in letters, appeared as an embarrassing affliction which struck sensitive souls in particular, nerves, which were the result of an excess of tension, of a restrained trouble which sometimes burst in the light of day, with convulsions, laughter and tears, could affect the individual in his identity and were the evidence of an inability to master oneself. But his medical status was subject to controversy since the matter concerned a problem which had no organic foundation. Nervous illnesses, or 'neuroses' were widely commented on in public, and this notion although prevalent was the object of mockery. Nervous attacks or crises particularly affected women. In this regard, they could be considered to be a diplomatic illness, simulated by the flirts, on the same basis as the tears of command. The *Dictionnaire des gens du monde* [dictionary of society], in the article on Tears dismissed both.

> *Tears*: Water too often ill-employed, for it remedies nothing. Resource which women have at their command to hide an infidelity or demand a cashmere shawl. Weapon which they employ with the greatest success after a nervous attack.[41]

'Nervous illness: constant grimaces' wrote Flaubert in the *Dictionnaire des idées reçues* [dictionary of commonly accepted ideas].

Flaunted symptoms, weapons of weakness against strength, nervous attacks and fits of tears represented a vision where the limits between illness and pretence fluctuated. Through these passages from laughter to tears, where sadness and inability to feel went side by side, romantic passion and a nervous attack could present curious similarities. These nervous contradictions demonstrated a sickly sensibility which was mostly shared by women and poets. But also, all these heart-rending scenes were laughed at, and associated with feminine coquetry: such was the reply of the bourgeois to romantic women, considering these tearful outbursts to be a noisy theatrical production.

8 Moral Studies

The novels of the first half of the nineteenth century, which, as we have seen, echoed personal torments and the exploration of a private suffering, also proposed the study of morals. The social comedy could oblige one to mask or play at emotions. The definition of male and female also became an issue through fits of tears. The ages of life could also affect the capacity to be moved and the quality of the tears shed. By including in novels the different scales of interpretation which were applied in the presentation of emotions, the writer supplied us with an account of the redistribution of the concept of tears between the identity of the individual and social conventions which is as precious as it is difficult to interpret.

A LACHRYMAL POCKET SOCIOLOGY

With Balzac, the novelist became the observer of social codes and the vivisector of souls which were prey to all the passions. A great admirer of Lavater and de Gall, he paid great attention to the association of physiognomy with characters. The traces of tears should be read accordingly like hieroglyphics. The story of a life was to be read in a face and with it the tears which had been shed. The Père Goriot had a swollen inner corner of the eye. His eyes, which had been previously so lively took on dull and iron-grey hues, and their red rims appeared to weep blood. The marks of unhappiness were imprinted on his physiognomy.[1] The old age of a mother guilty of adultery gave her face a particular character: 'The nature of her wrinkles, the folds of her face, her pale, distressed expression, all bore eloquent witness to those tears which, devoured by her heart, never fell to the ground'.[2] If each person's body tells the story of his passions, historical events can also model souls.

Balzac stressed a difference in sensibility between the generations. This, for example, was what he suggested by presenting two old men, who were marked by the behaviour of the *Ancien Régime*;

Pons and his friend Schmucke whose friendship and delicacy of feeling did not appear to Balzac to be comprehensible to his contemporaries.

> Indeed, it is a question of giving an idea of the excessive delicacy of two hearts [a hard thing for 99 per cent of readers in 1847]. [. . .] From an excessive tenderness for the pains of others, each of them wept for his powerlessness; and, as for their feelings, they were of a sensitivity which was developed to the point of illness.[3]

These two hearts, which harboured an anachronic sensitivity, a compassion without measure and a childlike naivety, would be constantly fooled, for the spirit of the times was not at all in accord with these effusions. Even in the eyes of Balzac, who was a verbose commentator who did not hesitate to analyse his readers, they passed for pathological beings. And this description labelled them as potential victims. In the opposite case, an old noblewoman could not weep with her niece, despite her good heart: 'for the Revolution had left the women of the old monarchy with few tears in their eyes'.[4]

The body was therefore a historical unit and was to be consulted like an open book, even when each person sought to conceal his tears from an outside world which was curious and hostile. The person who had encountered these sufferings which were meant to be hidden, knew how to behave: he 'comes into the world to lie to the world, to play his role in it, he knows where to find the wings to which he can retire to calculate, weep and joke'.[5] For if the world was a stage on which we must know how to act without displaying our emotions, and reserve them for the private sphere, the imposed restraint was written on our bodies and strangers could read our troubles through the mask of worldly presentation. Hidden sufferings would bend the course of a life and were deeply engraved on one's attitudes and facial features. The novelist would decode the symptoms there, study the psychology despite the roles acted out by the characters in public or in private. Society imposed the silence of the passions, but this self-refinement could not be achieved without leaving traces, as though the expression of feelings and of emotion, once contained, overflowed all the more, after they had torn the spirit apart. It was as though Nature avenged itself for the training necessary for social life. In order to play a public role, it was necessary to learn to control one's tears and to reserve them for the secrecy of one's room. When tears were about to flow, it was important to retire quickly but discreetly from the view of others, who appeared only to wait for this move to discuss one's case and the cause of one's emotion if one had allowed it to appear. This theme was recurrent in the novels of Balzac.[6] When the desire to cry was irresistible, such as that which took hold of Goriot at table in the pension Vacquet, a person would turn away, and could, like him, accuse his neighbour of having thrown tobacco in his eyes.[7] To weep in the sight of society was frankly humiliating for a man, but also dangerous for a woman who thus discovered her heart. Women were the first victims of this social hypocrisy. Suffering in marriage, they could only swallow their tears, for the law and morality forbade their cries. They could confide in nobody, nor could they weep with the consolation of friendship: 'a woman friend would have rejoiced in it, a man would have speculated',[8] everybody followed his own interests under the cover of morality, because society required peace in the home. If in certain respects, the private domain was a refuge, it provoked a series of suppressed sufferings and of restrained tears. For the domestic realm as a conditional term of the balance between public and private was subjected to the inquisitorial regard of society, which enforced the reign of the law of silence there. Nobody wished to hear anything through the walls of private life because the institution of marriage must be preserved at all costs. Society constantly set itself up as judge of domestic sufferings, without anybody ever being able to reply with normality because it was above all thirsty for scandal. Collective sorrow, and mourning in particular, was on the other hand merely a mean pantomime: it was only expressed by stereotypes. Society

laughed at sons who wept too much for their fathers; it abominated those who did not weep enough for them; then it amused itself, in measuring the value of the corpses before they were even cold [. . .] After a few lachrymose phrases which were the a-e-i-o-u of collective suffering, and which were pronounced with the same accents with no difference in feeling in all the towns of France at any time, each one would calculate the product of the succession.[9]

In the extreme case of a day of mourning in which the afflicted family wept, because it was the sanctuary of private pure and authentic feelings, society would criticise the excess of tears and weigh the inheritance. This elementary alphabet of proprieties, pronounced without excessive conviction appeared to be devoid of feeling and true tears. In it the family was simply an economic unit which led to opportunities for gossip. Society ridiculed the most profound feelings in the name of communal pleasantries.

The power of simulation, which the questioning of appearances placed at the forefront, redistributed the understanding of the signs of emotion. Thus, pity concerning the popular classes was partly modified: servants, peasants and the poor appeared to know too well how to arouse compassion among the well off. Did they not imitate simplicity of heart and spirit drawn by the lure of gain? In the novels of Balzac, servants, especially, knew the private life and character of those they served. If some were sincerely devoted, many imitated devotion and sadness to earn some money. They were prepared to humiliate themselves publicly to keep their place. Thus when the servants of the Président de Marville were ordered to go and excuse themselves to Pons, who until then they had mocked incessantly: 'they showed themselves to be what servants are, cowardly and ingratiating: they wept'.[10] Mme Cibot, the portress of cousin Pons and his friend Schmucke, could, concerning this, be a model of conduct. Anxious to be written into the will of the naive collector, she played the woman of the heart, direct and maternal, ready to use her savings to come to the aid of the two friends, and always moved to tears. She took on the attitudes of melodrama to prove her disinterest and her tenderness and wept while speaking of her husband who she would nevertheless not hesitate to poison. She played then the big-hearted woman of the people, but in fact she deliberately hastened the death of Pons by disturbing him further, most of all when he did not trust her.

'"These then are the consequences of the devotion of a poodle. Oh Lord oh Lord!" She burst into tears and collapsed onto a chair and this tragic movement caused the most unfortunate upheaval in Pons.'[11]

An 'atrocious actress'[12] in her tears begging 'with a very expressive pantomime'[13] la Cibot was presented by Balzac through the metaphors of the theatre, or rather of the melodrama, a popular genre and the model on which she appeared to base her exaggerated gestures.

Europe, Vautrin's henchman, who served Esther in *Splendeurs et misères des courtisanes* [splendours and poverty of courtesans], made use of the same pretence of attachment and false tears. Intimate enemies, servants entered into false relationships of the affections with their masters, while playing on the sentimental clichés attached to their position within the private sphere. This popular Machiavellianism haunted a bourgeois domestic realm which wished to be impenetrable to strangers.

Peasants also excelled in the art of playing the simple spirit who was quick to tears. Gothard, son of the farmer Michu, who was devoted to Laurence, the aristocrat of *Une ténébreuse affaire* [a dark affair], whose manoeuvres were watched by the police, was arrested. But on his interrogation by the policemen, he played 'the part of bursting into tears in the manner of idiots'.[14] To all the questions of the justice of the peace he replied with tears: 'In crying, he finally gave himself a sort of convulsive attack which frightened them and they left him. The little comic, perceiving himself to be watched no longer, looked at Michu and smiled.'[15] The young peasant's ability to act disarmed the authorities.

Skilled at compliments, the young Mouche of *Paysans* also knew how to cause emotion in the bourgeois in order to pick up a few coins while spying on his benefactors: 'Mouche understood admirably that he was acting for the entertainment of the bourgeoisie, the student of the père Fourchon then became worthy of his master, he began to cry'.[16] Among the peasants, the children themselves had learned to pretend, supplying the bourgeois with the clichés they expected.

Although the public still witnessed a few scenes of unalloyed charity in his novels, this moving episode appeared to be suspicious. There existed, in the novels of Balzac, a sort of disquiet concerning the popular classes who presented tears to the middle classes a little too easily to evoke pity in them. The acting was not just concerned with 'society', it infiltrated all social classes and perturbed the philanthropic relationship which had nevertheless known such fine hours. Thus uncertainty concerning the emotions presented by another came into play in social relationships: the men of the people wore the masks of melodrama to ape their feelings and fool the bourgeoisie.

MEN AND WOMEN ON THE LADDER OF THE AGES

This social comedy so denounced by Balzac had consequences for individual destinies. In this, the male and female roles were not defined once and for all, but were modified by advancing age. The capacity to be moved, the possibility of communicating one's emotions or the necessity to restrain them were graded according to sex and the stages of life.

In the course of her existence a woman wept in different ways. Thus marriage was a key stage which could often wound female sensibility even when, like the Marquise d'Aiglemont the woman had chosen her husband. Suffering from her husband's lack of sensibility and brutal sensuality, she was obliged to bite back her tears, while 'her most private wishes, the morals which in the past as a young girl she had dreamt of, troubled her'.[17] Her interior heartbreaks were without glory, her long melancholies were hidden, 'her bitter tears were shed aimlessly in solitude'.[18] In her terrible conflict and her solitary tears she could either devour her suffering or be devoured herself, 'either die or destroy something within herself, her conscience perhaps'.[19] Thus her girlish dreams which had made her weep so deliciously were lost in marriage. After years of restrained tears and interior battles which gnawed at her, she was finally undone by being unfaithful to her husband with a more sensitive man. Between the young girl, and the woman of 30 an abyss had formed: 'The first possessed only tears and pleasures, the second had only voluptuous experiences and remorse'.[20] Between these two ages of life, the worst which women had to endure was the indifference of the men with whom they lived. Thus M. d'Aiglemont slept peacefully at her side, undisturbed by the hot tears which his wife let fall.[21] This soldier did not hear the weeping and suffering of his wife. This solitary pain which flung itself against the barrier of the other's sleep shows how greatly and deeply her sensibility was disturbed. These tears which this man ignored or ridiculed would wound the maternal love of the Marquise d'Aiglemont for ever, she would regard her son with dry eyes.[22] The sensitive nature of women appeared thus to be perturbed by male behaviour. Even if they were not abandoned or ridiculed, women were often forced by delicacy not to cry. The role of mother and of wife demanded a calm and smiling face so as not to sadden the children in any way and not to cause any further worries to the husband.

However, when alone, they knew tears. Joséphine, worried over her husband's passion for science which threatened to deprive their children of the bare necessities because he was continually chipping away at their inheritance, experienced such a moment.

> Her expression, which would have moved the most careless of her children, was one of cold, enduring stupefaction, despite a few burning tears. Nothing could be more terrible to see than such extreme pain which overflowed only occasionally but which remained written on her face like petrified lava around a volcano.[23]

This suffering which could only overflow in solitude, consumed this woman from inside and threatened her health. Her burning tears did not comfort her because they were blended with insensibility which was proof of a hidden pain. On hearing her husband arrive she transformed her expression.

> At that moment the stricken lady listened and appeared to collect herself, she took her handkerchief, wiped away her tears, tried to smile and eradicated the expression of pain engraved in all her features with such skill that one might have thought that she was in that state of indifference created by a life free of worries.[24]

Swallowing back her tears, this loving wife succeeded in constraining herself to the extent of giving an impression of tranquillity which would not alarm her husband. For she intended to be his comforter, to bring him peace while she was suffering in secret, not for her own benefit, for she was all sacrifice, but for her children. 'The tears and the terror imprinted on her face at the beginning of the story of domestic drama which developed in this peaceful household were caused by the fear of having sacrificed her children for her husband.'[25] Torn between her role of wife and that of a mother, but committed to the preservation of the reign of calm and tranquillity in the bosom of her family, Joséphine was the living image of the tragedy which was to shake an apparently peaceful home, because she was already experiencing it on her own while displaying a serene face to everyone. Thus even inside the private world, this model wife could not express her troubles and her worries. Her silent devotion and suppressed tears nevertheless threatened to be her undoing, even to cause her death or her downfall. For in Balzac's works, one died of thwarted emotions. This hidden heroism which broke the hearts of women took on the dimensions of their excessive tenderness.

'"Come Léontine, there are times when women like us should not weep but should act" said the Duchess.'[26] Certain female characters exhibited a strength of character which was superior to their sex by resisting passive emotion. They, like men, would prefer to face up to the event rather than spoil themselves in useless tears. Laurence, the heroine of *Une Ténébreuse affaire*, appeared little inclined to tears, despite adversity: 'Her heart was of an excessive sensibility but she bore in her mind a virile resolution and a stoic strength. Her far-seeing eyes did not know how to weep.'[27] Intelligence, strength, self-mastery, qualities considered to belong to men, silenced the heart of this sensitive woman. However, in the story she would allow the reader to see her capacity for tears, for instance when she was told that her friends were saved:

> The joy of triumph sparkled in her eyes, she blushed, and tears rolled between her eyelids. Strong in the face of the greatest of troubles, this young woman could only weep for pleasure. In that moment she was sublime, especially in the eyes of the *curé* who, almost annoyed by the virility of Laurence's character, perceived in her the excessive tenderness of a woman which lay in her like the most deeply hidden treasure beneath a block of granite.[28]

Charged with the care of the spirit, and an observer of hearts, the *curé* was relieved at this sublime display of a femininity concealed under the granite of a virile personality. For if circumstances demanded the expression of a heroic temperament in certain women (Balzac, following his inclinations, reserved this quality for the nobility), they could not break into the treasures of emotion which belonged to the female heart. A tear sufficed to reveal this deep femininity.

The theme of the repentant courtesan which here sheds light on a whole world of the imagination concerning the armour of insensitivity and female nature, ran through many novels of the nineteenth century. They revealed the spirit of a young woman in love and penitent. Both culprits and victims, these women, branded with the seal of impurity, cleansed themselves of their sins in tears. The character of Esther in *Splendeurs et misères des courtisanes* sacrificed her life to Lucien de Rubempré, whose tears she drank lovingly.[29] She rediscovered in the convent the emotions of a novice and had only her tears to offer in expiation. Demanding towards herself, she wept with rage when memories of orgies come into her mind, while everybody admired her for her fervent piety.[30] Thus, despite external appearances and past sins, devotion, tenderness and excessive sensibility and the purity of the woman were revealed to any who knew how to read hearts.

When unscrupulous men spoke of women, they discussed the ways of seducing them, of making them believe that they were loved. Vautrin advised Rastignac, who he wanted to become a perfect lady-chaser:

I will not speak to you of the scrawls of love, nor of the nonsenses to which women are attached, for instance, the ploy of sprinkling drops of water onto the writing paper like tears when we are far from them, you seem to me to know the slang of the heart perfectly.[31]

The theme of the traces of tears in love letters, fully developed in the eighteenth century, was here an object of derision for men without scruples: they saw it only as a cliché, a sentimental stereotype, the childishness of women, but one with a guaranteed effect which they would all fall for. Men only made use of this slang of the heart through necessity, because so many women still saw poetic treasures in it. But for masculine pride it was far more chic to avoid effusiveness.

Beyond the behaviour of these hardened seducers, there was also a whole mastery of emotions which was at issue in the man's life. Balzac thus lingered over the last tenderness of a young man, which occurred as a farewell to the previous object of his reverence. Eugène, reading the letters of the Goriot family, was still prey to emotion: 'A few tears escaped his eyes, the final grains of incense thrown on the sacred family altar'.[32] This was the final homage to the values he must put aside if he wished to make his way in the world which were like the remains of his purity. A witness to the death and burial of Goriot, he would leave behind him there his final feeling of generosity:

The day was over, a damp twilight irritated the nerves, he looked at the tomb and buried in it his final tear as a young man, a tear drawn out by the sacred emotions of a pure heart, one of those tears which spring up as far as the heavens from the earth on which they fall.[33]

This pure and saintly sadness was nevertheless a farewell to the sensibility of youth. Knowing the morals of society, the young man knew that from then on he would have to silence it. Lucien de Rubempré, just before his suicide in prison, wept for an irreparable loss:

this similarity between his point of departure, filled with innocence, and the point of arrival, final degree of shame and degradation, was so well understood by the final efforts of his poetic fibre that the unfortunate burst into tears. He wept for four hours with the impassive appearance of a stone figure, but suffering from all his overturned hopes.[34]

This final self-appraisal – a retrospective glance into the past, and into innocence – attained the most profound personal suffering. The poet did not weep so much for his present situation as for the road which he had travelled since the time when he had dreamed of his life. Men, especially if they were poets, appeared thus to know a vast regret for the loss of an unchanged heart filled with hope, they wept for their lost illusions.

In novels, mature men practically never cried, or in such rare circumstances that the tears which they shed demonstrated the most important part of them, for instance, a deep affection. This was why Jacques Collin was moved when he learnt of the imprisonment of Lucien de Rubempré:

The idea of the misfortune caused by the weakness of Lucien, who must have lost his head because of the strain of secrecy, developed to enormous proportions in the mind of Jacques Collin, and guessing at the possibility of a disaster, the unfortunate man felt his eyes with tears, a phenomenon which had only occurred once in him since his childhood.[35]

The tears of one who had ceased to cry from an early age showed the strength of his character through the reference to the past as much as the fault in the armour of a man who was impervious to every test. His emotion showed no bounds on the death of Lucien: 'A torrent of tears came from his light yellow convict's eyes which had formerly flamed like those of a wolf starving from six months of snow in the middle of the Ukraine'.[36] The contrast between this wild animal's gaze and the excess of tears which quenched it, beyond the hyperbolic effect of style, revealed Jacques Collin's internal turmoil and the depth of the feelings which attached him to Lucien.

Michu, when he heard the lawyer pleading his boundless devotion for Laurence, whose farmer he was, could not contain his tears.

> On hearing himself rehabilitated by an eloquent voice, there was a moment when the tears fell from Michu's yellow eyes and ran down his terrible face [. . .] His behaviour was suddenly explained, mostly by his tears, which produced a great effect on the jury.[37]

The most terrible and impassive faces appeared to wear the truest tears, as though wild natures revealed their motives and their passion in a rare expression of emotion. Tears acted in this case as a sort of reversal of appearances and allowed the naked truth to be seen on a face in an exceptional and dramatic moment.

Restraint thus no longer had a role in Balzac once paternal feeling was aroused. The spy, Peyrade, although little inclined to sensibility, began to weep when he discovered that his daughter Lydie had been kidnapped.[38] For this cold man had felt all the treasures of affection for his only daughter. For Balzac, fatherhood was a passion and the Père Goriot was the most developed prototype of this. He wept a lot, but in addition, he placed a limitless value on the tears of his daughters. He wanted to retrieve Eugène's waistcoat on which Delphine had wept, she who had never cried when she was small.[39] We know his tragic end and the hot tears shed by the students who were then taken by the dying man for his daughters, which made him give 'a sharp cry of pleasure'.[40] Once the period of youth had passed, where men learned to master their emotions, maturity was indicated by a certain general dryness and by the individual outbursts reserved for the most profound characteristic, the most vital attachment of an individual existence. The fit of tears, by its very rarity thus revealed an unknown truth. We find here the concept that men, having learnt since adolescence to control themselves, shed more 'real' more deeply significant tears than women and children who were still practising a sort of blackmail through their tears. These unmasterable tears of the male adult could not be simulated, providing others with information which had not been scrambled by the reign of appearances.

But in parallel, family affections could be suffocated by a dominant passion. Balthazar, a tender husband and good father, was so immersed in his chemistry that he forgot his family for it. '"Come", he said on seeing the tears of his wife, "I have analysed the properties of tears. They contain a little phosphate of lime, sodium chloride, mucus and water"'.[41] Balthazar could only read a possible chemical breakdown in the tears of his wife: the scientific eye had replaced that of the loving husband. Concentrated in the channel of the dominant passion, his nervous fluid and sensibility were particularly badly distributed. Beyond this channel, the impassioned man displayed the most complete indifference to the most sacred of ties. In this, Balzac took part in the age of passions, where the ability to cry or to be moved by the tears of others could be diverted from natural feelings by an excessive polarisation of will, and not by a simple eclipse of reason.

THOSE TEARS WHICH WE MUST KNOW HOW TO CONCEAL

The heroes of Stendhal were generally of a natural sensibility, but they quickly learned to mistrust their emotions. The tears of youth had to be abandoned little by little: the young man was at first surprised by an uncontrolled ability to be moved, then he learned to restrain himself. This apprenticeship was bound up with the words exchanged between men. Thus the young Lucien Leuwen discovered to his cost that filial sentiment was not well received. Filled with gratitude and with tears in his eyes, he came to embrace his father:

'Ah! I see what it is' said M. Leuwen in considerable surprise, 'you have lost a hundred louis, I will give you two hundred; But I don't like to see tears in the eyes of a sub-lieutenant. Should not a courageous soldier consider first of all the effect that his demeanour produces in others?'[42]

This debonair but rather insensitive father could not understand such an impulse of the feelings, and imagined that his son had lost at cards. He was concerned above all to teach his son the expressions which were appropriate to his new career. Lucien learned from this misunderstanding: '"I must not trust my first impulses" he said to himself, "truly I can be sure of nothing concerning myself, my feelings only succeeded in shocking my father"'.[43] This worry of not knowing himself provoked a self-examination, and the application of restraint. It is interesting to note that this apprenticeship took place within the private circle of father and son, because inside it effusiveness was already misunderstood, displaced and even considered shocking. Despite this wish to conceal what he felt, Lucien Leuwen could not restrain his tears after having been shouted down by a crowd. He confided his anguish to his friend Coffe, asking him to preserve an eternal silence, but he was not any the less humiliated at having shed tears in front of him: 'Leuwen had the weakness to think aloud in front of Coffe: he had drunk in all shame, then he wept'.[44] The tears which were shed before a real friend whom he had known for a long time still caused him humiliation. His words of despair and lassitude were then no longer of any importance, he had shown his weaknesses and he had nothing else to hide.

The third example in this novel concerns women. Lucien Leuwen remembered, after his adventure with Mme Grandet, the comments which his cousin had made: 'Ernest was once mistaken when he predicted that I would never in my life acquire a woman without love as I should, except through pity, tears and all the things which that chemist of unhappiness calls the "passage of tears"'.[45] For to 'have' a woman while loving her, or at least while weeping, was to borrow her sentimental code and was not at all flattering inside the male world. It was better to make use of the dry method if one wished to talk among men and to boast of one's conquests. In front of his father, his friend and his cousin, this sensitive young man was brought back to the norms of virile behaviour. The formation of the male character in all its maturity necessitated the complete mastery of the emotions and the hardening of the heart, especially for anyone who wished to play a part in Parisian society: this was one of the springs of action of Stendhal's incomplete novel; the search for power whose path led by the conquest of women.

Julien Sorel was also possessed of a natural sensibility, he shed tears in solitude, and felt a mixture of shame and pleasure in surrendering himself to his emotion: 'Julien was ashamed of his emotion, for the first time in his life, he saw himself to be loved; he wept with delight and left to conceal his tears in the great woods above Verrières'.[46] He then reflected on the significance of this outburst of tears: 'I will only rely on the parts of my character which I have put to the test. Who could have told me that I would find pleasure in shedding tears!' This sensitive hero, animated by agreeable but unpredictable emotional impulses, then decided to contain the movements of his heart which surprised even him and which threatened him with an unfavourable verdict.

Julien, when imprisoned, could not restrain his tears before his father: '"What an undignified weakness", he said to himself in fury. He will exaggerate my lack of courage everywhere.' Furthermore this ability to weep was not a proof of cowardice but a part of his character. He had explained this before: 'It is easy to touch my heart, the most banal words, if they are spoken with the accent of truth, can move my voice to sympathy and even move me to tears. How many times have dry hearts been wary of me for this fault'.[47] Stendhal's hero often ran counter to the dominant mode and suffered for his capacity to be moved which was taken for a weakness. He assessed the elements of his character which could harm his success or his honour: the ability to be moved was one of these.

Another of Stendhal's characters, Octave, Armance's male hero, was harder on himself and less inclined to feeling, he knew shame before emotion. Thus he did not allow himself to be moved to tears on the day when he realised that he loved his cousin against his will: 'He could not weep. The shame which he found himself to be worthy of prevented him from feeling sorry for himself, and dried his tears.'[48] Shame and the need to harden oneself appear to have been the two essential motives for the inhibition of male tears. Young men were often obliged to vanquish their inclination and their taste for the sentiments, in order to succeed in taking part in an active life while knowing how to triumph over their tendency to emotion. This knowledge was acquired in the company of men, but also by a confrontation with the self which took the form of an interior monologue.

The need to save face also explains this absence of expressed emotion. In an unfinished novel, Vigny described a young man whose enemy proved to him that the object of his love had given herself to an old marshal.

> During my silence, he gravely drew out the address of the place and the times of the meetings, and proofs written in the hand of the unhappy young person, proofs which left no room to doubt the shameful truth. I was saved from the humiliation of shedding tears by a glance at the face of the man speaking to me which revealed to me his ferocious joy [. . .] I thought only of revenge.[49]

The necessity to act, to remedy the affront quickly triumphed over the affliction which could have caused shame in the young man. It was almost good luck to be able to fight a duel in such circumstances.

Did this need to harden oneself, to save face, really happen in life? The private papers of Alfred de Vigny might lead us to believe so:

> The cold and rather dark severity of my character was not natural. It was given to me by life.
>
> An extreme sensibility, suppressed from childhood by my masters, and in the army by the senior officers, remained locked in the most secret part of my heart.[50]

Stendhal and Vigny described the stages which obliged the young man to restrain his tears: military life was often presented as a moment of apprenticeship but teaching also played a role. The eyes of mature men were even more important in obliging him to work on his own character. Vigny's earliest education took place under the eyes of his mother, who, in weeping while copying a painting by Raphaël taught him about aesthetic emotion. But this age lasted only a short time: handed over to men, the young Vigny quickly learned to restrain himself, and to keep secret the sensibility which was part of him.

TO BE A WOMAN IN HER TEARS

Women were destined to follow the opposite path. Sometimes struck with insensitivity they rediscovered their 'womanly nature' in tears. For them, there was no other salvation than through the passage of tears.

The mineral metaphor which defined spirits which were strong and impassive in adversity was to be found under Gautier's pen. Musidora was 'one of those diamond natures which have brilliance without heat and invincible hardness'.[51] One can see in this the effect of the imagination of the surface and depths, of the hard and the liquid, which structured the portrayal of the individual, and of women in particular. A martyred childhood shed light on Musidora's lack of sensitivity, her heart must have armed itself very early because of it. Indeed, she did not weep over the death of her mother. The latter had rather inhibited the bonds of daughterly tenderness by having sold her at the age of thirteen to an old English lord and by having beaten her to make her hand over the money she had thus earned. She did not experience any emotion when one of her lovers committed suicide in despair, unable to bear her prodigalities. She lived as a courtesan, indifferent and calm in the midst of disorder and infamy. 'Her true existence was completely separate from her private thoughts and was totally external.' Her private and hidden part remained preserved by this double life, but she did not participate in her outside existence and nothing could move her. One evening, however, lying back on her couch, she wept at not having met Fortunio as she had wished to: 'the ice-floes of her heart, more cold and more sterile than a Siberian winter melted at the warm breath of love, and turned into a gentle rain of tears. These tears were the baptism of her new life'. These sacred tears which were caused by love, represented a second birth. Fortunio had succeeded 'in scratching Musidora's armour' for his spirit was as strong and resisting as hers. From this encounter between two diamond natures a metamorphosis was accomplished, 'a woman came out of the statue'. Her private existence which until then had been underground and paralysed, grew like 'a mysterious flower sown by Fortunio on the sterile rock of her heart', and her own tears watered it. This change from the solid state of the desert to a liquid germination marked the return to femininity. The courtesan, beautiful and insensitive, was transformed into a young girl: 'her love had all the divine childishnesses, all the adorable immaturities of a pure and virgin passion'. Armed and unaffected by debauchery, Musidora rediscovered through love all the purity of the woman-child: to weep was for her a baptism (or a first communion). Curiously then, although women were committed by nature to shed easy tears, some of them often found themselves needing to suppress them, by overcoming weakness in order to face up to difficult situations. However, and more than ever, these rare tears revealed the female qualities of the treasures of devotion and of purity. Deep femininity was defined by this ability to weep. Subjected to the control of external appearances in order to bear her surroundings without suffering, the depth of a woman's character remained defined by her ability to melt and to be moved. On the surface, roles, conventions, armour and shells were in opposition to the treasures which were deeply buried in the female spirit, over which writers were constantly enthusing.

NUANCES AND PSYCHOLOGY

The social codes were often considered to be responsible for interior sufferings, even when the conventions were apparently hypocritical. The individual suffered from society which demanded grimaces and false smiles, but also false tears, when it was not mocking those who wept. Even more, society life, where one's presentation of oneself was of the first importance, was paradoxically the arena for a savagery which was all the more ferocious for being invisible. Popular morals were not any more exalted. In the face of the ruling classes, the men and women of the people acted out a role to attract compassion, or appeared to be what they were not in the least: naive and devoted, with their hearts on their sleeves while they plotted the blackest of schemes. Social relationships therefore necessitated a general self-control, the discovery of intentions which were most often the opposite of those suggested by appearances, the development of a sort of defensive armour in the face of the external world.

This new regime of behaviour had an effect on both men and women. Women, who were more committed to the domestic circle, could indeed allow nothing to escape into the outside world and society concerning their private life, and had to present a welcoming face. In private, their sensitivity was sometimes mocked by men. Often victims, they wept alone. However, even those who by their strength of character managed to master their female emotions, would one day or another reveal their deep femininity in a fit of tears. For it was in the nature of women to be tender and sensitive despite all they endured and novels did not cease to exalt this delicate weakness.

The men who wept at their feet knew it well, but they sometimes laughed in the wings at this sentimentality which made tears necessary for the purposes of seduction. In order to face the outside world for which they were destined, more than women, men had to renounce the emotions of a sensitive heart if they did not wish to appear weak. If they sometimes wept in serious circumstances, the emotion which they expressed was all the more profound for being so rare, and this moment marked an important step in their lives.

In the nineteenth century torrents of tears and shared tears became rare: literary texts proposed different types of exposition. The vocabulary which was used was singularly diversified and the established code of the signs of expression was dismantled in favour of a relatively wide palette of expressive nuances. The eyes could be damp, the glance veiled, a tear could be furtively wiped away or suppressed, a sob could be smothered. Deep suffering led to rare and burning tears. These subtle notations, these tiny nuances of movement, were probably as much the signs of a transformation of the genre of the novel as of a social ethic of restraint. The fact that the observation and the description of people, of their physical appearance and their movements took on a sort of narrative efficiency, was probably related to a new conception of social relationships and of the encounter between characters. This exact reading of visible or proffered attitudes, this worried cathechism of information on the feelings of others, appears to have been without real precedent.

This impression appears to have been reinforced by psychological observation in which the act of weeping became individualised. The fit of tears became motivated in the text, even metaphorically. It revealed deep femininity, a true sensibility which had nevertheless been hidden until then, the dominant passion of a mysterious character. A face could bear witness to devoured tears, explained by a personal experience such as a husband without delicacy or a guilty relationship. Only an individual history could make certain expressions of emotion explicit: an unhappy childhood, overturned hopes or the dreams of a young girl held up to ridicule were thus called on to make an emotion intelligible and to give it a meaning. The ages of life each had their own tears: the young pure girl knew gentle and easy tears, the young man was still sensitive but he shed his last tears, there existed a psychology of youth which was not that of maturity or even of old age. All these instances where tears in themselves were not enough to shed light on the narrative but which took on meaning only in the context of an individual background, represented a psychologising of emotion. If the expressive nuances were described with such precision, it was perhaps because of the fugitive message which they concealed, and which the character gave off in spite of himself. The man who would have liked to conceal his motivations and his weaknesses, bore marks on his face and in his movements which betrayed him. Psychological motivation, which could sometimes appear verbose, nevertheless remained the necessary mediator for the understanding of certain scenes of tears. More important than the signs given off, tears now became symptoms deciphered by the expert eye of the narrator or the author.

The constant play between the surface and the depths between appearance and truth, was also recurrent. A character of granite revealed a profoundly buried treasure of tenderness, a diamond soul began to melt, delivering up an intimacy which had been preserved by general indifference. Anyone who had a grazed sensibility wore armour and the deepest pain could leave a legacy of dry eyes. On the other side of the coin, anyone who cried easily was only possessed of a surface sensibility. The expression which demonstrated the most emotion was sometimes only an expressive pantomime which concealed the blackest of intentions. Tears could be feigned and simulated. But a true pain could appear to be acted, and a false tear could move to emotion. Too much credulity or too much scepticism in the face of the tears of others were a constant threat to relationships, especially between men and women. One could neither trust appearances nor constantly question them. Truth was only revealed through a personal and profound knowledge of others, and sometimes of the self, because a tear could reveal what until then had been unknown, for instance: affection, or a characteristic. The truest sensibility thus became the most intimate and was therefore often the most hidden. Intimacy was depth, self-revelation was on the surface, play-acting or a shell. In novels, the significance of emotion through tears was no longer immediate, the narrator (the writer) had to decipher it in order to reveal the truth behind the appearances.

Part III

Crisis of Tears: Dangers of the Emotions

Part III

Crisis of Tears, Dangers of the Emotions

9 Against the Sickness of the Emotions

DISGUST WITH TEARS

Many people were tired of the romantic sobbing, which had set the tone for the first half of the century. Letters, memoirs and private diaries bore the evidence of it. Musset, cultivating irony when the fancy took him, made the singular declaration that he hated 'all these lovers, these dreamers in barques, these nocturnal lovers of lakes and little cascades, this nameless mob in which one cannot take a step without being inundated with verses, with tears and with diaries'.[1] He revolted against the Lamartinian snivellings, or he was perhaps attacking his own image, with a familiar act of derision, and a cruel laugh, turning on the tears which he had shed in such abundance. As for Mürger, he deplored the seriousness with which so many young people received the declamations concerning unhappy artists and poets. These desperate chants had turned the heads of those who did not even have any creative power:

> These are dangerous preachings, these pointless posthumous exaltations which have created the ridiculous race of the misunderstood, the weeping poets whose muse always has red eyes and unkempt hair, and all the impotent mediocrities who, locked in the prison of non-publication, call her an unnatural mother, and art a hangman.[2]

However he only attacked the parasites of art, who wept poverty. Delacroix was more virulent, he wrote in his diary on 14 February 1850 as follows:

> I am beginning to be furiously sick of the Schuberts, the dreamers, the Chateaubriands (this began long ago), the Lamartines, etc. Why is this happening? Because it is not true. Do lovers look at the moon when they hold their mistresses close to them? All in good time, when she begins to bore them. Lovers

do not weep together: they do not make a hymn to infinity, and describe little [. . .] This is the school of sick love. It is a sad recommendation and yet women pretend to be wild about these nonsenses.[3]

Delacroix would have liked to set about life quite differently from these insipid lovers. This sentimentalism took no account of reality but unfortunately women still dreamed of tearful declarations and of pale lovers. The war of the sexes was a war of codes, but it was also an aesthetic conflict.

Those who wished to revive literature reacted against the displays of sentiments, the outbursts of suffering souls which acted as a warning to creative activity. A reaction of the young generation of men of letters against their elders, this denunciation was made in the name of virility. Flaubert did not hesitate to assail the great literary figures of the first half of the nineteenth century. His profession of faith concerning truth, and analysis, which was in his view the major issue of the century, was accompanied by a deep mistrust of the works of Lamartine and of his advantageous poses. He told thus of his interview with the poet: 'before the final piece of verse, he took care to tell us that he had written it *in one breath only and while weeping*. What a fine poetic procedure!'[4] The taste for cold observation and mistrust of a poetry born of effusion were associated in Flaubert's mind with the virile values: 'The truth calls for hairier men than M. de Lamartine'. His distrust of the tearful posturing of the romantic poet went with a will to tell the truth which called for a male assurance. He also criticised Musset, who seemed to him to be a most unhappy boy:

I find the origin of this decadence in the common mania which he shared for mistaking sentiment for poetry. "The melodrama was good when Margot wept", is a pretty line but has a convenient poetry. "Suffering is enough to enable one to sing", etc. These are the axioms of this school and this turns everything into morality and nothing remains the product of art.[5]

The foremost quality of Art for him was illusion; tears which brought about emotion were of an inferior order from the aesthetic viewpoint. The tears which were shed were of less benefit to literary activity than a frenzied labour, in which there was no question of the artist's identity. Literature appeared to be deprived of strength when it was too concerned with emotions and confidences: 'Do you not feel that all is dissolving now through *letting go*, through the liquid element, through tears, through chatter, through milkiness? Contemporary literature is drowned in the rules of women.'[6] Unlike Michelet who was so in favour of all the female fluids, Flaubert saw physiological troubles in these tears which were repugnant to him. The proposition was clear, Literature must be purged of all feminine secretions which weakened it and must demonstrate a virility which cut to the quick.

The new aesthetic rebelled against the school of sentiments, as a school of women. This aesthetic concept passed into Flaubert's life, and into his relationships with women, whose tears he accused of sentimentality. Thus art met with private life and in a letter to Louise Colet Flaubert attempted, as much in the field of love as of literature, to convince her to abandon her old ideas:

if you weep, may my lips wipe away your tears! I would like them to sweep out your heart, to chase away all this old dust. [. . .] With the cult of the Virgin, the adoration of tears came into the world. Humanity has been pursuing a rococo ideal for 18 centuries now, but man revolts once again and he deserts the loving lap which has cradled him in his sadness. A terrible reaction is taking place in the modern consciousness against what is called love. This began with roars of irony (Byron etc.) and the entire century observes with the help of a magnifying glass and dissects the tiny flower of sentiment which felt so good in former days![7]

The piety of the virgin had contaminated humanity for too long. It was in the name of modernity, begun by the irony of Byron, that Flaubert no longer wished to bathe in sentiment and love, but to dissect these feelings, being prepared to present them in all their nauseating crudity. Without this, future generations would judge the stupidity of this literature of the nineteenth century severely:

The sentimental personality will be what will in the future make contemporary literature appear childish and rather stupid. Nothing but sentiment, nothing but sentiment, nothing but tenderness, nothing but tears! There will never have been such fine people.[8]

He therefore set out to fight against the sighs of the 'sentimental personality', and the tears which it caused, the whole 'female' and moralising element which dominated the literary stage and which he detected in the works of Louise Colet. He deplored on this count the woman's sentimentality which was to be found in the poetess, whom he wished to be at once a mistress and a friend:

> I believed from the beginning that I would find in you less female personality, a more universal concept of life. But no! The heart! a poor heart, a charming heart with its eternal graces is still there, even in the highest of women, even in the greatest. Men normally do all that they can to make it bleed. They drink in all the tears which are not shed by them with a refined sensuality, all those little tortures which prove to them that they are stronger. If I understood that pleasure, I would have every opportunity to enjoy it with you.[9]

Masculine pride loved to feast on the tears of women which men themselves did not have the right to shed: but Flaubert himself did not do so. Regretting constantly the emotions of Louise Colet, he did not like to cause her tears, and wished to see her changed into a 'new hermaphrodite', a woman in body and a man in mind.

The advice of Maxime du Camp to Louise Colet took a more direct route and rang a different note which was considerably less compassionate:

> Above all, you know, Gustave is a physical man and you only present him with a face disfigured by tears; he loves the most excellent harmony, and every time you see him, your beauty is twisted by tears and your soul and your heart only hold reproaches for him, of which some are unjust; consider, dear sister, and above all remember.[10]

Louise Colet was thus requested to suppress her tears and her complaints and to cut a fine figure, in other words to conform to her role as an art object, she should be beautiful and not cry. She had some difficulty in playing her part, and dreamed of expressions of emotion and tender consolations. She wrote thus in her diary of 6 May 1852: 'Ah! if Gustave loved me more, how I would open up my heart to him, how good for me it would be to weep with him and to have his sympathy! But what good would it do? I would only lose my attraction for him, no more.'[11] Flaubert's friends appear to have been very aware of the tears shed by Louise, who they called the Muse. Louis Bouilhet warned Flaubert thus:

> Do you want me to tell you what I feel? Do you want me to tell you straight out what she is working up to, with her visits to your mother, with her comedy in verse, with her cries, her tears, her invitations and her dinners? She wishes, she thinks to become your *wife*![12]

Thus the tearful scenes played by Louise Colet made her uglier, and worse, they were part of a war of attrition which was very involved (marriage was the height of horror for the two friends), and then these fits of despair took place. It was better to warn Flaubert, male solidarity demanded it, and to reprimand Louise so that she stopped weeping.

Condemning female sentimentality, Flaubert also attacked family affections in his letters. In a letter to Bouilhet, he denounced the family, which weakens the virile character and reduces vital energy: 'Curses on the family which softens the heart of the courageous, which drives one to every cowardice, to every concession, and which soaks you in an ocean of milk and tears'.[13] Flaubert and Bouilhet comforted each other: family emotions and their tears made the personality become more female, the creative man of action should therefore protect himself against them so as not to allow himself to be anaesthetised in the insipidity of the scents of women and the stupidity of good feelings. Flaubert nevertheless had some difficulty in applying his principles and those of his friends. He managed to preserve his countenance when faced with his mother's cry on the eve of his departure for Egypt by chewing on his cigar and turning on his heel, but he collapsed into tears in his room and wept for the entire night. Flaubert suffering a thousand torments did not allow himself to give in to any expression in front of others:

> I have such cramps of bitterness in my soul that I could die from them. I tell nobody because I have nobody whom I could tell. The others are worse than I, and in any case I am not used to showing my tears to others. I find it dumb and indecent, like scratching at a scab in public.[14]

Public tears were repugnant for the modest and the sense of ridicule prevented him from shedding them despite his suffering. The pains of the spirit were bitten back to the level of a physical illness which was connected to the physical body and was not at all spiritual. Flaubert's tears would remain without a witness, his emotion was secret. To others he appeared insensitive, but, when he was alone, all those tears which were contained took over again: 'everything irritates and wounds me; and since I contain myself in front of people, I am overcome from time to time by fits of tears and it seems to me that I will burst'.[15] This return of suppressed tears made the outburst all the more violent and was not soothing.

Flaubert was sometimes moved, but he also adapted himself to the person he was communicating with. When he wrote to George Sand, he declared that he read the letters of the master with tears in his eyes, being moved by them, or simply wishing to weep over them.[16] He was probably flattering the inclinations of his friend, proving his attachment to her through tears. But when he wrote to Bouilhet, he spoke of his friendly emotion with the distance of irony: 'This morning at twelve, dear and poor old thing, I received your fine long letter which had I wished for. *I made it damp.* How I think of you, there now! Inestimable rascal.'[17] Bouilhet would use the same tone, beginning his letter thus: 'Your letter brought water to my eyes'.[18] The joking was also a sort of modesty; it was with a smile, a wink, a play on words that the two friends allowed themselves to evoke their emotions and their reciprocal attachment. It was in the same mode that Flaubert told him of the transformation of his sensibility in Egypt:

> There is a development taking place in me (you would perhaps rather that I chatted to you about journeys, fresh air, horizons, blue sky?) I can feel myself daily becoming more sensitive and more emotional. A trifle can bring a tear to my eye. My heart is becoming a prostitute, *it gets wet* about everything. There are small things which touch me in the guts.[19]

This hesitation before confiding, this questioning of the progress of his personality, this joke about his easy tears which smelt of the classroom, all display a certain fear of ridicule. The comment, both mocking and friendly, belonged to a language between men. Male delicacy consisted in concealing sensibility in a crude language, in speaking laughingly of tears, to avoid all the overly-feminine insipidities.

If Flaubert associated his aesthetic pronouncements with a rejection of the emotions judged to be feminine, the Goncourts also made observations on women in tears, which they accompanied by a flawless physical determinism. For the Goncourt brothers, the ability to weep was particularly developed in women for essentially physiological reasons: 'In women, tears are simply a secretion of the nervous system'.[20] Feminine tears were simple regulations of the humours and properly speaking had no meaning. There was then no point in paying any attention to them. On the same count, their tendency for compassion, which was often spectacular, was only the result of their physical complexion:

> Women are an admirable charitable machine. They have their heart in their nerves: pity, the poignancy of a misfortune are a nervous attack for them. Because of this, the fit is brief: a man would linger in his thoughts and sadness for two days, whereas a woman sheds tears and nothing is left.[21]

Woman abandons herself to her nature: the nervous convulsions of charity are worn out by tears, rapidly evacuating sadness. Suffering which was more moral and thoughtful in men, was more profound. Women were only bodies, a machinery of nerves and moods. This habit of always relegating women to their physical determinations permitted the standing of male suffering to be increased; it was without tears and not easy to see, but it inhabited the soul. It seemed to them that women wept as they spoke, that is, in quantity and about anything: 'Women have the chattering of tears'[22] wrote one of them after having described a breakup with his mistress. Chatter was always the language, of others, of the woman, of the child: through this refusal to give any significance to the tears of women, these two hardened bachelors condemned the register which they refused to make use of beyond recall. Most often, according to the Goncourts, women did not know why they wept, some had the honesty to admit to it, but others gave false pretexts. They allowed them to give them because: 'It is always polite to allow it to be thought that one believes in the pretext which a woman gives for her tears'.[23] But the Goncourts, armed with their theories on nerves nevertheless continued to reflect on them. In the eyes of the two brothers, George Sand did

not escape this lack of discernment in tearful outbursts. Dining
in her company for the first time, they described her thus: 'She
listens, does not speak, has a tears for a play in verse by Hugo at
a falsely sentimental place in the play'.[24]

These destroyers of sentimentality were probably not representative of the taste of a larger public which caused successes in
the libraries and filled the theatres in 1850. Did the general feeling
remain attached to fine sentiments and the troubles of a beautiful
soul? The critical view of easy expressions of emotion and of the
nervous sentimentality of women was often reserved for private
diaries and correspondence. The Goncourts, or Flaubert were
careful of offending the public. But they were not second-class
citizens of the heart, their anatomical view, their physiological
and surgeon's approach, and their distrust of feminine weaknesses
imprinted on the literature of the second half of the nineteenth
century a movement in which fine feelings, the emotions of the
soul and moral beauties passed into inferior novels. The literature
of the feelings was far from being dead, but it lost its capital letter,
while that of Art grew without constraint, along with the demand
for a literature of vice, a baseness and of horror which transformed
them under the scalpel of style. Beyond aesthetic declarations,
the male discourse asserted itself in refusing to place any value
on the outbursts of women, which were a most embarrassing
natural function, and reserved rare and true tears for its own
use. Personal expressions of emotion had lost their prestige:
'Only communicate the experience which is to be drawn from
pain and which is no longer pain itself to your readers. Do not
weep in public',[25] Isadore Ducasse ironically proclaimed. It is
easy to believe that in 1870 there was still a long way to go for
the supporters of modernity.

AUTHORISED TEARS

Nevertheless, virile strength experienced relapses into weakness. Alcohol often served as a release for male sorrows which
were suppressed too much. The Goncourt brothers accordingly
described a drunken evening in which their friend Charles wept
on Edmond's hand because his mistress was cold-shouldering
him.[26] Inebriation perhaps allowed men to shed a few tears, without affecting their dignity too much, because it was admitted that

a drunken man was not in a normal state and that alcohol could make one sentimental.[27]

Along with this, the Goncourt brothers only appear to have wept over books when they were accounts of real mourning. This was the case of J-N. Bouilly, whose nickname was the tearful poet and who they considered to be an imbecile, but who wrote that these were: 'The only pages which a man who is not a woman cannot read without feeling tears in his heart and in his eyes'.[28] In this passage entitled *La Perte irréparable* [the irreparable loss]. J-N. Bouilly wrote of the death of his fiancée Antoinette, whom he watched die of consumption and whom he helped to fool her family over her approaching death, which occurred in 1790. The same judgement held for the *Histoire de ma vie* [story of my life] by George Sand, concerning the account of the death of her grandmother and of her mother: 'In the middle of the jumble of a speculative publication these are the scenes which exact admiration and sometimes tears'.[29] The death of dear ones, described in the form of autobiographies, appears to have led to the shedding of tears among their male readers. Further, the death of another was unbearable, and authorised male tears. Mourning remained a situation in which the tears of men were acceptable, even valued: true expressions of emotion were reserved for the funeral ceremony. Buloz, according to the Goncourts, shed 'true tears over the death of M. Planche' which proved a real sensibility.[30] At the burial of Jules de Goncourt, Saint-Victor and Gautier shed abundant tears, according to Flaubert who wrote to his niece Caroline: 'Théo who is accused of being a man without a heart wept in buckets. For myself, I was not very gallant.'[31] At that of George Sand 'Flaubert kept a little apart; he was not ashamed to weep' and burst into sobs, embracing Aurore the granddaughter of the woman of letters.[32] Expressions of mourning provoked the only tears which a man could shed with dignity in public. A dramatic and revealing moment, it demonstrated the depth of the feelings of those who appeared to be the strongest, the most insensitive. As the only breach in virile aridity, the scene at the cemetery was at the centre of presentable sensibility.

We find evidence of this in the private diary of Caroline Brame[33] where, on the death of her grandfather, everyone wept, both men and women. She consoled one of her bereaved friends by weeping in her arms, as though death authorised a physical closeness in shared tears. Not only one's intimates were cried for,

Marie Bashkirtseff[34] could write that on the death of the son of
Napoleon III in the depths of the African bush, all his entourage
had red eyes: although Marie was far from being a Bonapartist.
It was with a certain complacency that people expanded on the
troubles provoked by the announcement of this news: Marie wept
for three days, and a woman of her acquaintance was overcome
with nervous spasms which were fully commentated. It seemed
as though another's death could allow free rein to extensive
commentaries on one's own bodily excesses. In this respect,
mourning was like illness at the end of the nineteenth century:
it was the occasion for a proliferation of words on the organism
which surprises our contemporary modesty. Mourning and death
were, in short, the occasion for overwhelming tears.

THE WAY OF YOUNG GIRLS

If private diaries are to be believed, it appears that young girls had
not at all lost the taste for tears: they wept for sorrow or over their
weighty solitude, they shed tears of boredom. In Caroline Brame,
the memory of her dead mother and the anguish of passing time
led to frequent outbursts. For her, as for Marie Bashkirtseff, tears
rhymed with prayers. Religion was lived in tears by these young
girls who were rocked by chaste homilies. But tears could also
provoke prayers. Caroline wept at the feast of Easter, but she also
did so alone: 'Alone in my room, I weep, I pray'. She knew however that it was not good to nourish suffering, for piety required
more self-abnegation: she asked God to pardon her tears. Thus on
the day of her cousin's wedding: 'I must suppress in myself what I
am feeling; how many times have I had to restrain my tears! What
oh Lord, have I no courage!' The will to restrain herself appears
to have been guided by the necessity of showing herself to be
friendly, welcoming and not to cut a sorry figure.

Marie, on the other hand, did not hesitate to cultivate the
pleasure of tears, she even confessed in her diary that she hoped
to lose someone dear to her so she could drown herself in sorrow
and feel her existence more acutely: 'I would be in despair, I would
weep, moan, cry, and then this would melt into a long sadness. I
do not find this charming, I do not desire it, but I am obliged to say
that this would be to live, in consequence a pleasure.' She feared,
though, to reveal to others the degrading signs of femininity: 'I

hate being . . . sensitive . . . In a young girl it is close to . . . a number of trivial things.' A note which echoed the remarks of the Goncourts and which seems to demonstrate that the private secretion of tears, could evoke quite different ones in women. Marie did not want to be committed to the role of the young girl, which was why she dismissed her aunt shortly when she surprised her weeping: 'They must not see me weep, they would think that I am weeping for love and I would weep with vexation'. One can easily picture her wildly fighting between her desire for tears and her horror of appearing sentimental.

The counsels given to young girls on the occasion of a bereavement were even more revealing about the fragile balance of necessary gestures and of presentable sentiments: 'Know how to fulfil your obligations without egotism, without sensibility, without childish fear. Be strong women from now on, capable of bearing emotions, and even of braving a moving spectacle once that it is a question of doing your duty.' The rules of condolence distinguish the spirit from the letter:

> the code of sympathy for unhappiness has been treated in a phrase of Saint Paul, 'Weep with those who weep'. Of course this must not be followed to the letter. Whatever your natural goodness may be, you must fight against tears, and in any case, neither goodness nor sympathy call for such a display.

Compassion was a female virtue, but dryness was less to be feared than an excess of sensibility. The complacency which expressions of emotion could lead to was feared. It seems that the treatises of etiquette attempted to direct the waves of female sensibility and wished to make solid mothers of bourgeois families out of these diaphanous young girls, a role in which courage and a sense of duty were required more than easy emotion.[35] But women, unlike men, did not take part in all the rituals of death. According to books of etiquette, women did not enter cemeteries: 'the congregation accompany the cortege to the cemetery, women never enter it, at least in Paris, indeed they cannot take into it the vision of a lively sorrow and they must avoid any demonstration of insensitivity'.[36] Thus the problem of moderation (or of immoderacy) which was part of feminine emotion was suppressed: women, who wept too much, or were not sufficiently moved, would have broken up this ceremony where men wept among themselves, offering each other, for once, the sight of painful emotion. The time-space of the burial was required to be exclusively male, at least in good Parisian society.

The mistrust of the immoderation of fits of feminine tears and the necessity of crying on appropriate occasions on which there was no question of forcing oneself, outlined the shape of a new expressive model. Profusion was laughed at, and the rare tears which represented an irrepressible impulse were approved: men who wept less gained in prestige. If women had a great capacity to be moved it was better that they should not abuse it, because they were then thrown back onto their nature or onto their weak sentimentality: they were preferred to be courageous and smiling, even if when alone they knew how to sample, with piety or with delectation, the pleasure of tears.

10 The Disturbing Strangeness

BURSTING INTO TEARS

Fits of tears were often described, in the novels of the second half of the nineteenth century, as an explosion of pain which had been too contained. Sobs suffocated or were smothered, a convulsive shudder ran through the body, it was violently shaken. The soul was torn apart, allowing the accumulated tears to overflow. Explosion, tearing, trembling, shaking, suffocation, smothering, the body was overcome with crises, with convulsions with nervous spasms. It was threatened, disintegrated, filled with the symptoms of suffering, it was carried away. It was impossible to control it, to master it, to stop the fit. There then followed a state of dejection, of stupor, of confused and stupid sadness, of gloomy convalescence. On the occasion of these extreme manifestations one sobbed more than one cried. The hiccoughs cut off the breathing, the body was shaken from head to toe: we are far here from the gentle liquefications (bursting into sobs was not the same as melting into tears). The dominant image was that of explosion, of overflowing, in short it was a catastrophe, a tempest or an earthquake. Tears burst out instead of flowing away.

Men, in particular, sobbed more often than they melted into tears: it seems to have been easier to contain gentle expressions of emotion than crises. The body, through an uncontrollable spasm which reduced its ability to breath, appeared to revolt against too many contained emotions. One could attempt to smother a sob, but the sob would then strangle. It came from the guts, could not be commanded, and during the length of the attack, made the individual a stranger to himself, totally incapable of resistance or reflection. The violence of this physical explosion was a sudden witness to the limits of emotional resistance. A nervous upheaval, connected with fear, with despair mingled with anger, in the second half of the nineteenth century sobbing was related to the greatest suffering (this had not always been the case since, in the *Confessions*, Rousseau had said that he sobbed with tenderness).

This conception of the manifestations of the life of the emotions, like a journey to the limit, applied to a certain extent to the flowing of the tears themselves. They escaped mastery in the extreme cases at two levels: they were irrepressible and suffocating, but they could also be denied. One could wish for them: and only be torn apart more, especially if one was a man. They came from the depths of one's being like a raw and unpredictable force as though, having been held back too often, they were released without any assurance of their positive effects of release of tension and calming.

If women shared with men this tragic and convulsive aspect of tears, they had not lost their aptitude to dramatise, to act out their sufferings. Besides, they seemed better able to recover from their nervous attacks, which posed less of a threat to their integrity because they themselves were indeterminate and fluctuating in nature. The stronger and more wilful they were, the less this characteristic was in evidence. There should be no radical distinction between the ways in which men and women cried: the violent attack is an example of this. However, the aptitude for simulating and provoking tears clearly lay on the feminine side. The difference between the sexes was founded on the completely female ability to shed pretended tears. In parallel, the disturbing figure of the hysteric made its appearance, who mixed pathology and spectacle, presence and absence of the self.

MEN WHO SOBBED

A sense of humiliation dominated the male fit of tears. Dominique, the narrator of Fromentin's novel supported this: 'There are places in the world where I am humiliated at having displayed such ordinary sorrows, and shed such weak tears there'.[1] Even though Dominique had wept without a witness, he resented himself for having descended to the level of such effusions. These burning memories were evidence of the intensity of the shame he felt: the banality of his suffering was given the same status as a lack of virility; weakness and tameness were what made men afraid to cry. This association was important because the fear of experiencing a set emotion was part of a virile ideal of self-mastery.

The connection between the intensity of masculine constraint in public, and the explosion of tears in private sheds light on the element of violence which it manifests. This relationship was particularly clear, in Zola's *Oeuvre* for Claude, the painter artist, who had suffered the affront of the visitors to the Salon des Indépendants. He made a good impression but on going home where he found Christine who attempted to comfort him, he suddenly collapsed:

> He listened to her ardently stammering out these tendernesses, still without moving, and suddenly he fell down in front of her, he let his head fall onto her lap, and burst into tears. All his excitement of the afternoon, his whistled artist's defiance, his gaiety and his violence burst there, in an attack of sobs which suffocated him.[2]

The consolations proffered by the woman he loved made the defensive armour which he had maintained in public until then, melt away in a brutal attack which submerged and smothered him. Abandoning his proud and recalcitrant stance he found himself in all the nakedness of weakness.

The situations which led to attacks of tears in men were often related to defeat and humiliation. This was even more so when a woman was the cause of their tears; for the betrayed husband or wounded lover. In Feydeau's *Fanny* the male narrator was present, hidden in the shadows, during a night of love between his lover and her husband. This sight made him mad with pain and jealousy. The character suffered an attack which transformed him: 'I was still weeping. I had moved the window away, and with my nails clenched on my teeth, sweat on my face, with tears and with hiccoughs, stamping with fury, I looked into the room'.[3] He presented all the symptoms of the violent emotion which completely possessed him and yet left him with the strength to assess the extent of the disaster. He then began to run through the fields weeping and calling to his mother and rolled on the ground 'sobbing like a woman', destroyed by emotion and exhaustion.[4] His despair classed him with children and women, he was therefore in regression. His strength, his courage and his will abandoned him: he became ill from it. This revolution of his whole being in sobs was connected to his jealousy and a deep humiliation. Betrayed, wounded in his masculine honour and in his love, without being able to do anything legitimately (he was not the rightful lover), he lived through a complete defeat which was expressed by the attack of tears. A man wept when he could not act. The metaphors which illustrated male sobs revealed an image of the sealed body which began to explode. When Frédéric realised that he would have to give Mme Arnoux up for good, who was irrevocably lost to him and was leaving Paris following the ruin of her husband: 'he felt a sort of tearing apart of his whole being; his tears which had accumulated since that morning overflowed'.[5] This overflow of bursting tears followed an internal injury which threatened the integrity of his very being. The attack of the Comte Muffat, on learning through Nana his mistress that his wife was cheating on him was convulsive. He sought at first to reject this idea while walking in the street, but his comforting thoughts crumbled one by one: 'He was afraid and he burst into tears, suddenly in despair, appalled, as though he had fallen into an immense void'.[6] He was surprised by his violent agitation, and he attempted again to regain his footing, to reason coldly, but he was drawn even more into his collapse:

> Then, once more overcome by tears, despite his efforts, not wishing to sob in front of people, he threw himself into a dark and empty road, the rue Rossini where walking past the silent houses he wept like a child.
>
> 'It's over', he said in a low voice. 'There is nothing more, there is nothing more'.
>
> He wept so violently that he had to lean back against a door, his face in his wet hands.[7]

Plunged into nothingness, into a bottomless void, the Count, torn between fear and shame, could not hold back his tears born of the images which forced themselves into his mind. Hounded by the passers-by in his nocturnal wanderings, he sought refuge in the dark, shaken by sobs. All the values on which he had founded his honourable existence and which he constantly came out with among fine company foundered in a complete absence of meaning, of reference: he wept like a child afraid of the dark. It was in fact when everything seemed to sink into nothingness and absurdity that male restraint could not hold back emotion.

The tears of men had a sexual connotation: they indicated the sufferings of unassuaged desire. Léon, in love with Mme Bovary, could not declare himself to her: 'he tortured himself to find how he could *make his declaration* to her: and constantly hesitating between the fear of displeasing her and the shame of being faint-hearted, he wept from discouragement and desire'.[8] Or again Georges, the young man escaped from school, who had just seen Nana (who represented Woman to him) on the stage, could not find the stage door and fled 'with tears of desire and impotence in his eyes'.[9] The impossibility of seducing a woman they desired made these young men cry by calling into question the dignity of their virility. Conversely tears, in weakening their will and making the nervous tension increase, could also excite desire. When André met his wife again after their separation and when he allowed himself to weep, an infinite anguish caught hold of him:

> He was in a terrible state of nervous excitement. The shocks of the evening had broken him; he experienced a great weariness, a general bending of his mind which seemed to float in emptiness. Far from soothing him, his tears at first held back and then soon run dry had increased that obvious disease which must end in carnal release.[10]

The tears of the alcove in Huysmans turned into physical problems which the male character suffered and which increased his sickness. His destroyed intelligence, his weakened forces, his suppressed and then poorly shed tears only increased his anxiety. He then allowed himself to be directed by his desires, born out of trouble, while fearing at the same time that he would commit an irreparable mistake concerning the interest of his patched-up marriage. Tears were thus associated with nervous states, connected with a female presence which diminished the ability to make cold decisions: they were hardly glorious.

Even if, in a man, tears were taken for weakness, they could still hold for him the image of a demonstration which could sooth a torturing pain. Conrad, one of the heroes of the *Pléiades* by Gobineau, asked Harriet, the wife of his friend, to make him cry: only feminine compassion was likely to allow him to shed tears. Here again, the woman was the mediator of the world of tears. He was finally moved,

> but instead of doing him good, it only served to increase the intensity of his pain. He came to the point of no longer being able to master himself. Until then he had managed it, his strength had been barely sufficient, but it had been enough.

Taking refuge in the idea that tears which did not want to be shed, would flow one day and deliver him from his unbearable anguish, he managed to withstand and control them. But he found no comfort in these tears which come too late, on the contrary he experienced a general rout of his strength:

> Tears fell and only led to the tyranny of pain: they prolonged his torture, and they destroyed his resistance; then he was humiliated; humiliated, he handed over his weapons, he could do no more; he abandoned pride, dignity, the fear of blame; what! like a beaten slave, he lay down on the ground and asked for mercy.[11]

This male demand that the expression of emotion should always be put off, led to an attack which made him suffer all the more. To the stranglehold of anguish, dry but dignified, there succeeded shame, weakness and despair in uncontrolled tears which enveloped the will: he became the slave of an outburst which he had longed for. In crying, he allowed himself to be submerged by a pain which until then his strength had managed to contain, the tears were the sign of the defeat of his entire being. The fit of sobs, a sudden irruption of obscure forces, left him defenceless.

The fit of male sobs seems then in these novels to have been related to a deep humiliation, to an infinite despair, to a nervous tension or an unbearable anguish, when the universe which surrounded them and the hopes which made them live were crumbling. This abnegation in tears does not appear to have comforted them, but instead underlined the rout of the virile image. Outside the mastered stance which affirmed a character, men in tears found themselves reduced to femininity, to childhood, or to servitude. Strangeness inhabited the interior of the intimate, a disturbing strangeness: the encounter with another self did not liberate but completely destabilised.

WOMEN'S ATTACKS

To draw strength from their weakness women could adopt the course of tears. They seemed to know that men found it hard to resist them because the scene of tears haunted the male imagination. In *En ménage* [in the home] by Huysmans, André laid down his arms in the face of the tears of his wife, on the day when, having made herself particularly disagreeable she had driven away one of his friends:

> Once the door had closed, a terrible scene broke out. André shook his wife in a rough way: she took the course of fainting and tears. He ended by being contrite, fearing that he had gone too far, lifted up his wife, embraced her and almost offered her excuses.[12]

In reply to male violence there were these worrying signs which women knew how to cause in which their bodies gave themselves over to a tragic performance. Further, when André decided to leave his wife who had a lover, he said to himself: 'If I go back to my wife I will have to suffer a shower of hypocritical complaints and tears and I will perhaps be stupid enough to forgive her'.[13] It was better to avoid the scene where even if tears were expected, they were still likely to affect him. The roles were in place, with a woman ready to deploy the whole armoury of attacks, and a man who was evasive in order not to be caught by her. For the fight was without surprises, whether she was a wife or a mother, tears were a high female trump which she would make use of at every turn and at will. Huysmans thus compared the entry to the Ministry to that of the actors into a theatre: 'noble mothers, old ladies with rolls of flesh sagging under their tapes who had come to request pensions or aid, making ready their contrite expressions on the doorstep and preparing their tears'.[14] Women practised tears with art, in order to sway men to pity, through the image of a suffering weakness which it was difficult to resist. Thus when Frédéric Moreau decided to return to Paris, his mother first tried to reason with him, and then seeing that he was shrugging his shoulders, she tried to sway him with feelings: 'Then the good lady used a different method. In a tender voice and with little sobs, she began to speak to him of her loneliness, of her old-age, of the sacrifices which she had made'.[15] These lamentations and tears were repeated 20 times a day: it was a war of attrition, which, combined with the agreeable nature of a comfortable home began to send Frédéric's resolutions for departure back to sleep.

The fit of tears allowed women to comfort themselves quickly over the moral pain which strangled them for a moment. This remark was a commonplace of the time: tears appeared to be indispensable to the nervous economy of women. The *Grand Larousse* of the nineteenth century, in the entry on tears thus informs us that when women's lachrymal glands are emptied, they feel lighter and happier, and husbands can then count of a week of peace and good humour.[16] This ability to rid oneself of all their suffering through tears gave little substance to the sorrows of women. Nana on learning of the death of the young Georges, one of her lovers, comforted herself with tears.

> She was obliged to interrupt herself, suffocated by tears, falling across the couch in her pain, her head buried in a cushion. The misfortunes which she felt surround her, these miseries which they had caused, drowned her in a warm and continuous gush of tenderness; and her voice was lost in the low cry of a little girl.[17]

Her sadness did not tear her apart, but turned her to liquid, this picture is a good example of the difference between the manifestation of female suffering which flowed away in warm humours, and that of men who burst into smothering sobs. It was not only for him that she wept, it was for her own life, and the fear of being accused of his death, for her ruin, and more generally for the unhappiness of others. She soon dried her tears in a gesture of revolt, accusing men of clinging to her apron strings. When her maid admitted a visitor, neither pain nor anger remained: 'Zoé let Mignon in. Nana received her smiling, she had wept well, it was over.'[18] As irresponsible and as changing as a child, and otherwise a good enough girl, her sincere pain faded away without trace in her tears. She rapidly regained the 'carelessness of a superb animal', ignorant of the victims who surrounded her. Ignorant like a beast.

Women rid themselves through tears of an excess of tension: in *L'Education sentimentale* [education of the feelings] Mme Dambreuse, wounded by Frédéric's neglect, calmed herself by shedding abundant tears.[19] Unlike men, they tended to benefit from the attack, even if it was violent. It was the absence of tears which became disturbing, abnormal, critical. George Sand, in *Le Dernier amour*, published in 1866 developed this theme: Félice did not weep, exhibited no disorder of the mind, no failure of the will on the death of her brother to whom she had been very attached. The narrator, who was disturbed by this dryness, attempted to induce tears in her, but he was rejected with a movement of exasperation:

> 'She threw herself onto the sand of the path crying:
> Leave me, leave me here; you can clearly see that I need to cry!'
> The unfortunate girl did not cry. Her sobs were growls which appeared to frighten the wild place where we were.[20]

This woman whose pride and whose nervous will drove her away from the ease of weeping which women generally possessed, experienced the same suffering as men in her heart-rending tearless sobs. Her reactions were the signs of a nervous imbalance. The narrator, a wise man who loved her and wished to correct her, profited from the tears which she shed over her child which had died at an early age, to persuade her to resign herself to this sign of femininity:

> I saw a tear trickle down her cheek. It was the first time that she had cried for her daughter in front of me. She had never spoken of her to me except for with a dark suffering, and as she tried to conceal the tear from me:
> 'Go ahead and weep', I said to her, 'Be a woman, be a mother. I prefer you thus than tense and irritated'.[21]

In order to be a wife and mother, it was necessary to know how to give in to emotion, to avoid too much self-restraint so as not to risk being sad and irascible. The expression of emotion was necessary to the economy of female nerves and needed to be released now and then. On the other hand, Tonino, the young Italian who was trying to seduce Félice, wept in appeal to the narrator: he 'attempted some playacting. He bent his knee before me and wept real tears. He wept at will, as women do.'[22] We might think that, in a society which was haunted by the difference between the sexes, in which tears made up a characteristic which was becoming more and more clear, the characters who were strangers to this difference which literature allowed to appear were all the more fascinating. It was at least on this that the novelist was playing in mixing the roles while defining the rules: a woman who did not weep, a man who wept like a woman, were both abnormal beings.

Women also knew terrible attacks of tears which shook the body, these attacks could in this instance be the result of pathology. According to Charcot, the attack of sobbing and tears flowing in abundance represented the fourth or final stage of the great attack of hysteria.[23] In some patients, a fit of convulsive laughter could occur instead of a fit of tears. Flaubert in *Bouvard et Pécuchet* illustrated ironically this new concept of hysteria. Père Barbey's daughter displayed its symptoms: 'Her nervous attacks, began with sobs and ended with a tide of tears'.[24] Bouvard would cure her by rubbing her abdomen and by pressing on the area of the ovaries, like a student of Charcot. Mme Bovary was also, in a way, a hysteric. Suffering with some pleasure from her carnal desires, from her wish for money, and from the melancholies of passion, she would sometimes see a vague abyss filed with darkness open up in her soul which distressed her:

> She remained shattered, panting, motionless, quietly sobbing and with flowing tears.
> 'Why not tell the master?' the servant asked her, when she started these attacks.
> 'It's my nerves' Emma replied, 'Do not speak of it to him, you will distress him'.[25]

In Félicité's view, Mme Bovary was suffering from the same illness as the Père Guérin's daughter, who was discovered stretched out on her stomach weeping on the pebbles beside the sea. Marriage had cured her forever, she told her: "But in my case", Emma replied, "it was after my marriage that it happened"'. What were her unsatisfied dreams doing in a nervous illness? Flaubert, well-acquainted with the developments reported in medical literature, here opposed the traditional concept of the modern theory of hysteria. Hysteria was no longer simply a disease of the womb, the sexual desire of a young girl, it was linked with the imagination.

But hysteria took on many shapes which the doctors had difficulty in dealing with and which they saw practically everywhere. Thus Doctor Berger wrote about hysterical tears which were manifested by a lachrymal hypersecretion.[26] This occurred in cases of infection of the uterus and in serious illnesses, and pointed to a hysteria which had been hitherto unknown, or in other cases it could become the most annoying symptom of this ailment. These cases 'where the hysteria occurs in the form of a lachrymal ailment prove how right Charcot was to call it a simulating illness'. In this game of hide and seek between the hysteric and the doctor, the stakes were great: as the following curious deduction testifies: 'It is probable that in a certain number of cases of tears which did not respond to any treatments, in which the lachrymal gland was removed, these were only cases of hysterical tears'. The removal of the source of the tears was the best way of telling whether it was a question of this famous simulating illness: one cut into the living flesh of the hysteric would unmask her. There were nevertheless other ways of knowing if one was really dealing with the 'neurosis of secretion': if the weeping increased when she was at home and bored, and if it diminished when she was out in the street, or otherwise when she gave herself up to her favourite occupations ('riding, bicycle races', Berger wrote innocently, 'the female practice of this last sport, we know, is a part of the image of the modern woman who braves many sarcastic remarks') but also in the presence of the doctor in whom she was confident. Another symptom of this type of hysteria was that the patient suffered from weeping but could not shed tears in a psychic state of emotion. She wept too much, and without reason, she therefore could not be displaying the signs of a true emotion. In any case weeping and the dryness of the eye were both symptoms of this hysteria which confused accepted signs. Through excess, through omission, the hysteric never cried when she should. Suggestion and hypnosis were the recommended treatments: Freud was not there, but he was not far away.

THE EFFECTS OF SENTIMENTAL NARCOTICS ON WOMEN

A woman, a sort of Machiavelli in skirts, might act out her tears in order to avoid reproach and obtain favours, or be struck with hysteria in deploying her full potential of pretence, but she was also the victim of what would be called her sentimentality. Music, songs, poor literature, a Saint-Sulpician religion, moved her to tears. The sentimental clichés, which were always effective turned women's heads. From the top to the bottom of the social ladder, they all appeared to weep for trifles. Noble ladies were not excepted: 'The most trivial little piece by Mme Emile de Girardin, entitled "Joy causes fear" caused the shedding, every evening for nearly a year, of the most aristocratic of tears' the nineteenth-century Grand Larousse noted.[27] The female heart knew no class distinctions. And if the young daughters of good birth wept over piano tunes, the daughters of the people were moved by romances. Women wept over the first communion, a bride in white, commonplaces about motherhood, or stupidities about the country or little birds. They evoked this imagery for the pleasure of being moved, and writers denounced the dangers which this taste for sentimentality led women to run. For those whose imaginations were inflamed by tear-filled novels of love, were often running towards their doom. In the convent, the future Mme Bovary discovered the sentimental novel through the agency of an old woman born of a family ruined during the Revolution.

> It was nothing but loves and lovers, persecuted ladies who fainted in solitary buildings, postilions who were killed at every posting house, horses who were worn out on every page, dark forests, troubles of the heart, vows, sobs, tears and kisses, barques in the moonlight, nightingales in the groves, perfect gentlemen who were as brave as lions, as gentle as lambs, virtuous beyond belief, always good to look at, and who wept like urns.[28]

Emma found a passionate exaltation in these tear-filled novels which she was to think that she could live out with her husband. She thus wished 'to devote herself to love', reciting passionate verses in the moonlight, and singing melancholic adagios. Charles appeared 'neither more in love, nor more stirred up'.[29] He nevertheless loved her sincerely and in his own way, but she persuaded herself that her husband's passion was lukewarm because it did not show itself 'in the accepted ways'. Her imagination, filled with novels, separated her from Bovary who did not fit the picture of the lover of her dreams. The episode of the ball at Vaubyessard which followed this disappointment completed her plunge into disgust for the boring countryside, and her mediocre petit-bourgeois existence:

Was not love like an Indian plant, requiring prepared soil, and a special temperature? The sighs in the moonlight, the long embraces, the tears which fell on hands at parting, all the fevers of the flesh and the languors of tenderness, these could not be separated from the balconies of the great houses filled with leisure, from a boudoir with silken blinds and a thick carpet, flower-filled arrangements, a bed mounted on a platform, nor from the glitter of precious stones and of the braid of the livery.

To tears in the moonlight there were added the elegance and luxury of Parisian life. Emma's infidelities took place under these two signs. Léon pleased her from their first encounter by speaking of music, of novels, of poetry, showing himself to be sensitive to the stereotyped formulae for love and feeling. He thus corresponded to the literature which had nourished Emma's imagination:

'Have you ever had the experience', Léon resumed, 'of encountering in a book a vague idea which you have had, some hidden image which returns from afar, and which is like the entire expression of the most penetrating of your feelings?'
'I have felt that', she replied.
'That is why I love poets most of all', he said. I find that verses are more tender than prose, and they make one weep better'.[30]

If Emma preferred romances, she was not any less moved by this young man who loved to weep over books. Rodolphe, more resourceful, played the fine dark mysterious man, and the fashionable Parisian. Knowing her to be romantic, he said all that was necessary to make her weep and cast damp glances at her.[31] When alone, she remembered the heroines of the books she had read, and considered herself to be 'of the type of lover which she had so envied'.[32] Rodolphe, becoming tired of his mistress, of her romantic rituals, and most of all her plans for escape (another example of her romantic exaltation) decided to inform her of his departure by letter. Struck by a final scruple, he served up to her the most commonplace of love letters:

'Poor little woman', he thought with emotion. 'She will think me more insensitive than a rock; I should have shed a few tears over it; but it is not my fault that I cannot cry.' Then, having poured some water into a glass, Rodolphe dipped his finger into it, and he let a large drop fall from above which made a pale smudge on the ink.[33]

A large part of Mme Bovary's troubles came from her immoderate taste for moving and romantic situations and for stupefying literature, the literature of the chemist, rather than the literature of the doctor recommended by Flaubert, as Michel Butor points out.[34]

Edmond de Goncourt in *La fille Elisa* [the girl Elisa] also criticised the pernicious effect of novels, of which he noted the deleterious effect among the popular classes, especially among women. 'We involve our interest, our emotion, our tenderness, sometimes tears, in a human history which we know to be untrue. If we ourselves are fooled like this, how can the uncultured and honest woman of the people not be so?'[35] Works of the imagination which moved cultured readers could only disturb the lives of poor women. With the works from Bourlement's reading room, the girl Elisa became feverishly obsessed with a cheap image of the Orient, a Judea in which a low-grade neo-Catholicism was spread, 'the whole epic of the boulevard of crime, all the false knighthood, all the false lovers, capable of transporting a down-to-earth girl, who earned her bread with her love in the poverty of an ugly country town, into the blue of a third sky'.[36] The effect of this second-rate romanticism blended with melodrama soon made itself felt on her weak mind. The girl Elisa left her country town to run away with a travelling salesman to whom she showed a blind devotion, the idea of which she had caught in her reading. Disappointed in him when she learned that he was a spy her disgust was extended to all men. This was what reading-rooms and the education of the people resulted in. The tears shed over sentimental novels led more than one woman to her ruin, and the girl Elisa to crime and from crime to madness.

According to Huysmans, romantic ideas formed a reference for women of the people when grouped together. When the father of Désirée Vatard opposed her love for Auguste, the women from the workshop who would not have wanted him for their own daughters were moved by her fate:

An old store of novels and of songs on the misfortunes of couples in love welled up in them, without them being aware of it. The snivelling sentimentality of the people appeared; Vatard became a monster; had there been the need, they would have helped Auguste to fool him.[37]

Sentimental themes made up the unconscious memory of the women of the people and could drive them to undermine the authority of a father.

Mistrust of this popular imagination which was filled with the tears of sentiment, mainly in women, was especially expressed at the end of the nineteenth century. It was developed by writers, not only because these emotions appeared ridiculous but mostly because they were dangerous for morality and family order. While in the eighteenth century the tears shed over a novel represented a moral conversion, the effect here was the opposite: romantic emotions led women to immorality, even to their downfall. The literature of the feelings was now at the bottom of the ladder and sank back into sentimentality.

The religious expressions of emotion exalted by the Romantics did not escape the writers' knives, even if young girls still encouraged it. The emotion which they caused was merely sentimentality. Between woman and priest an excess of easy effusiveness was condemned. The dependence of women on men of the church came from their gentle and encroaching behaviour which led women to confide in them and place themselves under their influence. In a novel by Marcel Prévost, the Abbé Huguet, confessor to many Parisian society ladies, knew the hearts of women well: 'He willingly assumed those enveloping words, those sort of spiritual caresses which disturbed the nerves of women. Mme Sugère wept. He took her hand.'[38] It was then in causing women's tears through a skilful manipulation of their fragile nerves that priests succeeded in directing their consciences and in bringing about vows and promises. According to Zola, the Church had changed in this matter. In *La faute de l'abbé Mouret* [the Abbé Mouret's crime], Brother Archangias, whose God was severe and vengeful, exclaimed:

Religion is disappearing into the countryside because it is made too womanly. It was respected for as long as it spoke as a mistress without forgiveness . . . I do not know what they teach you in the seminaries. The new priests weep like children with their parishioners. God seems to be quited changed.[39]

It was not only pastoral care which adapted itself to women, it was the priests themselves who were tearful and lacking in virility. The Abbé Mouret was the prototype of this: 'feminised, almost an angel, cleansed of his sex, of his male scent',[40] spoiled in the cult of the virgin. We know of Zola's anti-clericalism and his genetic determinism which made the Abbé Mouret the victim of a weighty inheritance. We can note however that as for Flaubert or the Goncourts, the literary and ideological battle was fought in the name of the values of virility and that, from this point of view, tears were a sign of a sickly and insipid femininity. Along with these feminised priests, who were always ready to weep, religious objects took on a sentimental preciousness. Désirée Vatard thus became lost in contemplation before the windows filled with objects of piety and dull religious pictures, 'engravings full of little boys on their knees, prostrate women, swollen angels pointing to the sky; Mater dolorosa, manufactured according to Delaroche's formula, with tears in their eyes and their hands filled with rays of light'.[41] To capture the attention of women, nothing was as valuable as the sentimental drug. From the confessionals to the windows of Saint-Sulpice, religion became mannered in order to arouse emotion and assure itself of the fidelity of women who, through a strange quirk of their nature, so loved to weep.

DISTRESS AND THE LEARNED REPLY

In the novels of the second half of the nineteenth century men wept when nothing else was possible, in a violent attack which suffocated them with sobs, invaded their bodies and their whole being. The male personality was in retreat and they were thus propelled back into the terrors of childhood. Suffering was no longer only a private experience, but sometimes its opposite: a delicious testing of the dispossession of the self, of explosion and of internal anguish. Everything happened as though women, who were also familiar with these attacks of tears, generally recovered better from them. Was it because they were used to crying or was it because they felt themselves less threatened by the loss of their integrity? Unlike men, tears soothed them, as though their internal economy necessitated an outburst to re-establish nervous balance. This difference was founded on nature. This natural propensity to empty their tear glands led them to become drunk on sentimental novels. Women in tears also distressed men, a problem which was known at that time to doctors who dealt with sufferers from hysteria who were ill, while being capable of simulating the symptoms. Women cried naturally but it was difficult to distinguish the line between real tears born of the weakness of their nervous make-up and acted tears, weapon of weakness against strength. With the modern form of hysteria the woman was no longer as in Michelet both person and Nature, traversed by its tides, but a double figure whose body spoke but who was a psychological being. The personality of the hysteric was disturbed:[12] she wept unwillingly while pretending and could not find tears when she was in a position to shed them. Concerning this, the extreme situations which developed in the novels of this second half of the nineteenth century, and which presented disturbing figures of men and women in tears, expressed the inner truth of the subject, which he was unaware of and which his body in crisis revealed clearly in spite of him. Strangeness and otherness slipped into the very heart of intimacy and were manifested by tears.

But this worrying strangeness which Charcot revealed at the Salpêtrière was not the only approach to tears attempted by science. Evolutionism, with Darwin at its head, proposed a theory of emotions which married the innate and the acquired, the savage and the child, the man and the woman, finally a whole reading of the ages of life which would give a global explanation. To sob was natural to man, Darwin declared, but he had to describe the genesis of this.[43] New-born babies cried without shedding tears: the appearance of the first lachrymal secretions indicated, according to Darwin, an innate aptitude which took over an acquired habit in order to come to life. This proved that tears must have been acquired at the moment when man was separated from the common origin of anthropomorphous monkeys: the new-born child told him about primitive man. In any case, as he was able to observe in his own children, the character of tears was modified very early: originally connected to anger, they were soon reserved for sorrow. He thought that this habitual repression was transmitted through heredity in a more advanced age than that in which it was first exercised. Thus he underlined the human character of tears, but situated their progressive mastery from childhood onwards in the process of evolution in which the acquired became innate for future generations. He underlined that, in the adult man, physical pain did not cause tears, whether among barbarians or civilised peoples, who all considered it to be undignified for a man to display bodily suffering through any external sign. It was different for other emotions: thus savages still shed tears for 'futile reasons' while madmen abandoned themselves without any constraint to all emotions: the more they were affected, the more they would weep for any reason (with the exception of idiots). The lack of discernment in the cause of tears was therefore a feature of madmen and barbarous peoples. He observed notable differences among the civilised peoples of Europe, and allowed it to be understood that he placed the Englishman at the peak of progress, because he only wept 'under the pressure of the most poignant moral suffering' whereas 'in certain parts of the Continent men would shed tears with great ease and abundance'. As for women, he noted that habit had the power to increase the ability to weep, witness those natives of New Zealand who were proud of weeping copiously and at will to honour their dead. Among civilised people, an isolated effort with the aim of suppressing tears appeared to exercise little influence on the lachrymal glands, and even to have the opposite effect of that which was expected. He reported the evidence of an old doctor who faced with 'the attacks of unpersuadable tears which one sometimes sees among women' begged them not to attempt to contain themselves and assured them that nothing would comfort them more than a long and abundant secretion of tears. It was better for them to weep once and for all, rather than make a feeble effort, too exhausting for their poor strength, in attempting to control themselves.

For everything lay in a balance of energy. Doctor Féré who wrote a commentary of Darwin notes that the voluntary obstruction of the expression of pain through tears, cries and bewailings 'necessitates a considerable expenditure of energy'.[44] The energetic body was juxtaposed to the evolved body. From this model, women did not escape unscathed. Women did not have a superior emotionalism, they had a defective one.

General and specific sensitivity is not so great in the female sex, it is a well-known and proven fact. Their so-called perfected emotionality places them most often in the position of being unable to accomplish the appropriate act.

Acts were the measurement of everything and created a hierarchy of useful emotions. Resuming the traditional example of the Greek heroes who sobbed while remaining capable of acts of courage, he contrasted them to the anaesthetising tears of women. Good use of energy. . . .

Professor Mantegazza offered us a system of implacable logic, still in the Darwinian tradition.[45] He observed that men and women expressed their sufferings differently and that the differences became increasingly large 'according to the degree of elevation in the personal and ethnic hierarchy'.

> In general pain is expressed in women by stupor or by violent reactions; tears are very frequent. The nature of the man, more courageous and energetic gives him a more fighting character when expressing pain. Men address threats and imprecations to Nature and to God. The fist shaken at the horizon is the virile expression of several very lively pains.

The favourable stance of masculine pain was contrasted with the weakness mixed with potential violence of the woman. He noted however that compassion prevailed in the woman, that the predominance of charitable and religious feelings gave 'a character of pity and charity to the sorrowing mimic'. In man, on the contrary, egotism prevailed. 'Woman suffers, prays and does good; man is most often blasphemous and threatening.' Each had a role: the woman was so well made for suffering, and the man so prepared to defy it. But the Professor did not stop there because age also modified the expression of pain. Moral suffering appeared in the child when he discovered self-love, jealousy and love of ownership. He then wept and manifested expressive nuances in the tears. Tears became less frequent as he advanced in years and were replaced by other signs. 'In the most intelligent, we can see a dawn of feelings of a higher order appear, such as the sardonic or ironic laugh, and melancholy sorrow.' These aesthetic forms were refined in adolescence and attained in first youth 'an extreme beauty'. Romanticism was limited to the time of youth: irony and melancholy were more advanced forms than easy tears but they were not the end of the march towards adulthood. If the young man cried only rarely, the adult had usually completely unlearned how to cry. Self-esteem and the feeling of dignity moderated his expression of pain, but soon, with the weakening of the nervous centres, a tendency to weep made itself felt which indicated 'the first degrees of the downward curve of the parabola of life'. Old age was hardly glorified, because it accumulated the faults of the adult male and female: the expression of tears which represented a cowardly defeat was nevertheless limited by the growth of egotism. After the calm and melancholy sadness of adolescence, the bitter expression and threatening reaction of the age of virility, old age was characterised by plaintive moans and tears.

This reading of tears which manipulated age, sex and the degree of civilisation in order to assign a role to each individual and to create a hierarchy of the expression of emotion could appear to be disturbingly innocent but also dauntingly efficient.[46] The Darwinism of tears, which allowed no place for cultural differences, socio-historical changes, or the disturbing strangeness of tears, assigned a clear direction to their interpretation: the completed form of the expression of emotion was that of the civilised adult male, the others appeared unfinished or decaying. The extreme motifs of otherness which made up the madman, the savage or the old man were distinguished from childhood and adolescence which prepared the future of the adult man. Woman with her excessive and imperfect emotionalism was in a strange position. Compassion, a female quality, made the heart charitable, and was an attenuated sentiment in men, who were more likely to suppress 'natural' feelings. Despite her constitutional weakness which determined too frequent and lengthy expressions of emotion, a woman still had a right to certain tears: her emotions were necessary to the survival of the species (she made a good mother) and to the maintaining of social order (emotionally, she provided succour for the unfortunate).

11 The Tears of the Popular Novel

It is interesting to compare Eugène Sue's different treatments of his characters' tears according to which public he wished to move. Before writing *Les Mystères de Paris*, he wrote novels of the sea, filled with tears and romantic irony in which the portrayal of morality was reminiscent of Balzac. In *Arthur*, one of the works of his youth, the hypocrisy and mockery of society life occasioned particularly ferocious battles. Thus a widow's tears were considered to be false. In society a weeping wife was either an expert in artifice, or stupid and incapable of playing an interesting role in salon life. The lack of understanding of tears between men and women was thus situated at the heart of the story. Critical of the male attitude towards personal feelings, the novel revealed the ravages it made on women. But although women were often the victims, they also had the ability to attack and defend themselves:

> For there is a fight between the women of society, a passive but frenzied fight, in which flowers, ribbons, jewels and smiles are the weapons; a silent and consequently terrible fight, filled with cruel anguishes, with devoured tears, with unknown despairs.[1]

Constraint and irony were its tragic consequences, inhibiting effusiveness and suppressing tears. When Eugène Sue converted to the popular novel, he abandoned his sceptical figures with complex emotions and his pictures of the salons, and replaced them with finished characters in unambiguous tears. There were no half-measures, discreet tears or reversals of sensibility, no questioning of the signs of emotion. Morality separated the tears of villains from the emotional expressions of the good. Bad characters were at first impervious to the tears of tender creatures. Jacques Ferrand, the infamous notary, could thus

say to Mme de Lucernay who came to plead the case of her
profligate lover: 'If you have come snivelling here to move me,
there is no point.'[2] Worse! La Chouette who had noticed that the
passers-by bought more orgeat sugar from Fleur-Marie when she
cried, beat her savagely to make her do so. Even the Chourineur
was shocked by it.[3] The villains also shed hypocritical tears, as
Sarah did to make Rodolphe marry her, as did Mme Roland,
the evil stepmother with lying tears who interceded in favour
of her step-daughter in order to appear to be good, while
she was capable of administering poison,[4] as Tortillard did,
a corrupt child who imitated filial love after having kicked
his schoolmaster terribly hard under the table.[5] He thus made
villains imitate finer feelings, to encourage sympathy and sooth
distrust (although the reader was always warned that these tears
were false). Virtue always triumphed in the end, the bad would
be punished, and a number of them would weep in their turn.
Jacques Ferrand was thus condemned to weep at Cécily's feet.
She had been sent by Rodolphe, and was a girl of the Islands,
one 'of those enchanting vampires who, intoxicating their victim
with terrible seductions, squeezed the last drop of gold and blood
from him and left him, to use the lively expression of the country,
with tears to drink and his heart to gnaw'.[6] Most of all the cruel
schoolmaster whose repentance had been predicted by Rodolphe
when he blinded him, finally wept for his victims. Shut into his
blindness like a criminal in his cell, remorse invaded him making
his tears flow. They thus paid for their sins through bitter tears.
The good often wept, men and women alike, sometimes from
suffering, but also from tenderness, from pity, out of charity or
from happiness or gratitude. Fleur de Marie was almost always in
tears, either because she was overwhelmed by the goodness of her
benefactors, or because the memory of her past life tormented her.
Naive and melancholic, her angelic face was never more moving
than when it was bathed in tears. Her attitude contrasted with
that of Rigolette, who was always gay, but ready to feel moved
by the unhappiness of others and who would surprise herself by
weeping. The male heroes wept, and these expressions were a
clean break with those which we have encountered. Thus the
noble Rodolphe, whose sang-froid, courage and determination
were equal to any test, could not listen to Fleur de Marie without
a tear in his eye, so moving was she. The first time he took her to
the country she was charming in her innocence:

A tear came to Rodolphe's eye on hearing this poor, abandoned, mistrusted lost creature, who was without shelter and
without bread, cry out in happiness and ineffable gratitude to
the Creator, because she was pleased by a ray of sunlight and
the sight of a field'.[7]

He wept even more when Fleur de Marie, who still took him
for a fan painter, advised him to put his money in the savings
bank: 'I was moved . . . Oh I was moved to tears, as I told you
(he is speaking to his friend Murph). And I am accused of being
blasé, hard, inflexible. . . . Oh! no, no, thanks to the Lord I can
feel my heart beating ardently and generously once again.'[8] His
seeming impassiveness led to his sensitivity being doubted but
it was nevertheless revealed in gentle tears before the picture of
innocence and virtue. Friendship, like tenderness and pity, had
rights over his generous heart. When he was shut in a cellar and
could not rescue his loyal companion Murph, who was running
great risks, he wept in imagining the latter being struck down by
the assassin's knife. Murph was as tender and valiant as Rodolphe,
but his emotions made up one of the comic motifs of the novel: his
British phlegm and squire's pride prevented him from displaying
his emotion too openly: he would accordingly blow his nose
noisily while turning his back or hiding himself behind a curtain;
what the narrator called a semi-burlesque event, just to keep us
informed. He did not want Fleur de Marie to see him in tears,
and asked to delay going to look for her, protesting that he was
not made of iron, and rubbing his eyes with his 'Hercules' fists'.[9]
This fine English gentleman, a sort of hulking great brute with a
big heart, should not appear ridiculous but should simply make
us smile through our tears. Rather than his tender emotion, it
was his clumsy modesty which was funny. The good wept over
moral attentions and emotions, but excellent souls could convert
even the most hardened people through their tears. Fleur de
Marie thus made all the inmates of Saint-Lazare weep, most
of all the She-Wolf, who rebelled for a moment against this
proof of weakness but finally gave herself up to her virtuous
emotions.[10] Likewise Rodolphe made the Chourineur weep 'like a
deer' and converted him to good.[11] Tears thus made the vestiges
of goodness, which survived intact in the roughest of characters,
germinate. In this novel without psychological context or a mind
tormented by anything other than remorse in proportion to the sins

committed, or by the excess of scruples experienced by a pure soul like Fleur de Marie, the characters wept over fine feelings and a savings-bank morality. Pretence was obviously on the side of vice. There was none of the pain of worry which could plunge one into the abyss of subjectivity: too much suffering made one mad, as it did to the craftsman Morel. Misunderstood wives did not swallow back their tears, but contrived to make their husbands weep. This was the case of Mme d'Harville whose husband repented with delightful tears that he had bound her to his life of an epileptic and who, after the happiness of the reconciliation, committed suicide to sort everything out. There was no furious passion with its parade of burning tears and male distrust, lovers wept together from the top to the bottom of the social ladder. There were few dried up souls and many virtuous conversions in tears. To see them weep so with happiness, with gratitude and with pity, to hear their virtuous, naive and moving remarks, one could picture a relationship between Eugène Sue's novels and those of the eighteenth century. But we should rather look to the melodrama of the first half of the nineteenth century for a likeness: with its mixture of fears and tears, the defenceless victims, the horrible villains, the comic supporting actors, the heroes, the succession of violent actions and expressions of emotion which made up the main components and the rhythm of the two genres. Like the melodrama, the popular novel would still know innocent persecuted victims, who were then saved by the champion of Good, but virtuous discourses and the moral emotions (virtue, gratitude, pity) would tend to lose ground to the passions.

THE MYSTÈRES DE LONDRES AND *ROCAMBOLE*: THE ELEMENTS OF A TRANSFORMATION

Although the *Mystères de Londres* by Paul Féval were written only a short time after the success of Eugène Sue's novel, the second work was not a replica of the first. Here, tears were less the indication of fine feelings, and were more often the sign of a suffering love which resembled romantic passion: pure young girls who had not experienced bitter tears, discovered, on becoming women, the sobs and burning tears of secret and incomprehensible passions, of betrayed ties. Miss Trevor and the Countess of Derby were pale, with shadowed eyes, bearing the traces of weariness and tears.[12] Miss Trevor, who knew the torments of love, advised Miss Stewart in these terms: 'Never fall in love, you who smile so gaily, it leads to too much suffering! You learn to weep, you grow pale . . . and the night sends you such dreams!'[13]

Virtuous emotions were allowed to remain only if they concerned the family. Susannah thus discovered on reading the *Vicar of Wakefield*, the happiness of those who, unlike her, had known their mothers, and shed gentle tears over the idea of such touching ties. Loo and her father expressed a reciprocal attachment in tears, whereas Snail, the son, could not contain his emotion and reproached them for making him cry like a child.[14] Family feelings could move to tears, not moral platitudes. Rio-Santos himself, when he rediscovered his brother Angus in a pitiful state, 'had tears under his eyelids'.[15] This character, a seducer and superb outlaw who fought against England to save Ireland was, it is true, the prototype of the romantic hero. The memory of his only love evoked by the sound of a melody, led him to shed a tear 'through his lowered eyelashes'.[16] If good young women were moved to tears while rescuing some unfortunate, men only wept for despair or passion, and never to excess: their eyes were damp or their voices filled with tears. On the other hand there were still odious characters who remained unmoved by the tears of their nearest and dearest, such as White Manor who dragged his wife on a lead through the streets of London, moving the emotions of even the livestock dealers, and who cried out: 'All the better! all the better, if she dies in tears! All the better if she still lives to weep and suffer.'[17]

The same applies to *Rocambole* in which the negative characters who were not moved by tears, pretended a false suffering when it was necessary to their evil designs. In addition, M. de Beaupréau epitomised the coward who tyrannised the weak and wept at the feet of the strong.[18] Armand de Kergaz, the good hero, was no longer moved to tears by moral abstractions although he was always saving the unfortunate. He only wept once, when he found out that the woman he loved had been obliged, through need, to get rid of her piano. He rushed to supply her with one on which she picked out some Weber, 'her eyes filled with tears', drawing from the instrument 'those plaintive notes which have made so many tears flow'.[19] If young girls of good family wept while playing the piano and while praying, they could at least preserve their dignity in their pain. Hermine, believing herself betrayed by her fiancé Fernand did not shed any tears: 'Unmoving as though struck by lightning, she looked at M. de Beaupréau and her mother in turn with dry eyes, seeming by this look to attest that her life was shattered from that moment on and that the whole world had become indifferent to her'.[20] Eaten up inside with suffering, she would, however, end up weeping in her mother's arms who was in great fear that her daughter would decide to enter a convent.[21] Maternal love made her shed many more tears. The character who wept the most in the novel was the courtesan Baccarat, who loved the same Fernand. Knowing all the tears of passion, she collaborated with the powers of Evil, to the point of giving her sister Cerise over to the lascivious appetites of the terrible M. de Beaupréau. She would, however, range herself on the side of Good in the end, and would end up sacrificing herself for the happiness of the virtuous characters. She attended their triple marriage, weeping and praying, attired in the grey habit of a novice.[22] The loving and repenting courtesan expiated her sins in a convent with many tears. The appearance of passionate love led to the shedding of many tears. Pale heroines devoured by suffering, characters outside the law, came away from it enhanced and rehabilitated through the strength of their feelings, or of their personalities. These elements broke with the gossiping morality and with the transparency of hearts which were developed and greatly reinforced by repetitive outbursts of tears in the *Mystères de Paris*. The great-hearted male characters did not weep as easily as before. Their virile dignity seemed to demand rarer tears. If it still seemed base to remain indifferent to the tears of others, it was not necessary to show one's sympathy by weeping, it was better to act. Charity, compassion, gratitude, devotion and their procession of gentle tears had lost ground. It was essentially family feelings which led to virtuous expressions of emotion.

THE TEARS OF THE AFFLUENT IN THE POPULAR NOVELS
OF THE END OF THE NINETEENTH CENTURY

The popular novel preferred domestic dramas to the picture of the mysteries of the city and of its tragedies. When the publisher Degorce-Cadot announced a new collection of recent illustrated novels entitled Vices and Virtues he promised laughter and tears but added 'They will not be made up, like the *Péchés capitaux* [mortal sins] of Eugène Sue, of theses and political debates, they will really be true family dramas'. The main action was centred round a family whose honour was threatened. A young woman, whether guilty or innocent, would be condemned, and this blame would fall on her child whose parentage, at least in some cases, would be doubtful. The springs of action of these novels were illustrated by the beginning of a novel by Emile Richebourg, *La petite Mionne*:

> Wealth can do nothing for happiness, which is not to be bought like a piece of art or a luxury, most often the hapiness which we envy exists only in appearance. How many people smile who long to weep? For the sorrows which we conceal are the most cruel. How many bleeding wounds within families, how many dark mysteries, how many unknown dramas there are! And nobody is exempt from misfortune; it strikes the high-up as easily as those below.[23]

From the cushioned interiors of the rich were born sufferings and tears which did not penetrate to the outside world but which were revealed by the novel. We should not trust the appearances of well-being, because respectability obliged characters to conceal their sorrows which were all the more intense for being bitten back. But for once we were at the heart of the drama: we knew that the young countess Raymonde had been unfaithful to her husband with the gamekeeper. In her room the dowager countess was prey to the most atrocious agonies:

> 'Large tears had put out the dark flame of her eyes. But violent spasms swelled her breast and from the convulsive trembling of her lips, from the flaring of her nostrils, from her waxen pallor it was easy to guess at the terrible rending of her spirit.'[24]

In this fit of tears, this face animated with sickly contractions was the mirror of a tormented and threatened soul. This description of the dowager countess, destroyed by sobs, who would eventually run out of tears, was nothing compared to the suffering of her son when he learned the shameful news:

For two days, he was in a terrible state, his eyes were dry and brilliant, his body was constantly shaken by convulsive trembling, he would sigh heavily, would not speak, but uttered strange and incoherent words, I was frightened then that he would lose his reason. But little by little a redeeming reaction came about; he experienced tears and sobs which appeared to comfort him, and his nervous over-excitement was calmed, long hours of prostration followed, and the final result was a deep depression which still lingers.[25]

Pain thus followed a distressing course: a dry nervous attack on the verge of madness, followed by sobs which released this tension, then prostration, lifelessness, general weakness. The body possessed by grief was the object of a detailed description which had not existed before. If the violent attack took on new forms, it found the relief appropriate to the laws of the genre. The son and the mother fell into each other's arms. The count then sobbed like a child in his mother's breast:

'Yes, cry my son', she said, covering his forehead and his cheeks with kisses, 'Weep, weep again, it does you good to cry . . . But after your tears you must rediscover your energy and pull yourself together [. . .] Ah! They will be richly paid for, the tears which you shed now'.[26]

If it was good for this young man to comfort himself through tears, he must nonetheless hold himself ready for the hour of vengeance and in it show himself to be strong, inflexible, without a single weakness. Simultaneously, the count could nurse the scars of his heart by being charitable as his mother advised him: it was in wiping away the tears of others that his own would cease to flow. In contrast with such a deep despair, which motherly love attempted to ease by receiving the tears of her son and by setting out a line of conduct for him, the conduct of the young countess was almost devoid of humanity. Raymonde, the adulterous woman, demonstrated the characteristics of a wild beast, even when she began to weep:

She let a sort of growling be heard and tears burst from her sparkling eyes. But it was not at all the distress of remorse, nor a great pain which made these tears flow; it was rage which she cried for, because she could no longer fool herself, she was judged and condemned without the right of appeal.[27]

A stranger to repentance, the torments of the spirit and the tearing apart of the being, Raymonde's tears were of an inferior quality; those of fury in the face of a punishment which was nevertheless deserved. The attacks of tears born of deep suffering only affected the good. Villains were all surface and instincts. But the honour of families would make the sins of the mother rest on the child's head.

In Paul Decourcelle's novel, *Les Deux gosses* [the two children], the plot was identical in this matter; in Chapter 6, he made use of the same situation. A home which appeared to be calm and smiling led all those who passed by it to say to themselves 'How happy they must be in that beautiful house!' But if they had been able to see what went on 'behind the totally sealed shutters, behind the carefully drawn thick curtains', they would have lost their enthusiasm, for inside it there was

a prostrate woman, aroused by the violence of her sobs, despite the length of time that she had been crying. A mother on her knees before a prie-dieu, her eyes reddened by tears, gaunt with suffering. A man, his head in his hands, his mind on fire, his throat dry, his breast torn by his fingernails, lost, destroyed in his thoughts.[28]

This pretty and comfortable interior, this nest of happiness concealed one of those adulterous dramas which ravaged the bodies and souls of the rich. But on this occasion, the prostrate woman, Hélène, was innocent of the crime of which she was accused: all she had done was to help her sister-in-law, Carmen, to leave her lover by reminding them of their duty. Appearances were against her: she would be unjustly punished by her husband, and this would reach even to her child, whom he wrongly considered to be a bastard. Ramon, the husband, would always be divided between despair and anger. The few drops of Spanish blood which ran in his veins explained his impetuousness, his jealousy and the terrible refinement of his revenge. The quality of the blood would often motivate the personality of the characters in this novel. Changing his will after the dishonour which had just struck his family, he was described as follows: 'From time to time

he would stop, as though to reflect and large tears sprang from
his eyes. But he would immediately wipe them away nervously
with his finger and his face would take on its apparent calm'.[29]
His involuntary tears which were quickly dashed away did not
weaken his terrible determination: he would give the child to a
robber. During the following nights, for long hours, he would
turn over in his mind the proofs of adultery: 'And with tears
swelling in his breast he would weep, he wept all his tears.
He wept for his lost love, his destroyed hopes, his broken life,
his tarnished fatherhood. Then he arose and with a savage joy
he murmured: "I am avenged!"'[30] If the violence of his emotion
sometimes overwhelmed him, and made him shed manly tears,
he would soon desert them for anger or the joy of revenge. His
virile impetuousness prevented him from experiencing doubts
which sadness and gentle memories might have allowed to be
born. His blood always dominated painful emotion. Hélène, after
the drama which had upset her life, recovered slowly from a long
illness. She came out of it a changed woman:

> 'She was more beautiful than ever, if that was possible, but
> her large blue eyes, previously drowned in an eternal and
> placid happiness, today appeared to be veiled by a poetic
> melancholy. One could always feel a tear ready to fall from
> beneath her long-lashed lids'.[31]

Her face reflected simultaneously the charms of pain and the
calm of innocence: she was a model of the noble and touching
heroine. When the efforts which she made to convince her family
and find her child again were unsuccessful, she knew a moment
of despair:

> Nature was stronger than her will, stronger than her courage;
> she wept, she sobbed, asking God why he had not left her to
> die, almost blaspheming in the wanderings of her suffering.
> But she prayed . . . And in the depths of her despair hope
> arose[32].

Hélène, because she was a woman, would sometimes see
strength give way to nature, in other words to tears. Her revolt
did not last long, and faith succeeded it. It was not anger but
prayer which consoled her. Filled with female compassion she

too began to wipe away the tears of the unfortunate[33] and wept when she was alone over the photographs of her husband and son, a new image of family affection. Fanfan, the child who was abandoned to vagabonds and thieves escaped being perverted thanks to the friendship he bore towards his companion in misfortune. Although their tears were formally forbidden them by their persecutors[34], Fanfan and Claudinet would cry together to combine in their weakness and remind each other of the finer feelings and the elements of morality which they could remember: 'And then it was necessary for one of them to be there to wipe away the tears of the other, to raise up his friend when he was exhausted, to share his grief, and, very rarely, his small pleasures.'[35] These child martyrs who in their downfall preserved a core of purity and good education which they demonstrated by their reciprocal compassion, had a prominent role in the popular novels of the end of the century. These vestiges of finer feelings allowed the final recognition scene (how moving) of the reunited family.

The popular novel of the end of the nineteenth century, with these crises, these tears, the voice of blood and conscience, occurring in confined interiors, incorporated some new elements. These bourgeois families in crisis, despite the airs which they gave themselves and the comfortable buildings in which they evolved, were struck by misfortune like poor people. In their tears, the characters revealed their internal torments in a domestic frame where drama was born of adultery. In a mixture of psychology and of genetic determinism, the different ways of crying would illuminate the personalities of the characters, and the pictures of virility, femininity and childhood. This type of novel soon became reserved for female readers, however, because in them, family tragedy triumphed over adventure.

The gentle emotions of the virtuous characters in the *Mystères de Paris* contrasted with the false tears of the villains, suggested a means of moving from vice to virtue by their conversion through tears, from Bad to Good, from sin to repentance. This moralising, associated with scenes of action, presented strong similarities with the melodrama of the first half of the nineteenth century. Sentiment and evil went side by side, offering varied but simple emotions. In *Rocambole* and in *Les Mystères de Londres* the emotions of the characters were already presented differently. Fewer gentle tears were shed, pale heroines were even obliged

to restrain themselves. The passion which animated characters
of the romantic type, the outlawed hero, the repenting courtesan,
made different tears fall. Hidden pains, degrees of emotion and
storms of passion suggested a different reading of the feelings.
Men were in tears far less frequently. In the popular novels of
the end of the nineteenth century, tears were motivated by the
nature of the characters which was revealed under the test of
unhappiness and dishonour. Descriptions appeared of a critical
state, in which the body was possessed entirely by suffering.
Family feeling and sensitivity to childhood were developed in
tragedy, torments and painful memories. Thus popular novels
showed, through their treatments of tears, a redistribution of
emotions and of images of the body: tenderness crystallised
into loving and family relationships, characters in disarray
were overcome by tears, while the difference of the roles was
accentuated.

Condemned to a lending-library success, the popular novel
demonstrated a different treatment of emotion from that which
was present in the novels of Flaubert of Huysmans or of
the Goncourts. The novelists who produced them and the
romantic expectations of popular readers combined to give birth
to different literary forms of the expression of emotion. Moreover,
the characters did not weep in the same way in the *Mystères de
Paris* which was still a point of reference for the evocation of the
sentimentality of the popular novel, as they did in the works of
the end of the century. Beyond any literary sociology, the simple
reading of these values indicated a new face of emotion: the cards
were redistributed between virtue, love, the family as privileged
poles of expression. Virtue was no longer at the front of the stage
in the popular novels of the end of the nineteenth century, while
it was in the foreground of Eugène Sue's *Mystères de Paris*. Family
dramas gained the advantage. In the question of tears, the popular
novel evolved over half a century. At the same time a movement
of specialisation in the novel took shape which aimed more at
the areas of potential readership. Adventure and feelings were no
longer mixed so much. At the beginning of the twentieth century,
the detective novel, read by men, was distinct from the novel of
the feelings aimed at women readers and situated at the bottom of
the hierarchy of the genre (with the exception of the catholic lady
writers who aimed to moralise, the writers who composed these
were on the lowest rung of the profession).[36] This context sheds

light on the status of tears in popular novels, and in particular on Huysmans' passion in denouncing the bad influence of these works on women of the people. Finer feelings were transformed under his eyes into unhealthy sentimentality once the novel of the feelings began to be reserved for women.

12 The Social and Political Codes of Emotion

Recourse to direct evidence gives us a better grasp of the socio-cultural differences which were displayed in the treatment of emotion. The path to writing of authors who were paid labourers, is a means of access to it, even if the accounts of such a life are rare and hard to interpret. The autobiographical work of these craftsmen or of these workers is indeed not to be taken only from a sociological point of view because their focus is often political. Norbert Truquin, in his *Mémoires d'un prolétaire à travers la Révolution* [memoirs of a man of the people during the revolution] did not incorporate the experience of tears into his tale: the title of the work alone indicated that the Revolution of 1848 was at the centre of the story. Martin Nadaud, in *Léonard, maçon de la Creuse* [Léonard, mason of Creuse] told the story of the movement of a migrant worker between town and country, describing the rural society which he had left, but also situating his emotion in the context of political representation.

The movement of the delightful tears of the Saint-Simonian workers appears to have gone out of fashion in the second half of the nineteenth century. Amandine Vernet in a lyrical speech managed however to make the striking Cevenol miners weep.[1] Curiously, tears could tell us about politics, and questioned a changing world in which the step between the condition of the workers and the rural way of life was telescoped.

Vallès, professional writer, spent his childhood on the margins of two worlds. He was brought up in a family universe of bourgeois pretentions but as the neighbour of families of a lower class where greater expressions of emotion were permitted. Tears were an issue in the politics of the family: the parents of Jules Vallès invested money in his education and made him pay quite dearly for his cry of revolt and his dream of Socialism. But the child who had wept so much had learned to contain himself. This bourgeois education of the restraint of emotions, with the concern over the self-expression which accompanied it, would veil from then on the tears of Jacques Vingtras, Vallès' fictional double.

216

THE ABSENCE OF TEARS

Norbert Truquin, in his memoirs, barely described tears of pain or pleasure, any more than he did humanitarian emotions. Despite the ill-treatment which he had suffered in his childhood, and the overwhelming days of June 1848 in which he was a young participant, he did not weep, or at least felt no need to give an account of it in writing the story of his life. The Revolution of 1848 included in the title of his memoirs was perhaps the point of no return, a moment when many hopes faded away. Although he wrote at length on his opinions, he did not tackle the emotions of a sensibility in tears, and did not dream of sharing them with his proletarian brothers. He wrote only with amusement of the tears shed by one of his many chance companions, encountered in the entourage of a philanthropic entrepreneur whose generosity did not preclude distance from the objects of his philanthropy. Truquin criticised this master for not sharing a table with the workers: this established limit undermined the philanthropic relationship and turned it back into paternalism:

> Among us there was an old soldier, who had passed three spells in Algeria. He was an old villain who knew how to laugh with one eye and weep with the other. He had been skilful enough to extract a few old clothes from his employer (trousers and cardigans) which he immediately hastened to sell, and he always knew how to bring people's hearts over to him.[2]

The conniving wink of the worker who moved the employer with his tears was not lacking in spice; it was also an answer to the owner's attitude who gave everything while keeping his distance from the workers. The philanthropy of the industrialist was not that of the doctor Raspail who dreamed of sharing tears and knowledge. Truquin was in no way haunted by sentiment or emotion: he did not write of his tears. He did however insist, when there were scenes of tragedy in the course of his life, on telling of the leaning of the poorest of men towards compassion, which contrasted with that of the rich, who generally found good reasons for doing nothing. The social war was continued in the adventures he encountered and the family was not, in this tale of an abandoned and rediscovered child, a privileged place for sentiment. Doubtless a choice made in his self-portrayal, he preferred his original political vision to the display of his sensitivity.

The memoirs of Martin Nadaud allowed little room for tears of emotion or personal sufferings, nor for collective expressions of emotion. As Jean-Pierre Rioux notes in his introduction, 'he plunges into his life without reticence, without any recourse to states of the soul or intimate sorrows'.[3] He told us however of the tears which revealed his political opinions and explained the birth of his republican convictions. He spoke of the tears of the Parisian workers who, in 1849, were the victims of forced redundancy. He evoked the sufferings which were more moral than physical, experienced by these urban workers who were excluded from society. The protests of the Republic would be raised against what they endured, and following this, the social question. Nadaud's political emotion was based on a refusal to accept the injustice which smote the workers and the republicans. One can understand even better how the key scene took place in court, where the character of the lawyer symbolised the republican bourgeoisie ready to defend itself. On attending the trial of a tailor who had been caught with weapons in his hands in the insurrection of 1834 and who was defended by Crémieux, he began to weep.

I saw almost next to me his wife and his children who wept hot tears. The gestures of the lawyer, his abundant words, his eloquent movements had moved the listeners. I could not keep back my tears on hearing the condemnation of this man who appeared so dignified and proud.[4]

The dignity of the worker, the unhappiness of a family, and the eloquence of a lawyer combined to move him, and to form his conviction: 'I can say that from that moment the republican party had a sincere supporter in me'. The expression of tears at the trial indicated republican conversion. And this scene indicated the loyalty which a different type of philanthropy developed which was not the same as that of Truquin's industrialist; that of the defence lawyer, a liberal republican, future minister of Justice of the June Republic and a member of Gambetta's cabinet.

WEEPING IN LIMOUSIN

In fact, the tears presented in the memoirs of Martin Nadaud tells us of other things: of his family in Limousin, of his education and then of his training as a mason from Creuse working in Paris. This life, punctuated with departures and returns, with debts and with profits, suggested a micro-ethnology of tears in a rural setting which moved with the rhythm of seasonal migrations. It was also the celebration of the memories of a Limousine mason who became a republican Député and who told the tale of his initiation into the world. Women wept copiously over the absence of their sons, their brothers and their husbands, who were all masons, for a greater part of the year, even for two or three years. On the first departure of Martin Nadaud at the age of fourteen, the women of his family let out cries of pain, not tears, on leaving him. 'We then had to submit to the embraces of my mother, my grandmother and my sisters. It was a painful and difficult moment. I think that had we been laid underground, the cries of the women could not have been more anguished.'[5] For to go off was to leave the world of childhood and women, and to enter the world of men and the danger of death. The departure became a ceremony of mourning, with its ritual crises and its weeping women. Another farewell ceremony (this one in a carefully locked barn) was that with his childhood friends, who were going to Lyon whereas he was setting out on the road to Paris: 'Finally it was time for us to separate, before we had even dried our tears'.[6] Uprooted, accompanied by the cries of despair of afflicted women and the tears of his childhood friends, Nadaud left his village on a basis of lamentation. But the journey was an entrance into the world of men which he had to face up to bravely, by suffering the physical pain of a difficult march without tears: 'To console me my father said to me: "I made the journey to the Vendée when I was younger than you are, and I did not snivel as you seem to be doing"'.[7] Becoming hardened to pain, to the weariness of the body, was just as much a mark of his apprenticeship. To show himself worthy he had to know how to maintain a dry eye, and to follow the example of his elders: 'With a man as hard and courageous at work as Thaury, there was no question of being moved; he had to remain impervious and not snivel over a few breaks in the skin of his hands'.[8] On the occasions of the return of the Limousine masons, two sorts of tears were shed in the Nadaud household. These could be the tears of the pain of an unpaid debt, of humiliating usury, of the poverty which threatened the family, or the tears of joy when the migrant brought back money to honour the debt. Nadaud, the young Companion, wounded on the building sites during the season, came back with nothing to give to his family. His mother on learning that this interrupted work and the necessary medical care had used up the money which he had earned began to weep: 'Then she began to shed many tears. Between her sobs she told me the story of the difficulty in which we found ourselves.'[9] The family was in debt and it was necessary to find the money to marry off one of the Nadaud daughters. The father found a moneylender to whom he was obliged to pay an extortionate rate of interest. On the return road, Martin Nadaud saw his father in despair, already suffocated with tears, then he went into the cemetery and expressed his sorrow and his humiliation aloud, kneeling before the grave of his parents: 'in a voice broken with sobs he cried out: "To be reduced to borrowing at 30 per cent; ah! if it was known, my friends would no longer have the least confidence in me, and it would be the end of my creditors' trust, for they would be the first to send round the bailiffs"'.[10] This father in tears, threatened by the ruin of his family, called on his ancestors to witness his courage at work and his honesty. The tears of Léonard Nadaud were connected with a visit to the cemetery and a speech addressed to the family dead. This nocturnal scene was an important one; it impressed a sense of filial duty on the child's mind for ever. This was a rural tragedy in which fate struck with the blows of usurious demands.

He also described another return, that of 1842, which, since it occurred under more favourable auspices led to the shedding of more gentle tears:

> As one may imagine, it was not simply joy which the family felt on the arrival of the migrant, especially when he was considered to be the prop and the bread earner for almost everybody, it was delirium, because rather than laughing, everybody wept.[11]

Tears of joy punctuated happy homecomings. When Martin Nadaud got out his moneybags and placed them on the table in front of the assembled family, they embraced each other and wept: 'we looked at each other, sobs smothered our voices, we were weary with embracing each other'.[12] Collective effusions were the signal for the good times. Tears in Martin Nadaud's tale had particular functions. The almost ritual cries of the women, Léonard Nadaud's invocaton of the dead, the departures and the arrivals in joy or sorrow celebrated the images of a country family which lived in the rhythm of migration. The male apprenticeship of courage belonged to the world of work which forbade the tears of physical suffering and discouragement to the young masons. Finally, tears caused by injustice, which revolted the republicans, and the eloquent defence by the lawyer who pointed out the true guilty parties, marked Martin Nadaud's entry into politics. A privileged place of initiation into culture, in this life-story, the undertaking and the entry into a different sphere of recognition were begun through a conversion in tears. Rooted in rituals, family tears celebrated an abandoned country life, which the loyalty of his heart towards the republican ideal, displayed by his participation in emotional expression, came to replace.

Martin Nadaud and Norbert Truquin both painted a picture of the worker whose male courage made him refuse to shed tears in situations of physical suffering but they did not speak of the same uprooting, nor of the same encounters or hopes. For Martin Nadaud, the migrant worker was part of a rural pattern in which mourning, departures, arrival, joy and family distress gave tears their own configuration which he inserted into the length of traditions while republican emotion was the inscription of the present and his individual path in the story. Martin Nadaud did not fear to speak of tears shed in the family and for the Republic but Norbert Truquin did not evoke either nostalgia or dreams of causing tears. He did not make emotions the spring of action of a life story which was both heroic and political.

VALLÈS: A PETIT-BOURGEOIS EDUCATION IN THE NINETEENTH CENTURY

The part reserved for tears in Jacques Vingtras' education was interesting in more than one respect. The Vingtras parents, socially mobile members of the middle classes, but whose modest income obliged them to live in the same building as families of the people, attempted at all costs to distinguish themselves from their neighbours. The young child was therefore brought up in a different way from his playmates, and their domestic privacy did not ring with the same scenes. The child could thus compare the two ways of living emotion: how the Fabres and the Vincents, two working-class families who lived in the same building, cried, and how his parents attempted to establish an order, which was in any case often threatened, in his domestic circle. In the Vincent family, the father, who had left the conjugal home, wanted to take his son with him, but did not succeed in doing so. Jacques saw him weep at the corner of the street:

> I find fathers who weep, mothers who laugh, in my home I have never seen tears or laughter: they complain, they shout. This is also because my father is a teacher, a man of society, because my mother is a courageous and strong woman who wants to bring me up as she should.[13]

The concept of bourgeois dignity was against laughter which was noisy and vulgar: it inclined to seriousness. Tears, which were a weakness, should not be shown, because one's children should be given the example of courage and of strength. These displays were tied to the professional status of the father and the educational role of the mother. Also, in the eyes of Madame Vingtras, Madame Fabre and Madame Vincent were bringing up their children in a careless manner because they did not resist their tears. 'They did not dare beat their children because they would have suffered to see them cry! (My mother had more courage)'.[14] This mother who did not allow herself to be moved by the tears of her son, and who did this for his greatest good, would of course prevent him from such bad associations. To punish him she forbade him to go to the Fabres, and Jacques shed tears over what he perceived to be a cruel injustice.

> I sometimes wept when I was a child: you have encountered, and will encounter tears on more than one page, but I do not know why I remember the sorrow of that day with particular bitterness. It seems to me that my mother was committing a cruelty, was being wicked.[15]

The account of this childhood gives an insight into the educational principles of the Vingtras parents, who were characterised by a deliberate indifference to the tears of the young

Jacques. To forge his character, they did not believe in giving in to the 'blackmail' of the tears of a child. 'If something distressed me, disgusted me, could make me weep, my mother imposed it on me immediately: "Children should have no will, they should become accustomed to everything"'.[16] His mother did not falter, and even went so far as to provoke the tears of her child to subjugate him further. For his better development he had to seek pain and eschew pleasure: because he liked leeks, she would not give him any. '"Why should I not have any?" I asked, crying. "Because you like them", she replied, for she was a woman of good sense who did not want her son to have passions for things.'[17] There was no limit to the power of parents over their children, and the young Jacques was not the only one to suffer vexations over dictates which were often given out: 'My father could cause me blood and tears throughout my youth: I owed him obedience and respect'.[18] Curiously, when his parents left him alone for a while, he was so accustomed to blows that to receive no more made him sense himself collapse. 'I feel urges to weep! I am not beaten. It is perhaps because of this. I was used to suffering or to anger. I lived always with a slight fever.'[19] When he showed deep sorrow, as for instance on the day when a little girl he knew died from the blows of her father, his mother reproached him for crying too much. She accused him in advance of not being able to suffer as much on the day of her own burial. One should not shed too many tears over others; it was necessary to keep them for the members of one's own family. Jacques Vingtras also suffered from these contradictory orders which attempted to channel his emotion.

More generally, the young Jacques did not know what he had the right to display. During a marital quarrel over his father's infidelity to his wife, he took part in a tragic scene and, weeping over his mother's face, he knew for the space of a moment a gesture of tenderness: his mother called to him and clutched at his hand. But he remembered mostly the painful impression of the day following a scene because he did not know how to conduct himself following this domestic drama: 'A strange thing [I was] more frightened of being gauche, of coming forward or of weeping at the wrong moment, than by the unknown drama, the secret of which I did not know'. He was afraid of annoying them with an explosion of feeling: 'they are cross with you because you woke them up in the morning with your tears – *your fuss* – ghosts which should die with the final cry'.[20] The anguish born of the tragic event was banished; that of showing ill-timed tears, of exhibiting an unhealthy sentimentality occupied the front of the stage. The child was afraid that his emotion would be ill-received, that he was making an ill-placed gesture: the law of silence was to be imposed again. Anything which might recall the incident was dismissed as fussing; those annoying and ridiculous jeremiads of a badly brought-up child. This uncertainty concerning self-revelation appears to have been at the heart of the bourgeois education which the young Vingtras suffered. On the threshold of adulthood, on the occasion of his departure for Paris, he knew a moment of emotion when the train left the station, but did not allow himself to cry in front of the other travellers:

> And I, the proud one, the brave one, I felt myself go pale and I thought that I was going to cry [. . .]. I pretended to have a cold to explain my moist eyes and I sneezed to hide that I was about to sob. It happened to me more than once. I shall eternally conceal my inside emotions with the masks of carelessness and the wig of irony.[21]

He thus mocked at his despair as an unhappy journalist, who could not deal with subjects which were close to his heart in his articles: 'Yes you are as stupid as a pig! Ah! my children! what a thing this Vingtras is! Here he is pissing from his eyes because he cannot write an article on *la Sociale*, in Girardin's office!' Vingtras wanted to laugh at the ridicule of seeing himself cry. If the novel of childhood gave a large place to the tears which his parents caused him to shed,[22] those of youth and adulthood offered tears which were always refined by irony and were here presented both as a gesture of modesty and as a pretence. The enterprise of the autobiographical novel was filled with this distancing; he thus described the book as it was being written: 'Here it is before me. It cries, it weeps, struggling with itself in irony and tears'.[23] He illustrated how the history of tears, in nineteenth century bourgeois society was bound to the history of laughter. But of which laughter? That of humour, of irony and of sarcasm, which according to Bakhtin is a 'diminished form' of it (compared with the popular and carnivalesque laughter whose forms he studied in Rabelais) but which revealed 'the infinite inner character of the individual'.[24] We can then understand better through the story of Jacques Vingtras, why intimate emotion in the nineteenth century was a fight between laughter and tears. After the sufferings of childhood, and the harshness of adult life, Vallès used irony in order to keep a dry eye.

From his novels, we can evaluate the importance of the gap between a bourgeois educational model and a popular one in which the child was the stake. To mould a character, impose an image of firmness and deny family conflicts, were the constituent parts of the imperatives of a bourgeois education of emotion, which were not shared by everybody. Sensibility in infancy had not yet encountered the pedagogy of self-expression: the educational and social issue implied a training of the will which mocked at and distrusted tears. They made up the other side of the scenery of tender families celebrated by the theatre and literature, themes which in any case appeared more and more to come from minor genres and after-dinner performances. Ironic modesty was preferred to all demonstrations of emotion: it introduced a distancing of the self in the face of misfortune which precluded tears.

This modest tendency was perceptible in the way of writing about emotions, and was the sign from that time on of a socio-cultural difference: a series of expressions which were disappearing from the literature and private writings of the writers of the nineteenth century such as 'eyes damp with tears' or 'my voice was smothered by sobs' were to be found again in Martin Nadaud's book. The famous and too truthful correspondence exchanged around *Marthe* revealed equally well the different levels of language. The members of the family from which she came, a bourgeoisie shaded with nobility, did not employ the expressions which her husband, who was of more modest origin, used when he wrote: 'I shed abundant tears at the idea that I am denigrated and attacked'.[25] This way of writing of his emotional outbursts in letters although it had been born in literature and the epistolary art, ended by becoming popular or middle-class.

13   The Misfortunes of the Melodrama

FROM THE EMOTIONAL DRAMA TO THE MELODRAMA

The bourgeois drama which was defended by Diderot was addressed to a larger audience after the Revolution.[1] Thermidor saw the success of Jean Nicolas Bouilly, known as the tearful poet, and of Beaumarchais, who, in *La Mère coupable* [the guilty mother] made a sacrifice to the serious dramatic genre. Badly performed in 1792, this play was successfully revived in 1797. The introduction to the text, written at this time, still found praise for tears: 'Tears which are shed in the theatre over acted ills, which do not hurt as much as cruel reality, are very sweet. One feels better for weeping. One feels so good after experiencing compassion.'[2] Apart from the reference to cruel reality and to the pleasure of fiction, Beaumarchais was a direct successor of those predecessors who boasted of the good effect of tears in the theatre and defended the moral drama which painted bourgeois ethics. Although the plays filled the theatres, they did not lead to agreement. Geoffroy reproached the drama for basing itself on the romantic and on sentimentality, and deplored the disappearance of the experts.[3] The *Etrennes dramatiques pour l'année 1797* [dramatic firsts for the year 1797] declared that cultured men were reduced to poverty by the Revolution. For these men of taste, the decadence of dramatic art was the result of the rise of a new bourgeoisie whose riches were spread around the theatre during the final years of the century. The *Décade* of 30 March 1796 spoke of shop girls, boy locksmiths, or market porters, who would come there to idle away their time and display their jewels.

The history of tears in the theatre was to be marked from then on by the desire of certain people, supporters of the classical tradition, men of letters and 'cultivated' bourgeois, to distinguish themselves from the populace who, in the theatre, came in search of emotion and tears. Here again, Sénancour advocated a tempered sensibility:

There are those happy spectators who have no need of any great verisimilitude, they always believe that they are seeing something real; and however it is acted, it is a necessity for them to weep as soon as sighs or a dagger appear. But as for those who do not weep, they hardly go to the performance to hear what they could read in their own homes: they go there instead to see how it is expressed, and to compare the different performances of a passage given by the actors.[4]

The true theatre-lovers, knew the text and went to the performance not to seek emotion but to compare the expressive ability and interpretation of the actors, which was the main interest of the performance. To these connoisseurs of the dramatic art were contrasted the ignorant spectators, who were taken in by the illusion, who had no care for verisimilitude and who cried at old clichés, with no critical distancing. These two types of spectator embodied on the one hand the distinction which culture conferred, and popular credulity on the other.

THE MELODRAMA AND THE TRANSFORMATIONS OF ITS PUBLIC

Historians of the theatre are in agreement that the birth of melodrama took place around 1800.[5] A popular genre, it developed from drama, but was distinguished from it by its spectacular scenic effects. The tragic and sometimes frightening events were divided up by comic interludes and ballets. It was total spectacle, music prepared the entrance of the characters, or increased the dramatic tension by introducing the episodes of violent emotion. The movement and the action thus took on the dominant role, but sensibility allied with morality were indispensable to the making of a melodrama. The audience wept over the good characters, who were generally weak, dumb, blind, crippled or without defence, with the exception of the avenging hero who had every good quality.[6] Sympathy was thus born simply from the appearance of the good characters, and led to the shedding of torrents of tears when these touching victims found themselves in the most dangerous situations. In *La Fille mendiante* [the beggar maid], which played with a full box-office at the Ambigu theatre,

a blind princess, reduced to begging, found herself surrounded by
bandits who wanted to kill her, under the eyes of a dumb hermit.
To this were added moving declarations of virtue, maternal love,
filial piety and generous devotion. At a melodrama one shivered
with fear, one wept with pity, invariably over fine feelings.

Pixérécourt, the most successful author of melodramas (with
30 000 performances) said that he wrote for those who could
not read. Nodier, who wrote the preface to the former's works,
explained his success through the combination of the dramatic
intensity of his melodramas, with the personal experience of the
men of the Revolution who had acted out 'the greatest drama in
history' in the streets.

> For these spectators who smelled of gunpowder and blood,
> it was necessary to supply emotions such as those of which
> they had been deprived by the return to order. They needed
> conspiracies, dungeons, scaffolds, battlefields, powder and
> blood.[7]

The sensitive and moralising aspect was kindled, according
to Nodier, by the moral need of a people who had long been
deprived of religion. It is hard to judge this: one would need
to know the ideas of these spectators on the moral conventions
which were to be respected in fiction, if one wished to understand
better the receptive phenomenon which took place in this public.
Geoffroy, a dramatic critic, explained this inclination by what
would have been the popular image of sensitivity: 'to admire
and to weep over noble actions, which advocate goodness and
the sensibility of the heart; laughter is bourgeois and worse, it is
malicious: a chambermaid believes herself to have the feelings of
a princess when she weeps at a play'.[8] Geoffroy, illustrating the
opinion of the cultivated public, laughed at the display of fine
feelings, and compared the spectators to 'children who listen to
the tales of old women with a pleasure mingled with fright': the
flavours of folklore were not appreciated (*Débats* of 27 November
1804). But these propositions still remained in the minority. All the
fine society of the Chaussée d'Antin rushed to see the Boulevards,
and was not ashamed to be moved. On meeting Pixérécourt, the
countess of Corbières, wife of Louis XVIII's minister of public
education, exclaimed: 'I must thank you for the many tears which
you have caused me to shed!'[9]

While people rushed to the melodrama, the *Théâtre Français*, preserver of the classical repertoire, was emptying. The atmosphere there was cold. The young Stendhal used to go there and write down his impressions. On 6 June 1804 he wrote in his diary: 'As soon as Talma returned to normal (once yesterday) I felt moved. I had a young neighbour with a good and pretty face who wept. It was a rare occurrence.'[10] The public of tragedy had become, in a few years, very reserved. Benjamin Constant, in *Réflexions sur la tragédie* [reflections on tragedy] noted the lack of success of sentimental subjects:

> Tragedies based on love seem to me to be no longer of the type to draw a large public who could echo their emotions. I have realised that there are a few exceptions, but they are daily becoming more rare and the public appropriate to this sort of tragedy would be made up of young people of eighteen and young ladies of fifteen.[11]

In good theatres, one only wept over stories of love during one's tender years. People wanted only the sublime. Chateaubriand who was enjoyed in the aristocratic salons could give an account on this matter of an opinion current at the time. In an article on Shakespeare, reprinted in his 'Essai sur la littérature anglaise' he wrote thus: 'The most evil drama can cause a thousand more tears than the most sublime tragedy'.[12] To distinguish themselves from the spectators of the drama and the melodrama, the public of the *Théâtre Français* preferred not to be moved to tears, and loved to admire the masterpieces of the classical repertoire in silence. The bourgeois public, whom we have seen mix with the popular public on the boulevards, were already inclined to desert them in the years 1820–30. The bourgeoisie understood that cultural and symbolic capital was as important as material riches. Napoleon, the lover of order, had already called the public to heel in limiting the opening hours, and by closing nineteen theatres in 1807. He demanded good conduct of the spectators and from 1809, the *Courrier d'Europe* found the public more well behaved. It is probable that restored stability obliged even the newcomers to good society to seek respectability at the price of being bored by the performance: it re-established official theatres and their tragic repertoire.

Under the Restoration the bourgeois public developed a passion at the Odéon for Casimir Delavigne, who demonstrated a liberal and patriotic ideology in a classical taste. For the liberal middle classes Delavigne was to men what Scribe was to families. The public of the Gymnase drew the mothers and the young girls and boys of the middle bourgeoisie together. Between 1820 and 1830 Scribe's plays developed the moving and sentimental figure of the soldier of the Empire who would sigh over a charming young woman. It is hard to understand why the grenadier Stanislas in *Michel et Christine* (1821) could bring tears to the eyes of the audience. Emotion also had a political element, for the speeches of General Foy would be read during the interval. In contrast to the melodrama whose theatres they occupied, Scribe's sentimental vaudevilles suited their public who, until 1830 wished to wipe away their tears shed over Napoleon's good soldiers surrounded by their families. The fashion did not last long: Legouvé in his old age recognised that these soldiers of Napoleon's old guard and these colonels who had made him weep would later make him laugh.[13] Scribe contented himself after this with a defence of the bourgeois family and its economic interests, in particular against badly matched marriages, without making too much use of the emotions. Scribe and Delavigne, each in their genre, regrouped the bourgeois public who were gradually deserting the melodrama and were trembling at the excesses of romantic, dishevelled and immoral dramas. The young who defended Romanticism in any case wished to make a deliberate stand against bourgeois conventions.

THE ROMANTIC DRAMA

The first theoreticians of the romantic drama founded their wish for the restoration of the theatrical conventions on the need to redirect a vast public and to adapt themselves to the times. Mme de Staël deplored that tragedy could not be sampled by the people: 'Our fine tragedies do not interest the people of France, under the pretext that our taste is too pure and our feelings too delicate to bear certain emotions, the art is being split into two'.[14] She demanded for her part that there should be more pathos, a certain emotional power. The purism of the theatre-lovers thus led tragedy to be reserved for an élite. In the *Journal de la littérature et des arts*, Boutton the stage designer added:

There is not one grisette of the Carré Saint Martin, not one dumpy boutique holder of the rue de la Verrerie who would not prefer to weep over *La Pauvre famille* [the poor family], or be moved by *Le Chien de Montargis* [Montargis' dog] [by Pixérécourt] than to yawn over *Phèdre* or more modern tragedies over which it is more acceptable to be bored.[15]

The initiators of Romanticism, starting from this realisation, wished to change the theatrical conventions in order to move the public more. Stendhal in *Racine et Shakespeare* thus imagined the plays which Racine would have written if he had lived in the nineteenth century: 'Racine did not believe that tragedy could be written differently. If he lived now and he dared to follow the new rules, he would have done a hundred times better than *Iphigénie*. Rather than inspiring only admiration, he would have caused floods of tears.'[16] The contemporary necessity of existing, of inventing and moving was in contrast with the respect for classical conventions.

Some, such as Planche, who attacked *Chatterton* did, however, criticise the form of the romantic drama. In February 1835, Musset wrote an accusation in verse against him in the form of a sonnet:

Quand vous aurez prouvé, Messieurs les journalistes
Que Chatterton eût tort de mourir ignoré
Qu'au théâtre français on l'a défiguré
Quand vous aurez crié sept fois à l'athéisme

Sept fois au contresens, et sept fois au sophisme
Vous n'aurez pas prouvé que je n'ai pas pleuré
Et si mes pleurs ont tort devant le pédantisme
Savez-vous, moucherons, ce que je vous dirai?

Je vous dirai, sachez que les larmes humaines
Ressemblent en grandeur au flot de l'océan!
On ne fait rien de bon en les analysant

Quand vous en puiserez deux tonnes toutes pleines
En les laissant sécher, vous n'aurez demain
Qu'un méchant grain de sel dans le creux de la main.

[When, good journalists, you have proved
that Chatterton was wrong to die unknown
that he was distorted by the French theatre
when you have cried atheism seven times

contradiction seven times and seven times sophism
you will not have proved that I did not weep
and if my tears were wrong in the face of pedantry
do you know, midges, what I will say to you?

I will say, know that human tears
resemble the waves of the ocean in their greatness!
in analysing them we achieve nothing good

When you have got to the bottom of two full tons of them
on leaving them to dry, you will have tomorrow
only a wicked grain of salt in the palm of your hand][17]

The tears which were shed defied analysis and cold reason
was dismissed in favour of feeling. The romantics created a
radical opposition between critical ability and theatrical emotion:
this is why Musset defended the melodrama which made Margot
weep. A letter from Musset to Buloz sheds a little more light on
this feeling:

> Tell him, I beg of you if you should see him (Vigny) how much
> I admire *Chatterton*, and that I thank him with all my heart for
> having proved to all of us, such as we are, that despite the
> turpitudes which have made us blasé, depraved and stunned,
> we are still capable of weeping and of feeling what comes into
> our hearts.[18]

He thus thanked Vigny for allowing him to escape his incapacity
to feel which was imposed by the spirit of the times which numbed
and darkened hearts. It was on these foundations of emotional
lifelessness that the theatrical event, the romantic drama shaped
itself.

Hugo, who, in his preface to *Angelo, tyran de Padoue* [Angelo,
tyrant of Padua] proclaimed his intention to touch his entire
people, made the public cry profusely. The most moving scene
was that in which la Tisbé, played by Mlle Mars (the character

of an actress of popular birth who sacrificed herself for the good of her lover and of a great lady) encountered her rival, played by Marie Dorval. But it was not always very helpful for a writer to move the audience. Gustave Planche, with all the authority of a recognised critic found the effects too facile: 'How M. Hugo has sunk from the peaks of lyric poetry to the boards of the melodrama?'[19] The challenge was thrown down, to wish to write dramas for the people and to move them to tears, was to demean oneself in front of the true connoisseurs: one was writing in the sensational mode even if the character of la Tisbé had little in common with the virtuous heroines of the Boulevards. Thus between the romantic writer and the Parisian critics a conflict was acted out over the ability to move others. The dramatist risked, in wanting to move too much, being relegated to a minor genre. For in France the spectators rarely allowed themselves to give in to their emotions. The comparison formulated by George Sand leads one to believe that the Italians were more easily moved to emotion:

These good Italians are quite the opposite. They applaud everything, weep, laugh, they stamp their feet, they are exalted. Good and bad, everything suits them. Providing that one touches their sensitive fibre, little matter that it is with a broom. M. Dumas would please them excessively, and yet they weep in a most timely fashion at a simple and touching word by Kotzebue.[20]

The Italians wept easily, which did not prevent them from being sensitive to delicacy of feeling. Sand who smiled at this appeared to regret the excessive coldness of the French public.

THE PLACE OF THE ACTOR AND THE EVOLUTION OF GENRES

It was largely the actor's interpretation which would transform the melodrama. In 1823 three authors (Mrs Benjamin Antier, Paulyarse and Saint Amand) wrote in collaboration *L'Auberge des Adrets* [the Adrets Inn], a melodrama which used all the tricks of the genre, with its standard characters and the victimisation of the good by the bad. The role of the abominable bandit who killed a traveller and accused an innocent man, was that of Robert Macaire and was given to Frédérick Lemaître.[21] On this occasion, the actor was to subvert the character of the villain completely, transforming him into a truculent, mocking character, who fooled the police and slit the throats of his victims while joking. Instead of adopting the traditional attitude of the bloody bandit, who moved furtively with the air of a conspirator, Frédérick Lemaître strutted onto the stage, adopting the airs of a prince in his tattered costume. The play which was meant to make the audience tremble and weep became a comic success, and played to a full house until the twenty-fourth performance after which it was banned. This censure was due to an incident which is worth telling, because it concerns tears which were ridiculed. The play ended with Macaire's death. The wife of the prefect of police, on attending it, found herself so moved by it that she burst into sobs. During this episode, Lemaître would normally extract his written confession from his shirt (in this he avowed that he was the father of the future son-in-law of the innkeeper and the lover of the latter's mother, the woman whom he had unjustly accused of the crime which he had committed). Now, not passing up the opportunity of performing an actor's flourish, he took the confession on this occasion out of his shoe. The wife of the prefect, deeply shocked, accused Lemaître of having made her emotion ridiculous and destroyed her illusion. Madame the Prefectess did not like people to laugh when it was a crying matter. Because of this, if Lemaître's biographer is to be believed, the play was banned.[22] Revived in 1834, the play led to the birth of a literary and social type which broke completely with and demystified the characters of the melodrama: Baudelaire discerned in this 'great moral and literary signs'.[23] Robert Macaire was part of a certain genre of romantic hero in revolt against society, and an aristocrat of vice. Virtue and its procession of emotions would no longer have the success of the Boulevard of Crime.[24] Whether it was a question of a superb outlaw, or of an exceptional actor who transformed the role which had been given to him, Frédérick Lemaître offered a new attitude for the admiration of the public. The great actor displayed his ability to alter traditional texts and roles by subjugating the public. It was thus that Gautier defined the 'essentially modern' talent of Marie Dorval, who had a career of acting in melodrama and in romantic drama.[25] 'Madame Dorval's talent was completely passionate, not that she neglected art, but her art came to her through inspiration; she did not calculate her acting through gestures.' The art of the actor exceeded technical ability, the work of putting the character in context, inspiration was the extra ingredient of the spirit which denoted genius.

> She put herself in the character's situation, she became one with it, and acted as it would have acted; from the most simple sentence, from an 'oh! my God!' she could make electric and unexpected effects spring, which the author would not have suspected were there.

This rare capacity to embody the characters to the point that the actress was one with them, allowed her to transcend the dramatic text and to lead to effects of surprise and electrification of the audience. 'She produced cries of a poignant truth, tears to shatter the breast, intonations which were so natural and tears so sincere, that the theatre was forgotten and one could not believe in a conventional pain.' Her suffering appeared so real that theatrical conventions disappeared. Nobody in the eighteenth century would have evoked the sincere tears of an actress. This fascination with the authentic preserved the illusion of the spectator.

> When you have followed an actress in the transformations of her theatrical life, when you have cried, loved, and suffered with her under the names with which the fantasy of the poets baptise her, there becomes established between her and you a magnetism which it is hard not to believe to be reciprocal – she stands giving off rays, while you the spectator are lost in shadow.

The spectator drowned in obscurity wept with the actress who subjugated him to the point where he imagined a relationship, an affinity, a 'magnetism' between them. The circulation of emotion was no longer essentially within the audience, between spectators. This magnetism was no longer the electric imagination of the end of the century of the Enlightenment. All the artifice of the theatre disappeared, the actress became more real, more touching than nature. 'You were not vain painted ghosts at all, separated from us by a cordon of fire: we believed in your love, your despairs, never had personal sorrows clutched at our hearts and reddened our eyelids as much as yours did.' The expression of truth which was given off by the performance of the actress, involved an intimate participation which no obstacle, even physical, could hinder and which real life could not supply.

From the transformation of a melodrama by an actor to the fascination which the actress in a romantic drama could exercise, Frédérick Lemaître and Marie Dorval appear to have occupied the central spot in the theatre: they had contrived to make a career in the two genres. Rather than represent those types which were immediately recognisable to the public, they caused surprise and admiration, with their ability to take over a role and to modify it in a very personal way. Instead of engaging an accepted emotion, they excited a series of emotional shocks which made the audience cry in a very different way from before. In the eighteenth century the public came to the theatre to act out its emotion, moving scenes were foreseen, waited for and judged. In the nineteenth century it seemed suddenly moved by an accent, a gesture, a pose of the actor, which nothing could predict and which extended the theatrical illusion to such an extent that the theatre itself disappeared, leaving the spectator on his own with this actor or actress whose emotion was so real. The paradox of the spectator of the nineteenth century could be described thus, according to a formula adapted by Zouc on prayer, they wept 'all together and each for himself'. One can understand that so personal an emotion could involve a certain modesty and that contemporaries did not describe tears which were shed collectively so much as the emotions of their own sensibility. On this count it would be tempting to think that in literature and spectacle the same process of personalisation of emotion was taking place: where the romantic writer revealed the torments of his soul, the actor overwhelmed the audience with the truth of his gestures. Tragedy and comedy had taken the place of feeling: 'the public did not want just to be moved, they wanted to be surprised in laughter and tears. The public no longer offered itself the spectacle of sensibility when an actor attempted to capture the auditorium.

THE DEGREES OF THEATRICAL EMOTION

During the second half of the nineteenth century, people wept in the theatres and the tears of the spectators were still an indication of success. George Sand wrote in her diary in 1867, on the performance of *Messieurs du bois doré* [gentlemen of the golden wood] adapted from her novel by Paul Meurice: 'The play seems charming to me and very well acted [. . . it] is pleasing, it is a great success and the audience weep without being told to'.[26] At the performance of *Villemer*, adapted from the novel by Sand and performed at the Odéon on 29 February 1864, Flaubert was in the box of the Prince Napoleon in which the novelist sat. Was it to give her pleasure that he was seen 'weeping like a woman'?[27] His attitude here had feminine connotations, and this was probably based on a personal rather than an aesthetic level. Each time that Sand read him one of her plays, or he went to see them performed he 'wept like a calf' or 'many times'.[28] Should one read into this an effect of what he himself called his masculine hysteria? We know in any case that he was far from having a limitless admiration for the novels of the authoress. In a letter to Louise Colet, he wrote of his lack of enthusiasm for the literary or dramatic effects which led to tears:

> Emotion, which is often obtained by certain sacrifices of poetic detail, is quite a different thing and of an inferior order. I have wept at melodramas which were not worth fourpence and Goethe has never caused me to wet an eye, unless it was out of admiration.[29]

When he wrote, in a letter to Alfred Baudry, about the first performance of *Madame de Montarcy* a play by his friend Bouilhet, on 6 November 1856, it was not he who wept but the ladies:

> I will set aside the style which is tremendous, but I insist on letting you know that it is a dramatic success. The beautiful weeping ladies of the boxes, as Jean-Jacques called them, did not omit to weep, and towards the end there was such a display of handkerchiefs that one might have supposed oneself to be in a laundry.[30]

As was his custom, Flaubert adapted himself to the people he was writing for: complacent or aesthetic, ironic or moved, he wept while mocking at tears. The different ways of weeping in the theatre nevertheless appeared to be a long way from demonstrative excesses. The diary of the Goncourts included an observation on the tears of the Empress Eugénie at a performance:

From there I saw the Empress seated in profile in her box with her Marie Antoinette fichu, her face contracted with emotion and her eyes filled with tears, which she at first tried to hide behind her fan, and which she then decided to wipe away in a bourgeois fashion with the corner of her handkerchief.[31]

The anatomy of this movement told of all the ruses and the delicacies of a modest emotion: the aristocratic fan, then the corner of a bourgeois handkerchief. To have good manners, for a woman and certainly for an empress, also consisted of knowing how to cry discreetly in public. For if one could still shed tears in the theatre as a woman, one should not do so in the manner of the people.

Indeed, when the men of letters of the second half of the nineteenth century spoke of drama or melodrama, they took the position of amused observers and laughed at the audiences. The public of this sort of performance appeared frankly exotic to them, even barbaric. In his guide *Paris s'amuse* [on the town in Paris] dating from 1870, Pierre Véron thus described the attitude of the public of the Porte Saint-Martin in the way that a traveller would describe a primitive people.

In the middle of the nineteenth century there still exist primitive creatures moved to an incontinence of tears by the misfortune of a few heroines on the boards [. . .] Do not only go to this theatre to watch the tearful candour of these frank labourers, these honest petit-bourgeois [. . .] Leave them to enjoy their unhappiness. They are so happy in their despair![32]

The attitude of this naive frustrated and uneducated public made a contrast with the silent, restrained attitude of the cultivated public, who would only let themselves be moved by sophisticated emotions and who sulked at stereotypes. It was not necessary to look at the stage but at the auditorium: practising a comforting ethnography which recognised the marks of distinction and the pitfalls of an easy emotion, they amused themselves by watching those who did not know how to move. They did not experience the personal emotion of the attentive spectator who would furtively quash a tear in the darkness. The Goncourt brothers thus recorded in their diary an observation by their friend, the caricaturist Gavarni:

Find me something which is more comical than these fine people who, right after stuffing themselves, while they are still digesting, go and place themselves in a suffocating box, where, sweating and unable to fart, the women strapped into their corsets, they drink in tearful and sentimental dramas, holding against the drama the hiccoughs of digestion and emotion.[33]

In this work of the bodies of the middle classes, the disgust of tears was equal to that of the digestion, and unhealthiness was as much a description of the confined atmosphere as of the sentimental themes which were considered to be base and animal. This minor genre led to primitive emotions which were close to natural functions. The theme of the fight against the digestive theatre became common. The Goncourts themselves attacked this inferior taste for fine feelings and went further in noticing the permanent nature of the drama of the Boulevard:

For years, there has been only one and the same play on the Boulevard, a daughter and son, lost and found, making fatherhood and motherhood play every note in the scale, from the brass to the weeping ophicleide. Truly, we only see tears over a brat, and one might think that humanity had been suddenly overtaken by a rinforzamento of feeling for the fruit of its loins, and in it there are only fathers and mothers, altogether part of Parisian society.[34]

The recognition scene appeared to be a stupidity, and those movements of weeping family feeling though they pleased the public of the Boulevard, appeared ridiculous to men of letters. The Goncourts accused the playwrights of demagogy: they made use of the 'my mother' joke to make themselves popular. In the theatre, the sentimental themes were only used to make good entrances. The family emotions at the centre of the comedy of tears and of the domestic drama of the eighteenth century, were no longer appropriate to the cultivated public: they were reserved for the populace and the middle classes.

In the course of the nineteenth century, it appeared increasingly ill-mannered to go to the theatre to seek out the violent emotions of the melodrama and its tender, accepted and awaited scenes, which allowed the popular public to weep over the finer feelings.

240   *The History of Tears*

Distinguished tears became those which were not foreseen
because the power of the theatrical illusion was a result of this
ability to reveal emotion through an expression which was truer
than nature, in the individual spectator. The search for truth in
feeling which was so rarely encountered in real life found in the
theatre a form of experience which the darkness of the auditorium
made possible. One could see acted out there what Norbert Elias
calls the process of deformulating: distrust concerning accepted
expressions which provoked tears, was accompanied by a search
for formulations which would be exactly appropriate to a unique
and personal emotion.[35]

14 Conclusion

Although the body sent out signals through movements, postures, attitudes and manifestations which corresponded to systems of rules, although, it developed some sort of language, it was not exactly speech and even less literature. But the springs of these old tears are well and truly dried up. We can nevertheless detect traces of them, like the smudged ink on Lucile Desmoulins' notebook, or printed words: torrents of tears, damp glances, sobs. Through novels, memoirs, letters and personal diaries, enhanced by accounts of performances or of political events, by philosophical essays, by medical and scientific writings and books of etiquette I have looked for the elements which made up the transformation of the status of tears, between strangers and intimates, from the street to the bedchamber, from the public square to the boudoir, and which illustrated the function which they filled in the definition of male and female roles.

In the course of the eighteenth century a model of the circulation of the sentiments was mapped out. Tears accompanied the practice of reading, and were desired by a broad literary public which established a connection between the author and the reader by participating in expressions of emotion. This movement, which gained its full momentum in the second half of the eighteenth century, was accompanied by a flourishing of the type of novel in which feeling rubbed shoulders with horror. The growth in distribution of every type of printed material towards the end of the *Ancien Régime* underlined this tendency. Letters appropriated the language of tears and made use of it with pleasure: effusiveness was *de rigueur* in fiction and the epistolary art. These manners of writing, which were an important part of the spirit of the Enlightenment, developed the emotions to their highest point. In this circulation of tears, excess was acceptable, but the exchange had set forms according to the ties which held the characters and the twists of the narration: tears could be given, shared or paid for. To step outside these forms brought down charges of separation, treason, falsehood and even barbarity on one's head. As part of a preregulated circulation within the family, these tides of tears endowed relationships with an extra element of physical participation which symbolised a renewal of feelings and regards. The fusion of emotions was not general here; respect, duty, honour and virtue combined to create the limits of the sharing of tears. The scene of the mingling of the tears of love, the dreamed-of situation, was often at risk, as much from the demands of virtue as from those of social acceptability (or even of libertine parasites). Tears were then shed in the bosom of friendship to console the participants.

Theatre, with the coming of the fashion for the comedy of tears and for bourgeois dramas expressed an echo of the model of the emotions. The stage was the interior of a house: family feelings, sensitivity to childhood, to love, to virtue and compassion were exhaled there only to fall again as a rain of tears. In the audience, the assembled spectators wept openly, celebrating in this way the encounter of natural feelings with a scenography of sensibility. In the strange ruins of the model of courtly behaviour, the Town allowed itself the luxury of the natural. Faced with the exquisite ballet of loving families and the impulses of nature, the bourgeoisie and the nobility melted into tears, sharing the accepted emotions, which were also promoted by novels. The public of theatre loved to indulge itself in the spectacle of sensibility. The art of tenderness and the practice of the pitiful tale combined to make up the aesthetic rules of a social code of the *salons*. But sensitive spirits wished to avoid the pitfalls of a psycho-physiological definition of sensitivity, as well as the instability of excessive feelings, vapours and convulsions, to which men and women could be subject. The affectations of some women and the whims of children were excluded from the category of the valued forms of tears. Tears, the body's means of participation in emotion must not be ruled by it: the excessive mobility of a person's fibres was not a sign of a sophisticated sensibility.

The eighteenth century did not forget solitary emotion either. Very soon the pleasure of weeping, a mixture of gentleness and melancholy, was exalted, as though the subjective experience defined by the outburst could not have been conceived without external expression. Sometimes represented as flight, dissolution, or suspension of time, this experience threw the historical status of a particular form of subjectivity into question, a fragile and singular form which discovered its liquid image in expressions of emotion and a privileged place to appear in self-expression through writing.

On other counts, the sensitive model gave tears the dimensions of a universal language. Bonds were established between strangers around the contagion of the emotions, of compassion, of a feeling of humanity. Pity, a voice which left nobody unmoved, provoked exchanges of tears in a relationship of co-existence, and of emotion, which should not be reduced to the tearful philanthropy which has so often been the object of mockery. It was this idea which allowed Rousseau to criticise the limited nature of tears shed in the theatre. The denunciation of the abuses of the *Ancien Régime* and of the poverty of the people, led to a form of tenderness. The language of tears could both sooth and attack: it could not be reduced to the simple exaltation of supposedly bourgeois values, it was also a way of experiencing the present in one's thoughts.

The contagious effects which were a sort of mesmerism through tears, shed light during the French Revolution on the imaginary motif of collective tears. This extraordinary experience of the 'delicious moment', in which people would weep, unable to speak, in each other's arms, evoked the dream of a new social bond. Curiously these feasts of tears came about at the moment when the political system became based on the individual. These moments of emotion in the Assembly or in the street showed a growth of opinion concerning the model of the feelings, but also a new application of it. The entire public space became the scene for a sharing of tears, a phenomenon which could be called, to refer to Rousseau, a general sensibility. Once the federative enthusiasm had passed, tears brought together men of the Revolution who were divided by their opinions, for fleeting moments, allowing them to celebrate a unity which was threatened but always desired by the general expression of emotion. But the rhetoric of tears could also make exclusions. In the terms of the art of oratory, speculators and moderates who cost the people tears, or drank them in, were barbarians and vampires who should be punished. Furthermore, an inflexibility which was redefining the limits of pity, sometimes accompanied the models of widely diffused emotion which led to tears. The revolutionary tribunals, in the absence of a distinction between the public and private domains, condemned the man who wept too easily over the troubles of others. And the Jacobin who, working for happiness, found himself cut off from everyone, found consolation only in the bitter sweet pleasure of solitary tears while he was accused of being a blood-sucker in turn.

After the Revolution, writers attempted to redefine sensibility. Sénancour turned his attention towards sensuality and, excluding metaphor and an excess of demonstration, he defined it as the superior perceptive ability which called for a constant self-moderation. In their private diaries, Stendhal and Benjamin Constant questioned the signs of sensibility and the differences between appearance and reality of emotion. They observed the tears of women and the use they made of them to move men or to make them falter. Neo-catholic dolorism, in contrast to the emotional model of the Enlightenment, brought the Christian tradition of tears up to date, and it was also cultivated by Romanticism. Tears, which were an intimate experience, the sign of one's downfall and of a purifying expansion, were the accompaniment to prayer and were called the gift of God. With the growth of aesthetic emotion, this private suffering permeated published works and became inherent to literary activity. More generally tears were born of deep wounds. This revelation of a raw sensitivity was rare and did not benefit from being exposed. For it was necessary to wear protective armour in a social space where self-interest, false appearances and conventional emotions dominated. The circulation of tears was no longer in fashion, except among Companions and paid craftsmen encountered by the Saint-Simonians: they still dreamed of gentle tears shared with their brothers the workers, humanitarian waves and fluids in contrast to the learned physics of isolated atoms and social egotism.

The difficulty of interpreting the positions of others, of assuming the appropriate one to the situation, the tenuous nature of a contained emotion led to uncertainty towards others, especially in relationships between men and women in which the prejudices which were communicated and an ideal of restraint and modesty in true sensibility transformed the status of tears. Dramas, scenes, sentimentality and coquetry in women and cynical and hardening impulses in men, disrupted communication and led to misunderstandings. Tears became a nuanced mode of expression and had no value in themselves. The act of weeping, which was not without motive in the narration of the novel, revealed the individual nature of a character. One can thus better understand why tears could be as much the evidence of the capacity for simulation in women as that of their femininity or their deep sensibility (which was actually the same thing): the one concerned appearances and the other concerned truth. Between these two poles and once extreme youth was over, in which it was permitted that they should weep easily, women knew well the restrained tears which were imposed on them by their public image, and even better, their role of wife and mother in the domestic sphere: those suppressed tears could be read in their faces and were the signs of the sufferings endured in silence. The demands of public life forbade men the outbursts of sensibility and emotion which might give power into the hands of the observers. Young men who had not discovered all the aspects of their character, who were not yet hardened, learned this to their cost and to their greater shame. The man who wept easily was a weak man or a fool, whereas the tears of men who were used to controlling themselves could, in exceptional moments of truth, reveal their deep attachment and their dominant passion. Crisis situations, jumps of mood from laughter to tears, nervous attacks but also dry suffering, and an inability to weep, characterised the tears of the romantic sensibility which was permeated with dolorism and with the cult of the woman. They were part of a general process of the individualisation of emotion, as was the model of restraint and self-control of the bourgeoisie of the nineteenth century, but they were at the same time a reaction to this norm, displaying a 'structural romanticism' according to Elias. As it was used in published literature, so an image of the inner self was displayed in public, as a protection against the observation of strangers, but also as a ground plan for the social space. This phenomenon could be seen, to a certain extent, in the theatre where the expressive capacity of the good actor was praised, and a relationship of identification developed between the actor and the passive spectator whose personal emotion was no longer expressed in an ostentatious fashion, but to the contrary was regulated by the dictates of modesty.

In the second part of the nineteenth century, the reaction of some writers against the expression of pain and of personal emotion indicated a slowing-down of this movement. Private suffering was no longer of enough merit to be used as a literary warning. Art had higher demands. The expression of tears in literature represented a feminine attitude, and the exaltation of the weeping and sensitive woman created a more mundane image for her, more virile energy was necessary in order to write. Male dignity demanded that personal suffering should not be displayed, even though it could sometimes burst out in solitude, or very rarely on the death of a close friend or relative: these were situations which gave it some value. This desire to conceal states of the soul and emotions from the public probably stemmed as much from the impression that they could not be expressed by any one traditional sign (unless in a situation of ridicule), as from an ideal of self-mastery. Although women continued to intoxicate themselves with lukewarm lovers and fine feelings, and greatly loved to weep, it was their nervous constitution which was to blame for it: their unpredictable balance made it necessary for them to empty their lachrymal glands. It was as well that they should 'do so at church, reading novels, or playing the piano', over social matters and through sensitivity, as they did in their marriages. For by weeping at will, they could sometimes make a weapon of their weakness which was feared by men.

At the same time as they described this mode of male behaviour, novels displayed its destruction. The attacks of sobbing which men sometimes experienced, indicated the defeat of an individuality built on the control of the emotions. In the excess of his nervous despair, the man who sobbed found himself relegated to femininity and childhood. This return of suppressed tears, enlarged, with regrets, humiliations and accumulated anguishes, established a strangeness in the heart of intimacy and was not a soothing process. Women who were familiar with the fluid economy of tears which could provide a more favourable end for the attack, even turning it to good account, brought to mind the hysterics who so disturbed the doctors, because they were at the same time prey to illness and capable of simulating it.

During the same period, the cultivated public played the role of the bright minds going to watch the workers and the middle classes weep at melodrama and the Boulevard. The sentimentalism of the people was taken to be ignorance and stupidity, and was in no way an indication of the goodness of their spirit but was rather a sign of its frustrated nature and its savagery. The women of the people increased the disadvantages of crying, their easy emotions came from inanity. In addition, the tears which they shed over love and good feelings were dangerous and could lead to worse results. The study of popular novels which reflected the rapid modifications of the formulae of expression could lead some to perceive in it a differentiated resuming of the dominant models, all the more because the novel of feeling was reserved for women in the *Belle Epoque*. But Vallès, fighting between laughter and tears clearly perceived the differences which existed between the petit bourgeois education of the will which made up his model of domestic intimacy, the status which his parents finally gave to tears, and that which reigned among his working-class neighbours who did not put so much order in the expression of their emotions.

The changes in the value of tears as a sign of communication, the new divisions which these changes brought and the concepts which they illustrated heightened a transformation from the eighteenth century to the nineteenth. The communication of the emotions was one of the issues of the Enlightenment which crumbled away, giving birth to new forms. The redefinition of the political space which was both social and sexual was one of the great changing-points in the presentation of the emotions and modes of behaviour which we have attempted to trace along the trail of tears. From representation of the social tie to representation of the self, from communication to expression, from the private to the public, but also from femininity to virility and from identity to otherness, the movement was easier to evaluate at the end of the nineteenth century. The areas in which bodily expressions originated had changed: the rise of the intimate, which was not simply the creation of a protected private space, could sometimes transform tears into a strange sign, into a disquieting experience of the dispossession of the self. The gradual education of the character and a slowly acquired self-mastery were menaced by relapses into weakness or by disturbing symptoms. Although women retained the right to tears, the excess of their emotions and their sentimentality did not give them the finer role to play. Public expressions of emotion already demanded more modesty of them: it was in private, in secret or in the dark that they could savour their tears.

Notes

CHAPTER 1

1. Valincour, in his letters to the Marquise of M*** about the Princesse de Clèves asked his correspondant if she wept during the avowal scene. J-J. Roubine, 'La Stratégie des larmes au XVIIᵉ siècle' (see bibliography).
2. Madame de Sévigné, *Correspondance*, 15 January 1672.
3. Mlle Aïssé, *Lettres Portugaises* (see bibliography) p. 71 (letter XIV, October 1728).
4. Mauzi, *L'Idée de bonheur* (see bibliography), p. 12. He rightly protests against the concept of preromanticism which considered the literature of the second half of the eighteenth century to be a prefiguration of what followed, that is, Romanticism.
5. Dorat, *Les Malheurs* (see bibliography), p. 11.
6. Baculard d'Arnaud, *La Comtesse d'Alibre* (see bibliography), p. 96.
7. Fréron, *Année Littéraire 1766* (see bibliography), vol. II, p. 195.
8. Mornet, *Le Romantisme au XVIIIᵉ siècle* (see bibliography), p. 125.
9. In *Histoire des Idéologies*, directed by F. Chatelet, vol. III, chapter on Rousseau.
10. Madame Riccoboni, *Lettres de Milady Juliette Catesby* (see bibliography), pp. 55–6.
11. Joan-Hinde Steward, 'Les lettres de Madame Riccoboni à Sir Liston', in *Aimer en France* (see bibliography under 'conference'), p. 186.
12. Monglond, *Le Maître des âmes sensibles* (see bibliography).
13. Roger Chartier, 'Du livre au lire' in *Pratique de la lecture* (Rivages, 1985), p. 75.
14. Marmontel, *Mémoires* (see bibliography), vol. II, p. 180.
15. Madame de Graffigny, *Lettres de Madame de Graffigny* (see bibliography), p. 39.
16. Mercier, *Mon bonnet de nuit* (see bibliography), p. 139. In this concert of praises of the novel an opinion was developed which was later to dominate others and which originated with a doctor: 'Perhaps, of all the things which have spoilt the health of women, the most important has been the infinite multiplication of novels over the last hundred years', Pomme, *Traité des affections vaporeuses des deux sexes* (see bibliography), II, p. 441.
17. Diderot, *Eloge* (see bibliography), pp. 43–4.
18. Darnton, *Pratiques* (see bibliography), pp. 136–40.
19. Claude Labrosse, *Lire au XVIIIᵉ siècle* (see bibliography), p. 67. This work gives a particular analysis of the correspondance of the readers of Rousseau's famous novel with the author himself.
20. Labrosse, p. 96.

21. Labrosse, p. 86.
22. Mornet, p. 108. Daniel Mornet evokes the thousands of letters which Rousseau received in Montmorency and Motiers-Travers, in which his readers told him of their ecstasies and the floods of tears shed by them on reading his novel.
23. Labrosse, p. 87.
24. Labrosse, p. 87.
25. Labrosse, pp. 89–90.
26. Mirabeau, *Lettres à Julie Dauvert*, p. 130 (November 1780).
27. Darnton, pp. 142–3.

CHAPTER 2

1. Robert Muchembled, 'Les Sorcières, la loi et l'ordre', in *Annales* (March–April 1985), p. 295.
2. Gauchet and Swain, *La Pratique de l'esprit humain* (see bibliography), p. 504.
3. Certain writers, however, did not wish to abuse the novel genre. Thus Bésenval, in the 'Avant-propos' to *Le Spleen* (see bibliography), which nevertheless had an evocative title, declared: 'I have attempted to provide my unfortunate hero with some degree of sensibility in order to make him interesting. I did not wish him to be a weeper; one rapidly grows weary of the misfortunes of a character who is constantly bemoaning them.' 'Letter to M. Crébillon (fils), royal censor', (he was writing to Crébillon and his knowledge of the type of novel which the latter wrote perhaps influenced Bésenval's tone). Without a doubt there were degrees in the display of tears, but sensibility rarely lost its prominent position.
4. Bakhtin, *Esthétique et théorie du roman* (see bibliography), pp. 208–10.
5. Duclos, *Confessions du Comte de **** (see bibliography), pp. 270–1.
6. Marivaux, *Le Spectateur français*, in *Journaux et oeuvres diverses* (see bibliography), pp. 239–40.
7. Dorat, *Les Malheurs de l'inconstance* (see bibliography), p. 16.
8. Prévost, *Histoire du Chevalier des Grieux et de Manon Lescaut* (see bibliography), p. 164.
9. Rousseau, *La Nouvelle Héloïse* (see bibliography), p. 237.
10. Rousseau, *Confessions* (see bibliography), vol. I, p. 36.
11. Mirabeau, p. 66 (November 1780).
12. See Gelis, 'Et si l'amour paternel existait aussi' (see bibliography) concerning this episode.
13. Laclos, *Les Liaisons dangereuses* (see bibliography), p. 351.
14. Dorat, p. 335.
15. Cazotte, *Le Diable amoureux* (see bibliography), p. 373. According to Etiemble, this ending replaced the one originally intended by Cazotte, which ended with the fall of the hero.
16. Marmontel, vol. I, p. 14.
17. Marmontel, vol. I, p. 178.
18. Dorat, p. 268.

19. Prévost, *Manon Lescaut*, p. 58.
20. Dorat, p. 104.
21. Dorat, p. 348.
22. Rousseau, *La Nouvelle Héloïse*, p. 390.
23. Vauvenargues, *Correspondance* (see bibliography), p. 529.
24. All these quotations are from Diderot, *Correspondance* (see bibliography), vol. I.
25. Rousseau, *La Nouvelle Héloïse*, p. 7.
26. Dorat, p. 25.
27. Mme Riccoboni, pp. 55–6. The scene of the reading of the novel given in chapter 2.
28. *Lettres de Madame de Graffigny*, p. 271.
29. Madame Riccoboni, p. 66, and *La Nouvelle Héloïse*, p. 74.
30. Dorat, p. 332, Madame Riccoboni, pp. 68–9 and 93.
31. Dorat, pp. 65 and 102, *La Nouvelle Héloïse*, p. 62.
32. Dorat, p. 162.
33. Dorat, p. 79.
34. Crébillon, in *Écrivains du XVIIIᵉ siècle*, II, p. 1736.
35. Laclos, p. 428.
36. Mlle Aïssé, p. 304. (lettre XXI).
37. Diderot, *Correspondance* (see bibliography), I, p. 32.
38. Diderot, *Correspondance*, p. 46.
39. Mme Roland. Letter of 17 November, 1779, quoted by A. Grenet and C. Jodry in *La Littérature de sentiment au XVIIIᵉ siècle* (Masson), pp. 23–4.
40. Farge, *Vivre dans la rue à Paris* (see bibliography), p. 108.
41. Rétif de la Bretonne, *La Vie de mon Père* (see bibliography), p. 127.
42. Madame de Graffigny, *Lettres d'une péruvienne* (see bibliography), p. 257.
43. Mercier, *Mon Bonnet de nuit*, II, p. 8.
44. Damiens de Goricourt, *Dorval* (see bibliography), vol. I.
45. Laclos, p. 71.
46. Baudelaire, *L'Art romantique* (see bibliography), p. 211.
47. Diderot, *Jacques le fataliste* (see bibliography), p. 571.
48. Abbé du Bos, *Réflexions critiques sur la poésie et la peinture* in Gusdorf vol. VII, *Naissance de la conscience romantique au siècle des lumières*, p. 299.
49. Rousseau, *Essai sur l'origine des langues* (see bibliography), p. 91.
50. *La Nouvelle Héloïse*, p. 524.
51. Mulot, *Journal intime*, p. 54.
52. Quoted by Monglond, II, p. 339.
53. *Précis de l'histoire de la Révolution française* (1792, in *Oeuvres de Rabaut-Saint-Etienne*, Paris, Laisné, 1826), vol. I, p. 257.
54. Mercier, *Mon Bonnet de nuit*, I, p. 26.
55. I am relying here on Mauzi's *L'Idée de bonheur*, pp. 222 and 580, quoting Diderot, Holbach and Vauvenargues.
56. Mauzi, *L'Idée de bonheur*, p. 606.
57. Rousseau, *Discours sur l'origine et les fondements de l'inégalité* (see bibliography), p. 197.

CHAPTER 3

1. *Mémoires d'un homme de qualité* (see bibliography), I, p. 264.
2. Trahard, *Les Maîtres de la sensibilité* (see bibliography), vol III. 'Easily moved, he wept with emotion and admiration, with tenderness and generosity, he wept for no reason, through fear, through an unequal temperament, with despair and with anger, he wept in the temple, he wept at Vervay while contemplating Lake Geneva; he wept almost without noticing it, singing the tale of Olinde and Sophronie, he wept easily while helping a sick person, he wept with abandon and in solitude.'
3. Rousseau, *Les Confessions*, I, p. 204.
4. *La Nouvelle Héloïse*, p. 504.
5. Rousseau, *Correspondance générale*, vol. XI (May 1764), to Mlle Hemette.
6. Prince de Ligne, *Correspondance* (see bibliography), letter to the Princesse de Coigny (1787), p. 118.
7. Baculard d'Arnaud, *Les Épreuves du sentiment* (see bibliography), vol. III. *Lorrenzo*. In 'Liebmann, Anecdote allemande, dixième épreuve du sentiment', we encounter the following dialogue: 'You are sensitive Sir! You are therefore most unhappy! Yes, my sensitivity has caused me many troubles: but these troubles are dear to me; the tears which they have led me to shed are sweet to my soul.'
8. J.L. Le Cercle. 'Baculard ou l'embonpoint du sentiment', in *Approches des Lumières* (Klincksieck, 1974).
9. Loaisel de Tréogate, *La Comtesse d'Alibre ou le cri du sentiment* (see bibliography), p. 117.
10. Laclos, pp. 432–3.
11. Marmontel, I, p. 190.
12. See Pomme, *Traité des affections vaporeuses des deux sexes*, I, p. 15. 'Sadness, melancholy and discouragement poison all the amusements, their imaginations are troubled, they laugh, sing, cry and weep without reason.'
13. *Lettres de Madame de Graffigny*, p. 81.
14. Marmontel, I, p. 281.
15. *Les Confessions*, I, p. 314.
16. Diderot, *Rêve d'Alembert*, in *Oeuvres Philosophiques* pp. 356–7.
17. Diderot, *Lettres à Mlle de la Chaux*, in *Correspondance*, I, p. 126.
18. Diderot, *Oeuvres Philosophiques*, pp. 585–6.
19. Mercier, *Mon Bonnet de nuit*, II, p. 131.
20. Delisle de la Sales, *Philosophie du bonheur*, III, p. 126, quoted by Mauzi, p. 449.
21. Ariès, *L'Enfant et la vie familiale sous l'Ancien Régime* (see bibliography), p. 454. The first teeth of a child are thus 'honoured with the correspondance of a general officer' writing to his wife.
22. Collé, *Journal et mémoires* (see bibliography), III, p. 47.
23. Farge, *La vie fragile* (see bibliography), pp. 73–4.
24. *Emile* (see bibliography), pp. 21 and 45–6.

25. *Les Confessions*, I, p. 99.
26. *Les Confessions*, I, p. 75.
27. Philippe Lejeune, *Le Pacte autobiographique*, pp. 94–9.
28. *Emile*, pp. 573–4
29. *Jacques le Fataliste*, p. 672.
30. Diderot, *Oeuvres Philosophiques*, p. 585.
31. Galiani, 'Croquis d'un dialogue sur les femmes', in *Correspondance littéraire*, vol. IX (15 May 1772).
32. Chamfort, 'Petit dialogue philosophique' in *Maximes et pensées* (see bibliography), p. 364.
33. Marivaux, *Le Spectateur*, p. 162.
34. Marivaux, *La Vie de Marianne* (see bibliography), p. 168.
35. *La Vie de Marianne*, p. 151.
36. Laclos, p. 188.
37. Sade, *Eugénie de Franval* (see bibliography), II, p. 1478.
38. Baculard d'Arnaud, *Les Amants malheureux* (1746), quoted by Mornet, p. 8.
39. Bernardin de Saint-Pierre, *Paul et Virginie* (see bibliography), pp. 70–1.
40. Madame Riccoboni, p. 51.
41. Madame Roland, 'Discours sur la question proposée à l'Académie de Besançon, "Comment l'éducation des femmes pourrait contribuer à rendre les hommes meilleurs"' in *Une Education bourgeoise* (see bibliography), p. 167.

CHAPTER 4

1.   M. Leiris, *La Possession et ses aspects* (see bibliography), Introduction.
2.   Grimm, *Correspondance littéraire*, quoted by Linthilhac in *Histoire générale du théâtre* (see bibliography), Introduction.
3.   La Porte, *Anecdotes dramatiques* (see bibliography), I, p. 147
4.   J-J. Roubine, 'La stratégie des larmes'.
5.   Racine, *Bérénice* (1768), Préface de l'auteur.
6.   Quoted by Maurice Descotes, *Le Public de théâtre* (see bibliography).
7.   La Porte, I, p. 487.
8.   La Bruyère, *Caractères*, 'De la Cour, Remarque 2' (Paris, Flammarion, 1965) p. 202.
9.   Diderot, *Le Paradoxe sur le comédien* (see bibliography).
10. Argenson, *Notices sur les oeuvres théâtrales*.
11. Figure quoted by H. Lagrave, *Le Théâtre et le public* (see bibliography), p. 649.
12. Marivaux, *Journaux et oeuvres diverses*, p. 205. Everyone agrees that this was a performance of *Inès*.
13. Montesquieu, quoted by J. Ehrard, *L'Idée de nature en France* (see bibliography), p. 172.
14. Lanson, *Nivelle de la Chaussée et la comédie larmoyante* (see bibliography), I, Chapter 1.

15. According to Ehrard in his chapter on Destouches, *Littérature française 1720–1780* (see bibliography).
16. Lanson, p. 43.
17. Prévost, *Le Pour et le contre* (see bibliography), V, p. 358.
18. Collé *Journal et Mémoires*, III.
19. In *Théâtre du XVIIIᵉ siècle* (Pléiade) II, p. 1461.
20. Collé, III, p. 10.
21. Mercier, *Du Théâtre ou nouvel essai sur l'art dramatique* (see bibliography), p. 103.
22. Voltaire, *Lettres à d'Argental* (11 April 1767).
23. Diderot, *Entretiens sur le fils naturel*, in *Oeuvres esthétiques*, p. 115.
24. The taste for the horrific, which came from the English domestic tragedy was accepted by the French public only with difficulty because they disapproved of violence on stage: in 1734 Prévost displayed this in *Le Pour et le contre*. An audience only really developed for it in the second half of the eighteenth century.
25. Bachaumont, *Mémoires secrets* IV (3 February 1769).
26. Gaiffe, *Le Drame en France au XVIIIᵉ siècle* (see bibliography), Chapter I.
27. D'Alembert, *Oeuvres* (see bibliography), II, p. 397.
28. Bachaumont (22 October 1769).
29. Thus Rousseau in his essay on the origin of languages, wrote: 'To move a young heart, to reject an unjust attacker, nature lays down accents and cries', p. 96.
30. Diderot, *Entretiens sur le fils naturel*, p. 101.
31. *Entretiens sur le fils naturel*, p. 89.
32. Vigarello, *Le Corps redressé, histoire d'un pouvoir pédagogique* (see bibliography), p. 61.
33. F. Riccoboni, *L'Art du Théâtre* (see bibliography), p. 43.
34. Grimm, *Correspondance littéraire* (see bibliography) (July 1760).
35. Mercier, *Du Théâtre*, p. 203.
36. *Du Théâtre*, p. 215.
37. *Du Théâtre*, p. 213.
38. Mistelet, *De la Sensibilité* (see bibliography), pp. 15–16.
39. Mistelet, pp. 26–7.
40. Chamfort, p. 237.
41. See Gaiffe.
42. Rousseau, *Lettre à d'Alembert* (see bibliography), p. 119.
43. *Lettre à d'Alembert*, p. 123, note 1.
44. Diderot, *De la poésie dramatique*, in *Oeuvres esthétiques*, p. 196.
45. *Le Paradoxe sur le comédien*, in *Oeuvres esthétiques*, p. 311.
46. *Le Paradoxe*, p. 314.
47. *Le Paradoxe*, p. 376.
48. *Le Paradoxe*, p. 317. The actor François Riccoboni expresses the same ideas in *L'Art du Théâtre*: 'it has always seemed obvious to me that if one is unlucky enough to feel truly what one must express, one is in no state to act', p. 37, and later, he gives advice on mime: 'as for the mouth, it should move only to laugh, because those who lower the corners of the mouth to

weep in moments of affliction display a very ugly and inferior face', p. 77.

49. *Le Paradoxe*, p. 330.
50. *Discours sur l'origine et les fondements de l'inégalité*, p. 197.
51. Lagrave, Conclusion.
52. Lagrave indeed notes (p. 663) that nationalistic tragedies had a predominantly male audience.
53. Diderot, *Entretiens sur le fils naturel*, p. 122.

CHAPTER 5

1. Quoted by Soboul, *1789* (see bibliography), p. 118.
2. Marmontel, II, p. 227.
3. Archives Nationales C27 (181).
4. Quoted by Hirsch, *La Nuit du 4 Août* (see bibliography), p. 115.
5. *Mémoires de Bailly* (Paris, 1822), II, pp. 10–25.
6. Quoted by Hirsch, p. 115.
7. There has been a tradition, since Michelet of speaking of the tearful Lally-Tollendal. It seems to me, however, that his capacity for tears was in no way exceptional.
8. Quoted by Soboul, *1789*, p. 145.
9. Rétif de la Bretonne. *Les Nuits révolutionnaires* (see bibliography), p. 196.
10. *Journal politique national* (Tuesday 28 July, 1789).
11. Michelet, *Histoire de la Révolution française* (see bibliography), I, pp. 175 ff.
12. Michelet, *Histoire*, p. 209.
13. Archives Nationales C30 (250).
14. See Darnton, *La Fin des Lumières* (see bibliography).
15. Quoted by Monglond, II, Chapter 4.
16. Michelet, *Histoire*, p. 409.
17. Michelet, *Histoire*, p. 414.
18. We know how important Michelet considered the federation festivals to be. His father and grandfather had told him exalted tales of these, because they had lived through them. The role of the historian was to make these sublime moments come to life again, 'these feasts of nature, when the earth, in order to explain the sky, made it come down to earth'. But participation in the feasts of the dead came up against the limits of the individualism which Michelet took part in despite himself, he wrote in his diary on 20 November 1847, 'How is it that I am not the true priest, I who have held the holy of holies on the altar of the Federations this year? How can these sublime things, which have caused my tears, have so little intimacy within me? How is it that nature obstinately insists on reducing me to my own individuality?', *Journal* (see bibliography), I, p. 678.
19. Robespierre, article in *Défenseur de la Constitution* quoted by Reinhard, *La Chute de la Royauté* (see bibliography), p. 206.

20. Rei-hard, *La Chute*, p. 372.
21. *Gazette Nationale*, VII, p. 403, quoted by Michelet in *Histoire de la Révolution*, II, p. 486.
22. Louis Dumont, *Essai sur l'individualisme* (see bibliography), p. 96. An anthropological perspective on modern ideology. I am indebted to this book on all points.
23. Durkheim, quoted by Dumont, *Essai*, p. 99.
24. Gusdorf, VIII, *La Conscience révolutionnaire et les Idéologues* (see bibliography), p. 136.
25. This idea of suspension is to be found in Rousseau and in Kant. Rousseau in the Discourse on Inequality deliberately situates his argument outside time and space. In truth, the state of nature perhaps never existed in this form. It does not matter that the origin is suspended in fiction, so long as it allows us to think out the foundations. To found his metaphysical structures, Kant likewise suspends Reason. After the dogmatic step and the sceptical step, the critical step is not a step beyond, but a suspension in which Reason is brought to appear in judgement.
26. Article from the *Magazine Littéraire* (May 1984). Michel Foucault lecture based on two texts by Kant, 'Qu'est-ce que les Lumières?' and 'Qu'est-ce que la Révolution Française?'.
27. Rétif *Les Nuits révolutionnaires*, pp. 49 and 327.
28. Quoted by Mathiez. *La Vie chère et le mouvement social* (see bibliography), I, p. 34.
29. Quoted by Marc Bouloiseau, *La République jacobine* (see bibliography), p. 86, speech of 1 December 1792 to the Convention repeated twice a week for a month to the Observatoire section.
30. Soboul, *Précis d'Histoire* (see bibliography), p. 265, the following quotations are extracts from this.
31. Mathiez, I, p. 111.
32. Soboul, *Les Sans Culottes* (see bibliography), p. 226.
33. Michelet, *Histoire*, II, p. 73.
34. Ariès, *L'Homme devant la mort* (see bibliography), p. 145.
35. Archives de la Préfecture de Police. I thank Dominique Godineau who was kind enough to send me this text and the one which follows. See his thesis which will soon be submitted:'Les Femmes des milieux populaires parisiens pendant la Révolution–1793–Messidor an III'.
36. Lenoble, *Histoire de l'idée de nature*.
37. Gauchet and Swain, p. 396.

CHAPTER 6

1. Sénancour, *Rêveries sur la nature primitive de l'homme* (see bibliography).
2. We know what to feel means for Sénancour who figures as a transformer in the discourse on scent in A. Corbin's work, *Le Miasme et la jonquille* (see bibliography).

3. Sénancour, *Rêveries*, p. 142.
4. *Rêveries*, pp. 58–9.
5. *Obermann* (see bibliography) (Letter XV), p. 92.
6. *Obermann*, Observations, p. 27 and note.
7. *Obermann* (Letter XLX), p. 207.
8. *Obermann* (Letter XLX), p. 209.
9. *Obermann* (Letter XII), p. 86.
10. *Obermann* (Letter XV), p. 92.
11. Ballanche, *Fragments* (see bibliography), II (23 July 1808).
12. Speech by Chateaubriand, quoted in the Garnier edition of *Atala*, p. 269, note.
13. Chateaubriand, *Mémoires d'Outre-Tombe* (see bibliography), I, p. 404.
14. *Génie du christianisme*, II, Chapter 9 and *Lettre à Fontanes* (12 March 1800) in *Correspondance générale*, I, p. 114.
15. *René* (see bibliography), p. 208.
16. *Atala*, p. 51.
17. *Atala*, p. 140.
18. *Atala*, p. 140.
19. *Atala*, p. 100 note.
20. *Atala*, pp. 6–7.
21. *Atala*, p. 7, note to Préface.
22. *Atala*, p. 8, Préface.
23. The cult of art was accompanied in the young, who, like Chateaubriand, were fed it at an early age, by a strange relationship with reality, because contact with art made them live mainly on an imaginary plane, and with great agonies! In his youthful dreams of love, Chateaubriand was taken with violent fits of despair: 'Suddenly struck by my madness I threw myself onto my bed; I rolled myself up in my unhappiness; I sprinkled my bed with burning tears which nobody saw, and which flowed, in poverty, for a nothing', *Mémoires d'Outre-Tombe*, I, p. 157.
24. *Mémoires d'Outre-Tombe*, I, p. 119.
25. Perdiguier, *Mémoires d'un compagnon* (see bibliography), p. 124.
26. Perdiguier, p. 168.
27. Perdiguier, p. 191.
28. Perdiguier, p. 223.
29. Perdiguier, p. 394.
30. Rancière, *La Nuit des prolétaires* (see bibliography), p. 174.
31. Rancière, p. 195.
32. Rancière, p. 15.
33. Rancière, p. 115.
34. Rancière, p. 29.
35. Rancière, pp. 180–1.
36. Rancière, p. 238.
37. Raspail, *Revue élémentaire de médecine et de pharmacie* (15 February 1848), quoted by Rancière. 'Heretical knowledge and the emancipation of the poor' in *Les Sauvages dans la cité* (see bibliography under Les Sauvages), p. 48.
38. Rancière, in *Les Sauvages*, p. 434.

39. Didier *Le Journal intime* (see bibliography), p. 30.
40. Genette, *Figures II* (see bibliography), p. 165.
41. Stendhal, *Journal* (see bibliography) p. 234 (3 June 1811).
42. *Journal*, p. 46 (Vienna, November 1809).
43. *Journal*, pp. 227–8 (3 June 1811).
44. *Journal*, p. 637 (18 germinal an XIII, 8 April 1805).
45. *Journal*, p. 721.
46. *De l'Amour* (see bibliography), p. 89.
47. *De l'Amour*, p. 53.
48. *De l'Amour*, p. 79.
49. Cabanis, *Rapport du physique et du moral* (see bibliography), see also Jean Starobinski, *L'Oeil vivant*, II, 'Sur l'histoire des fluides imaginaires', pp. 196–213.
50. Esquirol, *Des Passions* (see bibliography).
51. Stendhal, *De l'Amour*, p. 78.
52. Stendhal, *Journal*, p. 532 (18 August 1804).
53. Constant, *Cécile* in *Oeuvres* (see bibliography), p. 173.
54. *Cécile*, p. 197.
55. *Cécile*, p. 147.
56. *Journaux intimes*, in *Oeuvres*, p. 250.
57. *Journaux intimes*, p. 359.
58. Stendhal, *Journal*, p. 385.
59. *Journal*, pp. 297–8 (23 April 1804).
60. *Journal*, p. 742.
61. *Journal*, p. 745.
62. *Journal*, p. 748.
63. *Journal*, p. 794 (9 September 1815).
64. *Adolphe* (see bibliography), p. 39.
65. *Adolphe*, pp. 104–5.
66. *Adolphe*, p. 151.
67. *Corinne ou l'Italie* (see bibliography), p. 52.
68. *Corinne*, p. 149.
69. *Corinne*, p. 252.
70. *Corinne*, p. 243.
71. *Corinne*, pp. 82–3.
72. *Corinne*, p. 355.
73. *Corinne*, p. 439.
74. *Corinne*, p. 416.

CHAPTER 7

1. Musset, *Les Confessions d'un enfant du siècle* (see bibliography), p. 31.
2. Preface to the 1840 edition of *Arthur* (see bibliography) p. 13.
3. Gautier, *Mlle Maupin* (see bibliography), p. 204.
4. *Mlle Maupin*, p. 129.
5. *Mlle Maupin*, p. 122.

6. *Mlle Maupin*, p. 140.
7. Bakhtin, *L'Oeuvre de François Rabelais* (see bibliography), pp. 47 and 53.
8. Musset, *Les Confessions*, p. 111.
9. *Les Confessions*, p. 71.
10. *Les Confessions*, p. 77.
11. *Les Confessions*, p. 55.
12. *Les Confessions*, p. 62.
13. *Les Confessions*, p. 144.
14. *Les Confessions*, p. 206.
15. Sainte-Beuve, *Volupté* (see bibliography), p. 80.
16. *Volupté*, p. 137.
17. *Volupté*, p. 148.
18. *Volupté*, p. 57.
19. *Volupté*, p. 77.
20. *Volupté*, p. 281.
21. *Volupté*, p. 271.
22. *Volupté*, p. 331.
23. George Sand, *Lélia* (see bibliography), p. 98.
24. *Lélia*, p. 23.
25. *Lélia*, p. 173. George Sand proposed the following maxim to Nisard who accused her of sowing a hatred of marriage in her books. 'A husband who avoids his duties with a gay heart, swearing, laughing and drinking, is sometimes less excusable than the woman who betrays hers while weeping, suffering and expiating her sins.' Guilty women are rehabilitated by the tears which they shed, whereas careless and insensitive men are less deserving of forgiveness. Letter published in *Revue de Paris* (1 June 1836). In *Lettres d'un voyageur*, LXII (Garnier Flammarion) p. 316.
26. *Lélia*, p. 147. Also the following quotations.
27. Vigny, *Mémoires inédites* (see bibliography), p. 70.
28. Maine de Biran, *Journal* (see bibliography), 42nd Cahier.
29. 'The Curé of Ars, more than any other, has the gift of tears: at the altar, in the flesh and in the confessional his face does not cease to flow with tears'. A. Corbin, 'La Vie exemplaire du curé d'Ars' (see bibliography), p. 12.
30. Odile Arnold, *Le Corps et l'âme* (see bibliography), p. 120.
31. Michelet, *Journal*, II, p. 75.
32. Bénichou, *Le Temps des prophètes* (see bibliography), p. 430.
33. Michelet, *Ma Jeunesse*. Private notes placed in order by his widow (Calmann Lévy, 4th edition, 1884), pp. 77–8.
34. *Ma Jeunesse*, p. 628.
35. Letters of 26 November and 12 December 1848, *Ma Jeunesse*, pp. 608 and 611, *Journal*, II, p. 219 (5 October 1853).
36. Michelet, quoted by Roland Barthes in *Michelet* (see bibliography), p. 129.
37. Michelet, *Journal*, II, p. 27.
38. Sand/Musset correspondence (see bibliography), pp. 31, 69, 97 and 230.

39. Sand/Musset, p. 77.
40. Sand/Musset, p. 200.
41. *Dictionnaire des gens du monde* (see bibliography), p. 127.

CHAPTER 8

1. Balzac, *Le Père Goriot* (see bibliography), pp. 39 and 47.
2. Balzac, *La Femme de trente ans* (see bibliography), p. 260.
3. Balzac, *Le Cousin Pons* (see bibliography), p. 24.
4. *La Femme de trente ans*, p. 50.
5. *La Femme de trente ans*, p. 109.
6. For Balzac in *Le Père Goriot, La Femme de trente ans, La Recherche de l'absolu, Splendeurs et misères des courtisanes.*
7. *La Père Goriot*, p. 90.
8. *La Femme de trente ans*, p. 111.
9. *La Recherche de l'absolu* (see bibliography), p. 177.
10. *Le Cousin Pons*, p. 107.
11. *Le Cousin Pons*, p. 306.
12. *Le Cousin Pons*, p. 305.
13. *Le Cousin Pons*, p. 360.
14. *Une Ténébreuse affaire* (see bibliography), p. 84.
15. *Une Ténébreuse affaire*, p. 175.
16. *Les Paysans* (see bibliography), p. 108.
17. *La Femme de trente ans*, p. 65.
18. *La Femme de trente ans*, p. 66.
19. *La Femme de trente ans*, p. 111.
20. *La Femme de trente ans*, p. 143.
21. *La Femme de trente ans*, p. 77.
22. *La Femme de trente ans*, p. 167.
23. *La Recherche de l'absolu*, p. 37.
24. *La Recherche de l'absolu*, p. 39.
25. *La Recherche de l'absolu*, p. 61.
26. *Splendeurs et misères des courtisanes* (see bibliography), p. 410.
27. *Une Ténébreuse affaire*, p. 58.
28. *Une Ténébreuse affaire*, p. 118.
29. *Splendeurs et misères des courtisanes*, p. 201.
30. *Splendeurs et misères des courtisanes*, p. 83.
31. *Le Père Goriot*, p. 113.
32. *Le Père Goriot*, p. 93.
33. *Le Père Goriot*, p. 253.
34. *Splendeurs et misères des courtisanes*, p. 379.
35. *Splendeurs et misères des courtisanes*, p. 500.
36. *Splendeurs et misères des courtisanes*, p. 597.
37. *Une Ténébreuse affaire*, p. 208.
38. *Splendeurs et misères des courtisanes*, p. 310.
39. *Le Père Goriot*, p. 145.
40. *Le Père Goriot*, p. 248.
41. *La Recherche de l'absolu*, p. 117.

42. Stendhal, *Lucien Leuwen* (see bibliography), p. 72.
43. *Lucien Leuwen*, p. 74.
44. *Lucien Leuwen*, II, p. 205.
45. *Lucien Leuwen*, II, p. 445–6.
46. *Le Rouge et le noir* (see bibliography), p. 52.
47. *Le Rouge et le noir*, pp. 490–500.
48. Stendhal, *Armance ou quelques scènes d'un salon de Paris en 1827* (see bibliography), p. 132.
49. *Féra*, episode of a novel in Vigny, *Mémoires inédites*, p. 322.
50. Vigny, *Journal d'un poète* (see bibliography), p. 62.
51. Gautier, *Fortunio* (see bibliography), p. 75 ff.

CHAPTER 9

1. Musset, *Poésies complètes* (Pléiade), p. 156, and also Mardoche, *Namouna*, letters from Dupuis to Cotonet.
2. Mürger, preface to *Scènes de la vie de bohème* (see bibliography), p. 30.
3. Delacroix, *Journal et correspondance* (see bibliography).
4. Flaubert, *Correspondance* (see bibliography), pp. 77–8 (letter to Louise Colet of 24 April 1852).
5. Flaubert, *Correspondance*, pp. 116–7 (letter of 26 June 1852).
6. Flaubert, *Correspondance*, p. 508 (15 January 1854).
7. Flaubert, *Correspondance*, II, pp. 549–550 (Letter to Louise Colet of 12 April 1854).
8. Flaubert, *Correspondance*, p. 557 (22 April 1854).
9. Flaubert, *Correspondance*, p. 366.
10. Flaubert, *Correspondance*, I, Appendix 3, p. 366 (21 February 1847).
11. Flaubert, *Correspondance*, II, p. 886.
12. Flaubert, *Correspondance*, II, p. 1234 (December 1853).
13. Flaubert, *Correspondance*, II, p. 601 (5 October 1855).
14. Flaubert, *Correspondance*, I, p. 385 (13 October 1846).
15. Sand/Flaubert, *Correspondance* (see bibliography), p. 284 (17 March 1870).
16. Sand/Flaubert.
17. Flaubert, *Correspondance*, I, p. 567 (15 January 1850).
18. Flaubert, *Correspondance*, II, Appendix 4, p. 1002 (14 August 1858).
19. Flaubert, *Correspondance*, I, p. 678 (Damas, 4 September 1850).
20. Goncourt brothers, *Journal*, I, p. 175 (March 1855).
21. *Journal*, p. 483 (3 June 1858).
22. *Journal*, p. 210 (10 September 1855).
23. *Journal*, p. 365 (1 January 1861).
24. *Journal*, p. 18 (12 February 1866).
25. Lautréamont, *Poésies I* (see bibliography), p. 375.
26. *Journal*, p. 83 (November 1852).
27. *Les Fruits défendus*, by Aurélien Scholl (see bibliography), begins thus: 'It is a well known fact that towards the end of supper, when men are inebriated, they enjoy themselves by discussing the immortality of the soul. The discussion is often very lively; one man

will shed tears while speaking of his mother; another, whose heart
is hardened, revels and exalts himself with blasphemy', p. 1.
28. Goncourt, *Journal*, I, p. 295 (21 November 1856).
29. *Journal*, p. 400 (1857).
30. *Journal*, II, p. 183 (1 December 1868).
31. Sand/Flaubert, p. 298 (7 March 1870).
32. Sand/Flaubert, p. 535.
33. *Journal intime de Caroline B* (see bibliography).
34. Bashkirtseff, *Journal* (see bibliography).
35. Maryan and Béal, *Le Fond et la forme* (see bibliography), chapters on
'corteges, mourning and condolences' and 'With the afflicted'.
36. Not a childish but an honest civility by Mme Emmeline Raymond
(Firmin Didot, 1865), p. 201.

CHAPTER 10

1. Fromentin, *Dominique* (see bibliography), p. 193.
2. Zola, *L'Oeuvre*, p. 187.
3. Feydau, *Fanny*, p. 167.
4. *Fanny*, pp. 171–2.
5. Flaubert, *L'Education sentimentale* (see bibliography), p. 438.
6. Zola, *Nana*, p. 209.
7. *Nana*, p. 210
8. Flaubert, *Madame Bovary* (see bibliography), p. 382.
9. *Nana*, p. 33.
10. Huysmans, *En Ménage* (see bibliography), p. 365.
11. Gobineau, *Les Pléiades* (see bibliograhy), p. 266.
12. *En Ménage*, p. 104.
13. *En Ménage*, p. 36.
14. *En Ménage*, p. 147.
15. *L'Education sentimentale*, p. 124.
16. *Grand dictionnaire universel du XIXᵉ siècle* (see bibliography), under
'Larme'.
17. *Nana*, p. 420.
18. *Nana*, p. 421.
19. *L'Education sentimentale*, p. 438.
20. Sand, *Le Dernier amour* (see bibliography), p. 114.
21. *Le Dernier amour*, p. 270.
22. *Le Dernier amour*, p. 172. Doctors also considered the absence
of tears in a woman was one of the signs of lesbianism. Christian
Bonello, 'Les Images de l'homosexualité dans le discours médical
au XIXᵉ siècle' (Thesis, Paris 7, 1984).
23. Charcot, *Oeuvres complètes* (see bibliography), I, p. 444.
24. Flaubert, *Bouvard et Pécuchet* (see bibliography), p. 886.
25. *Madame Bovary*, pp. 390–1.
26. Docteur Berger, 'Du Larmoiement hystérique' (see bibliography).
27. *Grand Larousse*, 'Larmes'.
28. *Madame Bovary*, pp. 324–5.

29. *Madame Bovary*, p. 331.
30. *Madame Bovary*, p. 367.
31. *Madame Bovary*, pp. 433 and 437.
32. *Madame Bovary*, p. 440.
33. *Madame Bovary*, pp. 447–8.
34. Butor, *Improvisations sur Flaubert* (see bibliograhy), p. 89.
35. E. de Goncourt, *La Fille Elisa* (see bibliography), p. 60.
36. *La Fille Elisa*, p. 61.
37. Huysmans, *Les Soeurs Vatard* (see bibliography), p. 363. On this same popular sentimentalism we can note in this work the different musical tastes of Désirée and Auguste, the young girl preferring the sentimental style and the young man inclining towards the military style: 'Désirée confessed to him that she loved sentimental songs, those songs which touch your soul with little birds flying upwards, trees which grow, lovers who weep [. . .] he preferred patriotic songs [. . .]. He knew one, 'The letter of the child' which brought tears to his eyes', p. 181.
38. Marcel Prévost, *L'Automne d'une femme* (see bibliography).
39. Zola, *La Faute de l'Abbé Mouret*, p. 45.
40. *La Faute de l'Abbé Mouret*, p. 174.
41. Huysmans, *Les Soeurs Vatard*, p. 164.
42. Swain, *L'âme, la femme, le sexe et le corps* (see bibliography).
43. Charles Darwin, *L'Expression des émotions* (see bibliography), pp. 163–7.
44. Charles Féré, *La Pathologie des émotions* (see bibliography), pp. 216, and 479.
45. Mantegazza, *La Physionomie et l'expression des sentiments* (see bibliography).
46. A certain type of Darwinism has continued to rage and the study of the 'expression of the face' is still plunged in this sort of anthropological and psychological totalisation. Behaviourism has taken over. Ekman, a specialist in non-verbal communication writes thus: 'A century after Darwin published his work on the expression of the emotions, it seems to me to be finally possible to put forward a conclusion: there are universal facial expressions in the human race', P. Ekman, 'L'Expression des émotions', in *La Recherche*, 117 (December 1980) p. 1415.

CHAPTER 11

1. E. Sue, *Arthur*, p. 174.
2. E. Sue, *Les Mystères de Paris* (see bibliography), p. 390
3. *Les Mystères de Paris*, p. 14.
4. *Les Mystères de Paris*, p. 271.
5. *Les Mystères de Paris*, p. 221.
6. *Les Mystères de Paris*, p. 663.
7. *Les Mystères de Paris*, p. 43.
8. *Les Mystères de Paris*, p. 59.

9. *Les Mystères de Paris*, p. 883.
10. *Les Mystères de Paris*, p. 420.
11. Féval, *Les Mystères de Londres* (see bibliography).
12. *Les Mystères de Londres*, p. 331.
13. *Les Mystères de Londres*, p. 335.
14. *Les Mystères de Londres*, p. 207–8.
15. *Les Mystères de Londres*, p. 196.
16. *Les Mystères de Londres*, p. 28.
17. *Les Mystères de Londres*, p. 275.
18. Ponson du Terrail, *Rocambole* (see bibliography), p. 141.
19. *Rocambole*, p. 200.
20. *Rocambole*, p. 130.
21. *Rocambole*, p. 266.
22. *Rocambole*, p. 484.
23. Richebourg, *La Petite Mionne*, p. 5.
24. *La Petite Mionne*, p. 19.
25. *La Petite Mionne*, p. 34.
26. *La Petite Mionne*, p. 47.
27. *La Petite Mionne*, p. 72.
28. P. Decourcelle, *Les Deux gosses*, p. 160.
29. *Les Deux gosses*, p. 164.
30. *Les Deux gosses*, p. 259.
31. *Les Deux gosses*, p. 245.
32. *Les Deux gosses*, p. 246.
33. *Les Deux gosses*, p. 379.
34. *Les Deux gosses*, p. 226.
35. *Les Deux gosses*, p. 312.
36. This is told to us by Anne-Marie Thiesse, *Les Infortunes littéraires. Carrière de romanciers à la Belle Epoque* (Actes de la recherche en Sciences sociales, no. 60, November 1985), and 'Mutations et permanences de la culture populaire: le cas de la lecture à la Belle Epoque', in *Les Annales*, I (1984). To understand the evolution and diversification of this genre, it is necessary to be aware of the way in which people followed novelists, the relationship to reading of the 'popular' reader, about which we are very ill-informed and which was probably not the same as that of a bourgeois reader according to the analysis of R. Hoggart, *La Culture du pauvre* (see bibliography).

CHAPTER 12

1. Michelle Perrot, *Jeunesse de la grève 1871–1890*, pp. 72 and 201. 'In the country of the Cénevol "desert", the coal miners of Gard arranged country rallying points [. . .] in the Robillac wood, five thousand workers heard the enflamed words of an ardent young woman who moved them to tears.'
2. Norbert Truquin, *Mémoires et aventures d'un prolétaire* (see bibliography), p. 132.

3. Introduction to Martin Nadaud, *Léonard, maçon de la Creuse* (see bibliography), p. 7.
4. *Léonard, maçon de la Creuser*, p. 168.
5. Ibid. p. 38.
6. Ibid. p. 39.
7. Ibid. p. 44.
8. Ibid. p. 60.
9. Ibid. p. 71.
10. Ibid. p. 75.
11. Ibid. p. 184.
12. Ibid. p. 185.
13. Jules Vallès, *L'Enfant* (see bibliography), p. 102.
14. *L'Enfant*, p. 104.
15. Ibid. p. 112.
16. Ibid. p. 54.
17. Ibid. p. 129.
18. Ibid. p. 174.
19. Ibid. p. 209.
20. Ibid. p. 205.
21. *Le Bachelier* (see bibliography), p. 8.
22. *L'Enfant* is in fact dedicated 'to all who have died of boredom in school, who have been made to weep at home, have been tyrannised by their teachers and thrashed by their parents'.
23. *L'Insurgé* (see bibliography), p. 47.
24. Bakhtin, *L'Oeuvre de François Rabelais*, I, pp. 47 and 53.
25. Marthe, *Lettre de Robert Caron d'Aillot à Charles de Cerilly* (Seuil, 1981) (25 November 1895), p. 116.

CHAPTER 13

1. Unlike Jean Duvignaud in *Les Ombres collectives* (see bibliography), who perceives the ending of privileges in the theatre to be the key date in the sociological transformation of the public, I think that the movement started up in the final years of the *Ancien Régime*, and that it was accentuated under the Revolution. In January 1774, Grimm was already deploring the changes in the composition of the pit (the wigmakers, labourers and kitchen boys already mentioned), when 15 years earlier it had been composed by 'honest bourgeoisie and men of letters, all of them having pursued their studies' but whose affluence had made them all rise to the second level of boxes, where their judgement had no influence.
2. Beaumarchais, *Un Mot sur la mère coupable*, performed on 16 Floréal year V (5 May 1797), in *Théâtre* (Garnier Flammarion 1965), p. 248.
3. Quoted by Charles Dedeyan, *Le Drame romantique en Europe* (see bibliography), p. 89.
4. *Obermann*, p. 131 (Letter XXXIV).
5. Descotes, *Le Public de théâtre*, p. 201, and Dedeyan p. 79.

6. J-M. Thomasseau, 'Le Mélodrame sur les scènes parisiennes' (see bibliography).
7. Nodier, Introduction to *Oeuvres de Pixérécourt* (see bibliography), I, pp. vii–viii.
8. Geoffroy in *Les Débats* (8 Thermidor an II).
9. Descotes, p. 233.
10. Stendhal, *Journal*, p. 501.
11. Constant, *Oeuvres*, p. 940.
12. Article of 15 Prairial an X, see *Atala*, p. 7, note 1.
13. Descotes, p. 285.
14. Dedeyan, p. 103.
15. Thomasseau, p. 467.
16. Stendhal, *Racine et Shakespeare* (see bibliography), p. 61.
17. Sand/Musset, p. 225.
18. Sand/Musset, p. 227 (27 February or 6 March 1835).
19. Quoted by Dedeyan.
20. Dedeyan, p. 129, (15 June 1834).
21. Thomasseau, pp. 17 ff.
22. Baldick, *La Vie de F Lemaitre* (Denoël), p. 43.
23. Baudelaire, *De l'Essence du rire*, in *Oeuvres complètes* (see bibliography), p. 371.
24. Baldick, p. 109, believes that from 1830 onwards, 'Sentimentality was in retreat in the face of passion, the hatchet in the face of the dagger, the brigands and the shepherds in the face of poisoners, adulterous couples and politicians'.
    Certain dramatists who did not know how to adapt to the new taste had this sad experience. Gautier cites the case of Bouchardy who developed finer feelings in his plays and who saw the public desert the theatres in which his dramas were played, while earlier he had had a certain success. Gautier, *Histoire du Romantisme* (1877, Editions d'Aujourd'hui, 1978), p. 180.
25. *Histoire du Romantisme*, pp. 274–5, the following quotations are also from this source.
26. Sand/Flaubert, p. 44.
27. Sand/Flaubert, Introduction.
28. Sand/Flaubert, Letter from Sand to Maurice and Lina, p. 231, and Letter from Flaubert to Sand, p. 284.
29. Flaubert *Correspondance*, II, p. 433, Letter to Louise Colet (16 September 1853).
30. *Correspondance*, II, pp. 645–6.
31. Goncourt Brothers, *Journal*, p. 662 (December 1869).
32. Quoted by Sennett *Les Tyrannies de l'intimité* (see bibliography), p. 158.
33. *Journal*, (March 1855).
34. *Journal*, (12 October 1860).
35. Norbert Elias, 'La Solitude du mourant dans la société moderne', in *Le Débat*, 12 (May 1981).

Bibliography

ORIGINAL TEXTS: EIGHTEENTH CENTURY

Aïssé, Mademoiselle, *Lettres Portugaises de Marianne Alcoforado avec les réponses, lettres de Mlle Aïssé, suivies de celles de Montesquieu et de Mlle du Deffand au chevalier d'Ayde* (edited by E. Asse, Paris, Charpentier, 1879).

Alembert, Jean le Rond d', *Oeuvres* (Paris, Belin, 1821-2), 5 vols.

Argens, J.B. Boyen, Marquis d', *Mémoires de la comtesse de Mirol ou les funestes effets de l'amour et de la jalousie* (La Haye, 1736).

Arnaud, François Thomas Marie de Baculard d', *Les Épreuves du sentiment* (Neuchatel, 1773), 4 vols.

Bachaumont, Louis Petit de, *Mémoires secrets pour servir à l'histoire de la République des lettres*, edited and continued by Pisandat de Mairobert and Mouffle d'Argenville 1777-89 (Paris, 1859).

Bernardin de Saint-Pierre, Jacques Henri, *Paul et Virginie* (1788, Paris, Garnier-Flammarion, 1966).

Bésenval, Baron Pierre Victor de, *Le Spleen* (1747, Paris, Flammarion, 1899).

Cazotte, Jacques, *Le Diable amoureux* (1722, Romanciers du XVIIe siècle, vol. II, Gallimard, 1980).

Chamfort, Sébastien, Nicholas Roch, *Maximes et pensées. Caractères et anecdotes* (1795, Livre de Poche, 1970).

Collé, Charles, *Journal et mémoires de Charles Collé sur les hommes de lettres (1748-1772)*, edited by Bonhomme (Paris, Firmin Didot, 1863), 3 vols.

Crebillon fils, Claude, *La Nuit et le moment* (1755), *Le Hasard au coin du feu* (1763, Desjonquères, 1983).

Les Égarements du coeur et de l'esprit (1736-38, Romanciers du XVIIe siècle, vol. II, Gallimard, 1980).

Damiens de Goricourt, A.P., *Dorval ou Mémoires pour servir à l'histoire des moeurs au XVIIIe siècle* (Amsterdam and Paris, 1769), 2 vols.

Delbarre, Th., *Zénobie ou la nouvelle Coelina* (Paris, An VII).

Diderot, Denis, *Dorval et moi. Entretiens sur le fils naturel* (1757).
Discours sur la poésie dramatique (1757-58).
Paradoxe sur le comédien [1767-1773?] (1830).
Hommage à Richardson (1766).
La Religieuse (1769, revised 1780, Editions 10/18, 1963).
Jacques le fataliste (1798, Oeuvres romanesques, Garnier, 1967).
Oeuvres esthétiques (Garnier Frères, 1956).
Correspondance 1713-84 (Minuit, 1955-77), 16 vols.

Dorat, C.J., *Les malheurs de l'inconstance* (1772, Desjonquères, 1983).

Duclos, Charles Pinot, Sieur, *Les Confessions du Comte de **** (1741, Romanciers du XVIIIe siècle, vol. II, Gallimard, 1980).

Du Deffand, Marie de Vichy Chamrond, Marquise, *Correspondance avec la Duchesse de Choiseul, l'abbé Barthélemy* (Paris, Michel Lévy, 1866), 3 vols.

Epinay, Louise Tardieu d'Esclavelles, Marquise d', *Lettres à mon fils* (Geneva, 1759).

Fréron, Élie, *L'Année littéraire ou suite de lettres sur quelques écrits de ce temps* (Amsterdam and Paris, M. Lambert, 1774–75).

Genlis, Madeleine Félicité, Du Crest de Saint-Aubin, Comtesse de, *Mémoires inédites sur le XVIIIᵉ siècle et la Révolution française depuis 1756 jusqu'à nos jours* (Paris, 1825), 10 vols.

Graffigny, Françoise d'Issembourg d'Happoncourt, *Lettres d'une péruvienne* (1747, Garnier-Flammarion, 1983).

Lettres de Madame de Graffigny suivies de celles de Mmes de Staël, d'Epinay du Bocage, Suard, du Chevalier de Boufflens, du marquis de Villette etc (1879, Slatkine reprint, 1972).

Grimm, Diderot, Raynal, Meiter, *et al.*, *Correspondance littéraire, philosophique et critique* (Paris, M. Tourneux, 1877–82).

Laclos, Pierre Ambroise François, Choderlos de, *Les Liaisons dangereuses* (1782, Garnier Frères, 1980).

Lafitau, J.F., *Moeurs des sauvages américains comparées aux moeurs des premiers temps* (1724, La Découverte, 1979).

La Porte, de, *Anecdotes dramatiques par J.B. Clément de Dijon et l'abbé de La Porte*, vols I and II (1775).

Ligne, Charles Joseph, Prince de, *Correspondance* (Mercure de France, 1965).

Loaisel de Tréogate, J.M., *La Comtesse d'Alibre ou le cri du sentiment, anecdote française* (La Haye and Paris, Belin, 1783).

Dolbreuse, ou l'homme du siècle ramené à la vérité par le sentiment et par la raison, histoire philosophique (Amsterdam and Paris, Belin, 1779).

Marivaux, Pierre Carlet de Chamblain de, *La Vie de Marianne* (1731–41, Garnier 1963).

Journaux et oeuvres diverses (Classiques Garnier, 1969).

Marmontel, Jean François, *Mémoires* (Paris, M. Tourneux, 1891), 3 vols.

Mercier, Louis Sébastien, *Du Théâtre ou nouvel essai sur l'art dramatique* (Amsterdam, 1773).

Les Tableaux de Paris (1781–88, Maspéro, 1979).

Le Bonheur des gens de lettres, discours (London and Paris, 1766).

Mon Bonnet de nuit, suite aux Tableaux de Paris (Paris-Neuchatel, 1784), 4 vols.

Mirabeau, Honoré Gabriel Riquetti, Comte de, *Lettre à Julie Dauvert écrite du donjon de Vincennes* (Paris, 1903).

Mistelet, *De la Sensibilité par rapport aux drames, aux romans et à l'éducation* (Amsterdam and Paris, Mérigot le jeune, 1777).

Mulot, F.V., *Journal intime de l'abbé Mulot, bibliothécaire et grd Prieur de St-Victor, 1777–82* (Paris, 1902).

Pomme, Docteur Pierre, *Essai sur les affections vaporeuses des deux sexes* (Paris, Desaint et Saillant, 1760).

Prévost d'Exiles, Abbé Antoine François, *Mémoires et aventures d'un homme de qualité* (1728–32).

Histoire du Chevalier des Grieux et de Manon Lescaut, (vol. VII of *Mémoires*, Amsterdam 1731, Paris 1733, Garnier 1965).

Le Pour et le Contre, ouvrage périodique d'un goût nouveau (Didot, 1733–40), 20 vols.

Histoire d'une Grecque moderne (Amsterdam, 1740, Garnier, 1965).

Rétif de la Bretonne, Nicolas, *La Vie de mon père* (1779, Garnier, 1983).

Les Nuits révolutionnaires 1788–1794 (Livre de Poche, 1978).

Riccoboni, François, *L'Art du théâtre, à Mme *** suivi d'une lettre sur l'art du théâtre* (1750).

Riccoboni, Marie, Jeanne Laboras de Mézières, Madame, *Lettres de Juliette Catesby à Milady Henriette Campley son amie* (1759, Desjonquères, 1983).

Roland, Marie Jeanne, pseudonym Manon Philipon, Madame, *Une Éducation bourgeoise au XVIIIe siècle, extraits des Mémoires* (Editions 10/18, 1964).

Rousseau, Jean-Jacques, *Discours sur l'origine et les fondements de l'inégalité* (1755, Garnier-Flammarion, 1971).

Essai sur l'origine des langues (written 1755, Paris, Aubier, 1974).

Lettre à d'Alembert sur les spectacles (1758, Oeuvres Complètes, 1851, vol. III).

Émile ou de l'éducation (1762, Classiques Garnier, 1961).

Julie ou la Nouvelle Héloïse ou lettres de deux amans habitans d'une petite ville au pied des Alpes (1761, Garnier Frères, 1960).

Les Confessions, (1782–94), 2 vols.

Le Contrat social, (1762, Seghers, 1971).

Sade, A.F., Marquis de, *Eugénie de Franval* (1788, Romanciers du XVIIIe siècle, vol. II, Gallimard, 1980).

Vauvenargues, Luc de Clapiers, Marquis de, *Correspondance*, in *Oeuvres Complètes* (Hachette, 1968).

Villaret, Claude, *Considérations sur l'art du théâtre à M. J-J. Rousseau citoyen de Genève* (Geneva, 1759).

Voltaire, François Marie Arouet de, *Correspondance*, vol. III (January 1749–December 1753) (Gallimard, 1975).

Romans et contes (1759, Garnier Frères, 1960).

ORIGINAL TEXTS: NINETEENTH CENTURY

Anon. *Dictionnaire des gens du monde* (3rd edition, 1821).

B., Caroline, *Le Journal intime de Caroline B*, study by Michelle Perrot and Georges Ribeill (Arthaud, Montalba, 1985).

Ballanche, Pierre, Simon, *Fragments* (1808, Renouard, 1819, Slatkine reprints, 1967).

Balzac, Honoré de, *La Femme de trente ans* (1831–40, Albin Michel, 1957).

Le Père Goriot (1834, Garnier-Flammarion, 1966).

La Recherche de l'absolu (1834, Folio, 1976).

Une Ténébreuse affaire (1841, Livre de Poche, 1963).

Splendeurs et misères des courtisanes (1844, Folio, 1978).

Le Cousin Pons (1846, Livre de Poche, 1963).

Lettres à une étrangère (1846–47, Calmann Lévy, 1950).

Les Paysans (1848–55, Livre de Poche, 1968).

Bashkirtseff, Marie, *Journal* (1873–84, Mazarine, 1980).

Baudelaire, Charles, *Civilité non puérile mais honnête de Mme Emmeline Raymond* (Firmin, Didot, 1865).
Oeuvres Complètes (Seuil, 1968).
Berger, Professeur Emile, *Du Larmoiement hystérique* (offprint from *Progrès Médical* [5 October 1896], Paris, 1896).
Cabanis, Pierre Jean Georges, *Rapports du physique et du moral de l'homme*, (Paris, Crepert, An X), 2 vols. With the analytic table of Destutt de Tracy (1844).
Charcot, Jean-Martin, *Oeuvres complètes*, edited by P.M. Bourneville (Paris, A. Delahy and E. Le Crosnier, 1885–90), 3 vols.
Chateaubriand, François René, Vicomte de, *Atala* (1801, Garnier, 1976).
Mémoires d'Outre-Tombe (1850, Biré Garnier).
René (1802, Garnier Frères, 1878).
Constant, Benjamin, *Adolphe* (1816, Garnier-Flammarion, 1965).
Oeuvres, écrits autobiographiques et journal intime (Pléiade, Gallimard, 1975).
Courier, Paul-Louis, *Correspondances* (in *Oeuvres Complètes*, Pléiade, Gallimard, 1951).
Decourcelle, P., *Les Deux gosses* (1896, Livre populaire Arthème Fayard, no date).
Delacroix, Eugène, *Journal et correspondance*, edited by P. Carthion (Egloff, 1944).
Esquirol, E. *Des Passions considérées comme causes, symptômes et moyens curatifs de l'aliénation mentale* (1805, Paris, Librairie des Deux Mondes, 1980).
Féré, Charles, Doctor of Bicêtre, *La Pathologie des émotions. Etudes physiologiques et cliniques* (Paris, 1892).
Féval, Paul, *Les Mystères de Londres* (1844, Livre populaire Arthème Fayard, 1909).
Feydeau, Ernest, *Fanny* (1858, Stock, 1948).
Flaubert, Gustave, *Madame Bovary* (1856, La Pléiade, Gallimard, vol I).
L'Education sentimentale (1869).
Bouvard et Pécuchet (1881, La Pléiade, Gallimard, vol. II, 1982).
Correspondance (Pléiade, vols I and II, 1980).
Flaubert/Sand, *Correspondance 1863–1876* (Flammarion, 1981).
Fromentin, Eugène, *Dominique* (1863, Classiques Garnier, Paris, 1936).
Gautier, Théophile, *Mlle Maupin* (1833, Imprimerie Nationale, 1979).
Fortunio et autres nouvelles (1837–39, Romantiques l'Age d'Homme, 1979).
Gobineau, Arthur, Comte de, *Ternove* (1847, in *Débats*, Librairie académique, Perrin, 1929).
Histoire du romantisme (1877, Editions d'Aujourd'hui, 1978).
Les Pléiades (Editions 10/18, 1982).
Goncourt, Edmond de, *La fille Elisa* (1877) and *La Faustin* (1881) (Editions 10/18, 1979).
Goncourt, Edmond and Jules de, *Journal. Mémoires de la vie littéraire* (1851–96, Fasquelle et Flammarion, 1959), 4 vols.
Huysmans, Joris-Karl, *Marthe* (1876).
Les Soeurs Vatard (1879, Editions 10/18, 1975).
En Ménage (1881, Editions 10/18, 1975).
A Rebours (1884, Garnier-Flammarion, 1978).

Lautréamont, pseudonym, Isidore Ducasse, Comte de, *Poésies* I (in *Les Chants de Maldoror*. *Oeuvres Complètes d'Isidore Ducasse*, Renaissance, 1967).

Maine de Biran, François Pierre Gonthier, *Journal*, edited by H. Gouhier (Neuchatel-la-Baconnière, 1955), 2 vols.

Mantegazza, P., Professor at the National History Museum of Florence, *La Physionomie et l'expression des sentiments* (Paris, 1885).

Maryan, M., and G. Béal, *Le Fond et la forme, le savoir-vivre pour les jeunes filles* (Paris, 1896).

Michelet, Jules, *Journal* (1828–74, NRF Gallimard, 1959–76), 4 vols.

   Histoire de la Révolution française (1847, Pléiade, Gallimard, 1952), 2 vols.

Mürger, Henri, *Scènes de la vie de bohème* (1851, Julliard Littérature, 1964).

Musset, Alfred de, *La Confession d'un enfant du siècle* (1836, Folio, 1980).

Nadaud, Martin, *Léonard, maçon de la Creuse* (Maspéro, 1977).

Perdiguier, Agricol, *Mémoires d'un compagnon* (Maspéro, 1977).

Prevost, Marcel, *L'Automne d'une femme* (Paris, Lemerre, 1893).

Ponson du Terrail, Pierre Alexis, Vicomte de, *Rocambole, l'héritage mystérieux* (1859, Classiques populaires, Garnier, 1977).

Richebourg, Emile, *La petite Mionne* (Dentu, 1884).

Sainte-Beuve, Charles Augustin de, *Volupté* (1835, Garnier-Flammarion, 1969).

Sand, George, *Lélia* (1833, Classiques Garnier, 1960).

   Consuelo ou la comtesse de Rudolstadt (1843, Editions de la Sphère, 1979).

   Le Marquis de Villemer (1861, Casterman, 1976).

   Le Dernier amour (1866, Coll. Ressources Paris, Geneva, 1980).

Sand/Musset, *Correspondances 1833–40, Journal intime de George Sand 1834* (Editions du Rocher, 1956).

Scholl, Aurélien, *Les fruits défendus* (Victor Havard, 1885).

Sénancour, Etienne Pivert de, *Rêveries sur la nature primitive de l'homme* (1799, Merlant, 1910).

   Obermann (1804, Editions 10/18, 1965).

Staël, Germaine de, *Corinne ou l'Italie* (1807, Garnier Frères).

Stendhal, pseudonym, Henri Beyle, *De l'Amour* (1822, Folio, 1980).

   Racine et Shakespeare (1823–25, Garnier-Flammarion, 1970).

   Armance (1827, Garnier Frères, 1950).

   Le Rouge et le noir (1831, Livre de Poche classique, 1831).

   Souvenirs d'Egotisme (written 1832, Folio, 1983).

   Lucien Leuwen (incomplete first edition 1855, Folio, 1973), 2 vols.

   Journal (in *Oeuvres intimes*, Pléiade, 1955).

Sue, Eugène, *Arthur* (published in parts, 1837–39, first book edition 1840, Paris, Desforges, 1977).

   Les Mystères de Paris (1840, J.J. Pauvert, 1963).

Truquin, Norbert, *Mémoires et aventures d'un prolétaire à travers la Révolution* (written Valparaison, 1897, Maspéro, 1977).

Vallès, Jules, *L'enfant* (published in *Le Siècle*, 1878, first book edition 1879, Livre de Poche, 1972).

   Le Bachelier (1881, Livre de Poche, 1972).

   L'Insurgé (1882, Livre de Poche, 1972).

Vigny, Alfred de, *Mémoires inédits. Fragments et projets* (Gallimard, NRF, 1958).
Journal d'un poète, collected by Louis de Ratisbonne (1855, Editions d'Aujourd'hui, 1891).
Zola, Emile, *La Faute de l'abbé Mouret* (1875, Harpon et Flammarion, 1890).
Nana (in parts, 1879–80, first book edition, 1880, Livre de Poche, 1972).
L'Oeuvre (first published in *Gil Blas*, 1885–86, first book edition 1886, Livre de Poche, 1971).
Le Rêve (1888, Garnier-Flammarion, 1975).

SECONDARY SOURCES

Aghion, Max, *Le Théâtre à Paris au XVIIIᵉ siècle* (Bruges, Paris, 1926).
Albert, Maurice, *Les Théâtres des boulevards 1781–1848* (Paris, 1902).
Arendt, Hannah, *La Condition de l'homme moderne* (Calmann Lévy, 1961).
Ariès, Philippe, *L'Enfant et la vie familiale sous l'Ancien Régime* (Seuil, 1973).
L'Homme devant la mort (Seuil, 1977).
Arnold, Odile, *Le Corps et l'âme. La vie des religieuses au XIXᵉ siècle* (Seuil, 1984).
Atkinson, Geoffroy, *The Sentimental Revolution. French Writers (1690–1740)* (London, 1965).
Bakhtin, Mikhaïl, *L'Oeuvre de François Rabelais et la culture populaire au Moyen-Age et sous la Renaissance* (Gallimard, 1970, collection TEL 1982).
Esthétique et théorie du roman (Gallimard, 1978).
Barthes, Roland, *Michelet*, (Seuil, 1975).
Fragments d'un discours amoureux (Tel Quel, Seuil, 1977).
Bénichou, Paul, *Le Sacré de l'écrivain (1750-1830). Essai sur l'avènement d'un pouvoir laïque dans la France moderne* (Corti, 1973).
Le Temps des prophètes. Doctrines de l'âge romantique (Gallimard, 1977).
Benrekassa, Georges, *Le Concentrique et l'excentrique. Marges des Lumières* (Payot, 1980).
'Sphère publique et sphère privée. Le romancier et le philosophie interprètes de Lumières', *Revue des sciences humaines*, 182 (1981–2), pp. 7–20.
Bergson, Henri, *Le Rire. Essai sur la signification du comique* (1900, PUF, 1975).
Bernard, Michel, *L'expressivité du corps* (Delarge, 1976).
Bouloiseau, Marc, *La République jacobine 1792–1794* (Points Histoire).
Brissenden, R.F., *Virtue and Distress. Studies in the Novel of Sentiment from Richardson to Sade* (London, 1974).
Butor, Michel, *Improvisations sur Flaubert* (Editions de la Différence, 1984).
Chartier, Roger, editor, *Pratiques de la lecture* (Rivages, 1985).
Conference: *Le Préromantisme*, conference at Clermont-Ferrand, June 1972 (Klincksieck, 1975).
Conference: *Aimer en France 1760–1860*, in *Actes du Colloque international de Clermont* (1980).
Corbin, Alain, *Le Miasme et la jonquille. L'odorat et l'imaginaire social. XVIIIᵉ XIXᵉ siècles* (Collection historique, Aubier, 1982).

'La vie exemplaire du curé d'Ars', in *L'Histoire*, 24 (June 1980) pp. 7–15.

Csuros, Klára, 'Les Larmes du repentir, un topos de la poésie catholique du XVIIᵉ siècle', *Revue XVIIᵉ siècle*, 151 (April–June 1986).

Darnton, Robert, *Bohème littéraire et Révolution. Le monde des livres au XVIIIᵉ siècle* (Gallimard-Seuil, 1983).

  La Fin des Lumières. Le messmérisme et la révolution (1968, Perrin 1984).

Darwin, Charles, *L'Expression des émotions chez les hommes et les animaux* [The expression of the emotions in Man and Animals] (Paris, Reinwald, 1974).

Dedeyan, Charles, *Le Drame romantique en Europe* (SEDES CDU, 1982).

Descotes, Maurice, *Le Public de théâtre et son histoire* (PUF, 1973).

Desgranges, Charles, M., *Geoffroy et la critique dramatique sous le consulat et sous l'Empire, 1800–1819* (Paris, Hachette, 1897).

Didier, Béatrice, *Le Journal intime* (PUF, 1976).

Duby, Georges, *Histoire et mentalité*, in L'Histoire et ses méthodes (Pléiade, Gallimard, 1973).

Dumas, Georges, 'Les Larmes', *Journal de psychologie* (1920), pp. 45–8.

Dumont, Louis, *Homo hierarchicus* (Gallimard, 1969).

  Homo aequalis I Genèse et épanouissement de l'idéologie économique (Gallimard, 1969).

Essai sur l'individualisme (Seuil, 1983).

Duvignaud, Jean, *Les Ombres collectives. Sociologie du théâtre* (PUF, 1973).

Ehrard, Jean, *L'idée de nature en France à l'aube des Lumières* (Flammarion, 1970).

  Littérature française, vol. IX 1720–50 (Arthaud, 1975).

Elias, Norbert, *La Civilisation des moeurs* (1939 and 1969, Livre de Poche, 1973).

  La Société de cour (Calmann Lévy, 1974).

  La Dynamique de l'occident (Calmann Lévy, 1975).

Esprit, 'Le Corps entre illusions et savoirs', in *Esprit* (February 1982).

Evans, David Owen, *Le Drame moderne à l'époque romantique 1827–1850* (1923, Slatkine reprints, 1979).

Fabre, J., *Lumières et romantisme* (Klincksieck, 1963).

Farge, Arlette, *Vivre à Paris dans la rue au XVIIIᵉ siècle* (Collection Archives, Gallimard-Julliard, 1979).

  La Vie fragile. Violence, pouvoir et solidarité à Paris au XVIIIᵉ siècle (Hachette, 1986).

Fauchery, Pierre, *La Destinée féminine dans le roman européen au XVIIIᵉ siècle* (Colin, 1972).

Flandrin, J.L., *Le Sexe et l'Occident* (Seuil, 1981).

Fontaine, Léon, *Le Théâtre et la philosophie au XVIIIᵉ siècle* (Versailles, 1878).

Foucault, Michel, *Les Mots et les choses* (Gallimard, 1966).

  Histoire de la folie à l'âge classique (Gallimard, 1972, Coll. TEL, Gallimard, 1976).

  L'archéologie du savoir (Gallimard, 1977).

  'Un cours inédit (1983) remanié par l'auteur', *Magazine littéraire* 207, (May 1984).

Furet, François, *Penser la Révolution française* (Gallimard, 1952).

Furet, François, and Jacques Ozouf, *Lire et écrire. L'alphabétisation des Français de Calvin à J. Ferry* (Minuit, 1977), 2 vols.

Gaiffe, Félix, *Le Drame en France au XVIIIᵉ siècle* (Paris, 1910).

Gauchet, Marcel and Gladys Swain, *La pratique de l'esprit humain. L'institution asilaire et la révolution démocratique* (Gallimard, 1980).

Gélis, Jacques, 'Et si l'amour paternel existait aussi', in *L'Histoire*, 31 (February 1981), p. 96.

Genette, Gérard, *Figures II* (Tel Quel, Seuil, 1969).

Ginisty, Paul, *Le Mélodrame* (Paris, Aujourd'hui, 1983).

Goffman, I., *Les Rites d'interaction* (Minuit, 1975).

Gouvert, Pierre and Daniel Roche, *Culture et Société* vol. II of *Les Français et l'Ancien Régime* (Armand Colin, 1984).

Granet, Marcel, 'Le Langage de la douleur en Chine', *Journal de Psychologie* (1922), pp. 97–118.

Grothuysen, Bernard, *Philosophie de la Révolution française* (1956, Gallimard, TEL, 1982).

Gusdorf, Georges, *La Conscience révolutionnaire: Les Idéologues*, vol. VIII of *Les Sciences humaines et la pensée occidentale* (Payot, 1978).

Hazard, Paul, *La Pensée européenne au XVIIIᵉ siècle*, vol. I (Paris, 1946).

La Crise de la conscience européenne (Idées, NRF, 1968), 2 vols.

Hirchmann, A.O., *Bonheur privé, action publique* (Fayard, 1983).

Hirsch, J.P., *La nuit du 4 août* (Archives Gallimard-Julliard, 1978).

Hobson, Harold, *French Theatre since 1830* (Dallas, Riverrun Press, 1979).

Hoggart, Richard, *La Culture du pauvre* (Minuit, 1981).

Isolti Rosowsky, Guiditta and Pierre Sorlin, 'Lire les textes, écrire l'histoire', in *Littérature*, 47 (October 1982).

Knibiehler, Yvonne and Catherine Fouquet, *La Femme et les médecins. Analyse historique* (Hachette, 1983).

Lambrosse, Claude, *Lire au XVIIᵉ siècle. La Nouvelle Héloïse et ses lecteurs* (Presses Universitaires de Lyon, 1985).

Lagrave, Henri, *Le Théâtre et le public dans la première moitié du XVIIIᵉ siècle* (1969, Klincksieck, 1973).

Lanson, Gustave, *Nivelle de La Chaussée et la comédie larmoyante* (2nd edition, Paris, 1909).

Larthomas, Pierre, *Le Théâtre en France au XVIIIᵉ siècle* (PUF, 1982).

Lasch, Christopher, *Le Complexe de Narcisse. La nouvelle sensibilité américaine* (1979, Laffont, 1981).

Leiris, Michel, *La Possession et ses aspects théâtraux chez les Ethiopiens du Gondar* (Le Sycomore, 1980).

Lenoble, Robert, *Histoire de l'idée de Nature* (Albin Michel, 1969).

Les Sauvages. *Les Sauvages dans la cité. Auto-émancipation du peuple et instruction des prolétaires au XIXᵉ siècle*, various authors (Champs Vallon, 1985).

Lévi-Strauss, Claude, *Anthropologie structurale*, I, II (Plon, 1973).

Linthilhac, *La Comédie*, vol. IV of *Histoire générale du théâtre en France*, eighteenth century (Flammarion, 1909).

Lipovestsky, Gilles, *L'Ère du vide. Essai sur l'individualisme contemporain* (NRF, Gallimard, 1984).

Lough, J., *Paris Theatre Audiences in the seventeenth and eighteenth century* (OUP, 1957).

Mathiez, Albert, *La Vie chère et le mouvement social* (Payot, 1975), 2 vols.

Mauss, Marcel, *Sociologie et Anthropologie* (1950, PUF, 1968). Preface by Lévi-Strauss, see especially Part V, 'Une catégorie de l'esprit humain, la notion de personne, la notion de "moi"'.

'Réponse à Georges Dumas. L'expression obligatoire des sentiments dans les rituels oraux funéraires des populations australiennes', *Journal de psychologie* (1921), pp. 425–34.

Mauzi, Robert, *Littérature française*, vol. x, 1750–78 (Arthaud, 1977).

L'idée de bonheur au XVIIIᵉ siècle dans la littérature et la pensée française (1960, Slatkine reprint, Geneva and Paris, 1979).

Monglond, André, *Le Maître des âmes sensibles*, vol. II of *Le Préromantisme français* (Corti, 1966).

Monsacre, Hélène, *Les Larmes d'Achille. Le héros, la femme et la souffrance dans la poésie d'Homère* (Albin Michel, 1984).

Mornet, Daniel, *La Romantisme au XVIIIᵉ siècle* (Paris, 1912).

Muchembled, Robert, 'Les Sorcières, la loi et l'ordre', in *Les Annales* (July–August, 1985).

Nebout, Pierre, *Le Drame romantique* (Paris, 1895, Slatkine reprints, 1977).

Ozouf, Mona, *La Fête révolutionnaire 1789–1799* (Gallimard, 1976).

Perrot, Michelle, 'Note critique: fait divers et histoire au XIXᵉ siècle', in *Les Annales* (July–August 1983), pp. 911–9.

Les Ouvriers en grève. France 1791–1890 (Mouton, 1974, Seuil, 1984).

Perrot, Philippe, *Le Travail des apparences ou les transformations du corps féminin (XVIII–XIXᵉ siècles)* (Seuil, 1984).

Peyronnet, Pierre, 'La Mise en scène au XVIIIᵉ siècle' (Thesis, Paris III, Paris, 1974).

Rancière, Jacques, *La nuit des prolétaires. Archives du rêve ouvrier* (Fayard, 1981).

Reinhard, Maurice, *Le Révolution démocratique*, in *Cours de la Sorbonne* (typescript, 1959), 3 vols.

La Chute de la royauté (Gallimard, 1969).

Robin, Régine, *Histoire et linguistique* (Armand Colin, 1973).

Roubine, Jean-Jacques, 'La Stratégie des larmes au XVIIIᵉ siècle', in *Littérature* 9 (February 1973).

Sartre, Jean Paul, *Esquisse d'une théorie des émotions* (Hermann, 1939).

Qu'est-ce que la littérature (NRF, 1970).

L'idiot de la famille. Gustave Flaubert de 1821 à 1857 (NRF Gallimard, 1971).

Sennett, Richard, *Les tyrannies de l'intimité* (Seuil, 1979).

Serres, Michel, *Hermès I. La communication* (Minuit, 1976).

Sigaux, Gilbert, *Le Mélodrame, choix et notices* (Levallois-Perret, 1969).

Soboul, Albert, *1789* (Editions Sociales, 3rd edition, 1973).

La civilisation de la Révolution française (Arthaud, 1970–83), 3 vols.

Précis d'histoire de la Révolution française (Editions Sociales, 1975).

Comprendre la Révolution française (Maspéro, 1981).

Swain, Gladys, 'L'Âme, la femme, le sexe et le corps. Les métamorphoses de l'hystérie à la fin du XIXᵉ siècle', in *Le Débat*, 24 (March 1983).

Thiec, Y. J. Le Bon, 'La Révolution française et la psychologie des révolutions', *Revue de sociologie* XXII – 3 (July–September 1981), p. 413 ff.

Thomasseau, J-M., 'Le Mélodrame sur les scènes Parisiennes, de Coelina (1800) à l'Auberge des Adrets (1823)' (Service de reprographie des thèses, Lille, 1974).

Thuillier, Guy, 'Les Larmes dans l'administration', in *Pénélope*, 10 (Spring 1984), pp. 132–5.

Tocqueville, Alexis de, *L'Ancien Régime et la Révolution* (1856, 2 vols, NRF Gallimard, 1953, reprinted 1980).

Trahard, Paul, *Les Maîtres de la sensibilité française au XVIIIe siècle* (Paris, 1931–33), 4 vols.

Van Gennep, Arnold, *Manuel du folklore français contemporain* (A. Picard, 1943–46).

Les Rites de passage (Paris, Nourry, 1909).

Vernant, J.P., *Religions, histoires, raisons* (Maspéro, 1979).

Vigarello, Georges, *Le Corps redressé. Histoire d'un pouvoir pédagogique* (J.P. Delarge, 1978).

Vovelle, Michel, *Idéologies et mentalités* (Maspéro, 1982).

La Chute de la monarchie, 1789–1792 (Points Histoire).

Woronoff, Denis, *La République bourgeoise de Thermidor à Brumaire, 1794–1799* (Points, Histoire).

Zeldin, Th., *Anxiété et hypocrisie*, vol. V of *Histoire des passions françaises* (Encres, 1979).

Index